TRANSYLVANIA
AND THE
HUNGARIAN-RUMANIAN PROBLEM

a symposium

TRANSYLVANIA
AND THE
HUNGARIAN-RUMANIAN PROBLEM

a symposium

compiled by the Danubian Research and Information Center

Edited by
Anne Fay Sanborn
and
Géza Wass de Czege

Library of Congress Catalog Card Number: 79-53679
International Standard Book Number: 0-87934-021-5

DR
280
T7

Printed by:
Patria Publishing Company Limited
6 Alcina Avenue, Toronto, Ontario, Canada M6G 2E8

TABLE OF CONTENTS

INTRODUCTION

Since the principle of true progress demands a constant betterment of all conditions that regulate man's relations to his political, social, cultural and economical environment, it is mandatory that we keep careful vigil over the quality of human existence resulting from our fast changing world. However, governing ideologies on one side, and economical necessities on the other, tend to push toward the establishments of larger and larger political units, in which the smaller nationality groups are more and more engulfed into the strangulating webs of centralized and self-serving administrative policies of the ruling majorities. It is important, therefore, that we pay special attention to the fate of those minorities which were created by the political changes of this century, in order to detect and remedy unnecessary sufferings caused by infringements on the rights of these people who were placed by force under the rule of others.

The ideal solution would be, of course, if progress and prosperity within these newly created political units would be secured by a willing and multilateral cooperation between the coexisting nationality groups inhabiting the same country, with each group enjoying complete cultural and administrative freedom.

The greatest obstacles to such desired human progress seem to be man's inborn tendencies for intolerance, and prejudice, nurtured and used much too often by unscrupulous political leaders. The results of such practices culminate usually in a distorted self-image of the ruling majority, an extreme stage of nationalism, called chauvinism, thereby creating intolerable situations through oppression and sometimes even extermination of subdued nationality groups helplessly at the mercy of an aggressive majority nation.

It should be the obligation of all those whose position enables them to notice, observe, research and evaluate any such abuses, to make their findings known to the rest of the world in order that definite steps may be taken on the international, political, and economical level toward the elimination of these dangerous frictions, thereby ensuring a better future for all mankind.

Such a trouble-spot seems to be in our days the ever increasing problem of Transylvania. The symptoms of the problem are given in this book by a distinguished group of scholars, knowledgeable of the complexities of East-Central Europe, who have done extensive research concerning the multiple aspects of this problem. In their opinion the situation in Transylvania has outgrown the limits of a local conflict, and gained international proportions during the recent years.

It must be pointed out that the prevailing situation concerning the nationality groups inhabiting Transylvania is especially aggravated today by the unfortunate attitude of the Socialist Republic of Rumania trying to influence world-opinion on one hand by focusing attention on a much advertised mock-anniversary of a "two thousand year old Rumanian statehood" while on the other hand trying to eliminate the native Hungarian population of Transylvania - torn off from Hungary only sixty years ago.

In this symposium we shall examine the validity of the Rumanian claim to "all the lands between the Black Sea and the Tisza River", based on a so-called "Daco-Roman theory" of historic continuity. Since the existing international literature concerning this subject is so voluminous that it would be impossible to condense it into one single volume, we shall bring here, under the chapter marked "Research" excerpts from well documented, and recently published works, while listing in our bibliography all the available international material on the subject, thus leaving it to the conscientious reader to double check the validity of all data, if so desired.

We shall begin with an authentic survey and condensation of the geography, culture and history of Transylvania, with special attention to the diversity of the inhabiting population, as well as the influence of these nationality groups on each other during their many centuries long coexistence within the ancient framework of the Carpathian Basin.

We shall also expose the "Transylvanian problem" as seen from different perspectives, in order that the proper in-depth dimensions as well as the complexity of the situation may appear. We shall try to point out certain obvious directions in our conclusion where possible solutions to the problem may be found.

Today, when so many scholastic manifestations are tinted by ideological phraseologies and influenced by political aspirations, it is vitally important to establish documented and untarnished facts, especially concerning issues of political controversy, where millions of human lives are at stake.

The purpose of this symposium is exactly this: to furnish factual information and background research concerning the Transylvanian problem. The task of compiling this work was immense, and as our bibliography indicates, the material was extensive and scattered. Acknowledgement is due to each and every member of the Danubian Research Center for the gathering of material and the scrupulous evaluation of all the documentation used in this extremely complex and sensitive subject, striving to establish scholastic facts by separating unbiased data from myth, national zeal and political expediency.

Albert Wass de Czege
Moderator

I. THE FACTS

GEOGRAPHY

The name "TRANSYLVANIA" is the Latin translation of the original Hungarian name "Erdely" (formerly "Erdoelve" as it was used in the 10th, 11th and 12th centuries A.D.), meaning "Land beyond the forest". The word Transylvania appeared for the first time in the 17th century, when the official language of Hungarian public life and administration became Latin. Formerly, the Romans called the same territory the "Province of Dacia" after the previous inhabitants, the Dacs, who were conquered and completely exterminated by the Roman legions.

The Vlach immigrants (today called Rumanians) entering the country first in small bands, and later in large masses as refugees, took the Hungarian name "Erdely", and changed it to suit their tongue into "Ardeal". The Germans who were brought in as settlers by the Hungarian kings during the 13th and 14th centuries named it "Siebenburgen", because of their seven administrative districts with a centrally located fortification (Burg-Burgen) in each.

The territory known today as Transylvania includes Transylvania proper, part of the Banat, part of the Great Hungarian Plain as well as the former "Partium", totalling 24,027 square miles. On the North, East and South it is bordered by the high mountian ranges of the Eastern Carpathians, and the Southern Carpathians, also known as the "Transylvanian Alps", which form the natural frontiers of the Carpathian Basin, and at the same time the cultural frontiers between Western and Eastern civilizations for more than 1,000 years. To the West and the Northwest the land lies wide open, forming one undisturbed geographical unit with the rest of the Carpathian Basin.

A single glance at the map will show clearly that geographically Transylvania is but a part of that basin. This very fact determined its role within the European community for more than 1,000 years, economically, culturally, and politically.

The fertile plains and river valleys of Transylvania, as well as the rolling hills of the central basin and the gold, silver, coal and salt mines of the mountain regions invited the early Hungarian settlers from the 9th century on, making the land an economically and culturally important part of Hungary from 890 A.D. until 1920.

The city of **KOLOZSVAR**, meaning the "Fort of Kolozs" (called Cluj or Napoca by the Rumanians) was established in 987 A.D. by Kolozs, commander of the Hungarian armies in the East. The city became for many centuries the administrative capital as well as the cultural center of Transylvania. Its fine Gothic architecture makes this remarkable city even today, in spite of the new political borders, a part of the West.

Population in 1910: 60,808 of which 50,704 were Hungarians; 7,562

11

Rumanians and the remainder Germans and Jews. In 1930 the population grew to 100,844, of which 54,776 were Hungarians; 34,836 Rumanians. By 1966 the total population of the city became 167,930. Due to forced evacuations of the native Hungarian population by the Rumanian government, to the relocation of Rumanians from across the Carpathians, and mostly to the politically motivated census, the ethnic ratio cannot be safely established.

The same is true concerning the rest of the Transylvanian cities: **NAGYVARAD** (today Oradea), population in 1910: 64,169 of which 58,421 were Hungarians, was the first royal fort and monastery in Eastern Hungary, established in the year 1008. Population there today is near 120,000.

BRASSO (Brasov) was built in the 13th century by German settlers. Population in 1910: 41,056; 17,831 Hungarians; 11,786 Rumanians. Population today is 125,000.

MAROSVASARHELY (translated into Rumanian "Targu Mures") meaning "Marketplace on the Maros River" was established in the 13th century as a free market place for the Hungarian farmers of the Maros valley, and grew into a cultural center during the 17th and 18th centuries. Population in 1910: 25,517; 22,790 Hungarians and 1,717 Rumanians. Population today is 79,877.

ARAD established first in the 12th century on the edge of the Great Hungarian Plain, played an important role in Hungarian history. Population in 1910: 32,986; Hungarians, 30,410; Rumanians, 1,118. Population today, 109,832.

TEMESVAR (today Timisoara) meaning in Hungarian "Fort on the Temes" River), had in 1910 a population of 72,517 ; 28,552 Hungarians and 7,566 Rumanians, 19,465 Germans. The city played an important role in the economy and the industrial development of the Hungarian Kingdom.

Beginning with the 15th century, the educational institutions of the Transylvanian cities, especially those of Kolozsvár, Nagyvárad, Nagyenyed, Zilah and Gyulafehérvár became important centers of Hungarian culture, and gained world-wide recognition.

There are more than two hundred mineral springs, thermal baths and well known health resorts throughout Transylvania. The richness of its natural resources as well as the beauty of its landscape, made it desirable to immigrants as well as conquerors through all recorded history.

CULTURE

As an integral part of the Hungarian Kingdom, Transylvania was drawn into the Western Christian Culture Circle at the beginning of the eleventh century. The architecture of old Transylvanian cities, such as Nagyvárad/today Oradea/, Kolozsvár/today Cluj-Napoca/, Brassó/ today Brasov/ or Dés/ today Dej/ bear witness to this fact.

Besides a few scattered ruins of Roman fortifications, destroyed by the retreating Roman legions in 271 A.D., no sign of any kind would indicate a trace of an older established culture preceding the arrival of the Hungarians. Not even the legends, folk tales, ballads or folk songs of any one of the cohabiting ethnic groups suggest anything of this kind, except the oldest Hungarian/ Székely/ legends which date back to the time of Attila and the empire of the Huns.

If we examine the folk art, which is the most tell-tale expression of early influences, we find that the embroideries and architecture of the Transylvanian Germans relates to the embroideries and architecture of those districts of Germany where these settlers came from in the 12th and 13th centuries. In the same way, the folk art of the Transylvanian Rumanians is identical with those of Moldavia and Wallachia, and they clearly show the Slavic influences, the Bulgarian, Greek, and even the Albanian motifs, picked up by the migrating Vlach herdsmen on their way from the Albanian border to their present location. On the other hand, the famous art creations of the Transylvanian Hungarians, like those of Kalotaszeg, Csik, Háromszék, Udvarhely carry a basic similarity with those of other parts of Hungary, and clearly relate back to ancient Turanian/ Scythian/ motifs.

Due to the close relations of the medieval Hungarian Kingdom with the West, talented Transylvanians found their ways to the early Universities of Europe as early as the 12th and 13th centuries. The very first student whose name became officially registered at the University of Oxford in 1193, was Miklós of Hungary, son of Kende, nobleman of Transylvania. During the 15th century there were three famous Hungarian doctors on the faculty of the University of Bologna, and one of them, Peter Paul Apáti of Torda, later founded the "Free Collegium of the Noble Sciences", established in his hometown, Torda, then moved to Kolozsvár/ today Cluj/ by King Mathias. After the two Hungarian Universities were established, Pécs in 1367, and Buda in 1389, many Transylvanians sent their sons there, some of whom, after returning home, founded one by one the "Collegiums" of High Learning in Nagyenyed, Gyulafehérvár, Kolozsvár, Nagyvárad, Brassó, Arad, Zilah and Marosvásárhely.

Due to the ecclesiastical domination of Rome as in other Western empires, the official language of science and administration in the

Hungarian Kingdom was Latin. Therefore it was only in 1527 that the first book was printed in the Hungarian language in Kolozsvár. In 1598 there were already 24 printing establishments in Transylvania, publishing by that date 382 books, of which 368 were in the Hungarian language.

There were 18 Transylvanian Hungarians enrolled at the Wittenberg University in the year of 1586. Many Transylvanian Hungarians were teaching at famous Western Universities, while several Western scientists, such as Martin Opitz, John Alstead, Henry Bisterfeld and Isaac Basire taught in Transylvanian colleges during the 16th and 17th centuries.

In 1545 the complete translation of the Bible appeared in the Hungarian language, printed in Kolozsvár. Shortly after, in 1582, financed by Hungarians and translated by Hungarians, the Bible was published in the Vlach language.

In the 14th century two Transylvanian Hungarian brothers, Márton and György Kolozsvári, were famous sculptors. Most of their works were demolished through the many wars, except the well known statue of St. George in the city of Prague, which is today recognized as one of the greatest monuments of Gothic sculpture.

Thus Transylvania, as part of Hungary, became the center of Hungarian culture. During the most troubled times of Central European history, when the conflict between Catholicism and Protestantism set fire to the emotions, in Transylvania the Hungarian preacher and philosopher Ferenc Dávid/ 1535-1579/ was able to found and establish the Unitarian Church, and persuade the Congress of Torda in 1568 to declare, for the first time in the world, the *freedom of religion.*

It is indeed not accidental that man's God-given right to choose his own religion and to worship freely and undisturbed was first recognized and legalized in Transylvania. This was a direct result of the Hungarian concept of freedom, as well as the respect toward the freedom of others, which permeated the entire Hungarian state-concept, and enabled the Hungarians to rule the Carpathian Basin successfully for a thousand years. This secured free development to every ethnic group which asked permission to settle within the Hungarian borders.

Even after 1711, when Hungarian political independence was completely lost to Habsburg oppression, Hungarian culture in Transylvania not only kept in step with the cultural evolution of the rest of the country, but in many instances it became the guiding force of spiritual and cultural resistance. In fields of sciences, art and literature, Transylvania became the torch-bearer to the rest of oppressed Hungary. The same phenomenon repeated itself after 1849, when the Liberty War was crushed by the combined forces of Austria and Russia, and the darkness of revengeful oppression fell upon Hungary for the second time.

It might be interesting to note that the first English-Tibetan dictionary was published in 1834 by a young Transylvanian Hungarian explorer, Sándor Kórósi Csoma. The era between 1820 and 1867 is also regarded by many as the "golden age" of Hungarian national literature, brought forth by Habsburg oppression. Many of the great names in Hungarian literature were from Transylvania, such as Ferenc Kazinczy /1759-1831/, Ferenc Kölcsey /1790-1838/ Mihály Tompa /1817-1868/ and others.

In 1867 the "reconciliation between Emperor Franz Joseph and the Hungarian nation opened the gates toward industrialization and economic upswing. Though economic progress was much slower reaching into Transylvania than other parts of Hungary - due to distances, lack of roads etc. - the revitalization of the Hungarian culture reached a new peak in Kolozsvár and other Transylvanian cities. During the glorious years of the "millennium", Transylvania proudly celebrated its thousand-year-old cultural heritage within the framework of the thousand-year-old Hungarian national frontiers.

When in 1919 the Rumanian army occupied Transylvania, and the brutal persecution of Hungarian officials, clergymen, educators and other intellectuals began with unprecedented Balkanic ferocity, Hungarian stamina was put to the test.

Within a few weeks all geographical locations were re-named, from cities down to the most remote villages. Kolozsvár was changed overnight into Cluj, Nagyvárad into Oradea, Temesvár into Timisoara, etc. Many names were simply translated, such as Disznós into Porcu, Medvepatak into Ursu, Nagybánya into Baia Mare, Szentegyed into Sinte Jude, etc. Streetmarkers were replaced and streets renamed. Those who were born and raised in one of the Transylvanian towns, and lived there all their lives, suddenly had to change their old established home-address to a new one, in a foreign language they did not even know how to pronounce.

City halls, court houses, district offices, post offices, railroad stations were filled with new officials, imported from across the mountains, who did not speak the language of the population. Huge signs appeared everywhere: VORBITI NUMAI RUMUNESTI! Speak only Rumanian. Those citizens who were unable to obey these signs because they did not speak the Rumanian language, were refused service, abused, and sometimes even beaten by the new police.

The urban intellectuals of Transylvania suffered the most. Put out of their jobs, many of them were forced to leave the country. Others shifted into commerce or industry. Some of them became laborers, while many rallied around the only bulwarks left for Transylvanian culture: the churches, church-affiliated schools, and other cultural institutions, such as libraries, museums, civic societies, benevolent organizations, etc. which were not yet dependent on the State.

Rigid censorship was instituted by the Rumanian government toward

Hungarian publications of any kind. In spite of this, by 1926 Transylvania had more Hungarian monthly periodicals, weekly publications and daily newspapers than ever before. It was the automatic reaction of Hungarian national consciousness taking refuge in culture against the brutal oppression of a foreign and inferior civilization.

Gy. Zathureczky writes in his book "Transylvania, Citadel of the West" /Danubian Press, 1967/ page 46: "The Transylvanian /Hungarian/ Press, suffering under heavy censorship, lost its provincial character and rose to European level. The Transylvanian Literary Guild and the Transylvania Helicon gathered the writers and established a Hungarian Publishing Co-operative. A new and specifically Transylvanian literature was born. Struggling against poverty, and harassed by Rumanian authorities, the Transylvanian Hungarian stage reached an unprecedented peak against all odds."

In spite of the brutal political and economic oppression of a Balkan force, Transylvania remained part of the Western Culture. Just as an Austrian journalist aptly observed in the "Wiener Tagblatt", July 27, 1934: "Travelling through Transylvania one cannot help noticing that while the policeman on the street corner speaks only Rumanian, within the walls of old town houses there is a very lively Hungarian cultural life going on, discussing with foreign quests Western ideas, Western literature, Western art, sometimes in three or four languages at the same time - none of which happens to be the language of the policeman down on the corner..." Further down he stated: "The very fact that in those highly cultured Transylvanian circles everyone knows the names of German, French, English and American writers, scientists, actors, painters, but no one seems to know anything that goes on in Bucharest, shows clearly that in spite of the so-called 'peace treaties' the cultural boundaries between East and West are still firmly drawn on the ridges of the Carpathians..."

Even 20 years after the Rumanian take-over, Transylvania supported 38 periodicals in the Hungarian language, 5 Hungarian literary societies, and 12 Hungarian publishing houses. Twenty-seven Hungarian writers in Transylvania had one or more books published in foreign countries, while the Hungarian theatre of Kolozsvár was regarded by talent scouts all over the world as the springboard to fame for talented actors and actresses. Hungarian painters of Transylvania frequently toured Europe with their exhibits, and the Hungarian folk art of Kalotaszeg, Csik, Háromszék and Udvarhely reached the foreign markets with their embroidery and wood carvings.

In spite of the political oppression and the strong economic discrimination, the dominant culture in Transylvania remained the Western oriented Hungarian culture, followed by the German in the German districts. Those few Rumanian authors, poets and artists who were

16

born Transylvanians, were absorbed by Bucharest and the "Regat" /Old Kingdom/, and had no contact whatsoever with the representatives of either the Hungarian or the German cultural circles in Transylvania. The name of Octavian Goga, the excellent Rumanian poet, who though born in Transylvania, became known only among Hungarians and Germans after he was selected by the king of Rumania to be the prime-minister of the country.

In August 1940, when Northern Transylvania was returned to the Mother Country, it took only one day for such cities as Kolozsvár, Nagyvárad, Marosvásárhely to wipe off every trace of a Rumanian occupation, and turn back into the thriving Hungarian cities they had been for hundreds of years.

However, after World War II when the Russian army handed Transylvania over to the Rumanian government as a compensation for Bessarabia, all this changed drastically. Hungarian publishing establishments were shut down. Within the new Rumanian framework one single state-owned publishing establishment was formed to "serve the Hungarian cultural needs", not in Transylvania, but in Bucharest. This establishment, named "Kritérion", was allowed to publish only government-approved material, mostly translations from Rumanian and Russian, and only a few ideologically sterilized Hungarian authors in limited editions.

Today the Hungarian population of Transylvania is completely isolated from the West, not just politically and economically, but also culturally. No publications of any kind are allowed to enter. Even Hungarian language Bibles, donated by American Presbyterian Churches to the Transylvanian Calvinist Church were recently confiscated and burned.

Public monuments, statues, historic markers were systematically destroyed and replaced with new ones, reflecting the new Rumanian-dictated atmosphere. Old tombstones are destroyed, ancient churches "remodelled" in such a way that they lose their Hungarian character. The entire history is re-written, and the newly created false "history" is systematically introduced to the new generations. Even those very few Hungarian-language schools which are still left to operate must teach this falsified history to their pupils, according to which Transylvania is the "original homeland" of the Rumanian people, and the Hungarians were the "intruders" who ruled the native Rumanians by terror.

According to the law, the presence of two Rumanian children in any school suffices to have the language of instruction changed from Hungarian to Rumanian. In schools where the language of instruction is Rumanian, the children are forbidden to speak Hungarian among themselves, even during recess. Those children who disobey this rule are severely beaten by their teachers. Since the Rumanian government has already brought more than 600,000 new Rumanian settlers into Transylvania from Bessarabia, Bukovina and other parts of "old Rumania" while in the same time deporting more than 300,000 Hungarians from their native land, it is clear that there is a well-planned cultural genocide going on, fully using the "unlimited possibilities" and brutalities of a totalitarian regime.

In order to destroy every trace of the past, the Rumanian government first nationalized, then systematically destroyed every old document preserved in Church archives, museums, libraries or private homes. It is indeed fortunate that many of the ancient Transylvanian documents, dating back as far as the 11th century, were transferred to the Hungarian National Archives in Budapest, some before World War I, and others during World War II. Thus, in spite of all the Rumanian efforts to eradicate the past, the true history of Transylvania can still be proven by thousands of ancient documents and the traces of the once great Western-oriented culture of the Hungarians in Transylvania can still be found in libraries and museums, not in Hungary alone, but also in Austria, Germany, Italy, France, England and the United States of America.

The Rumanian culture is entirely different from that known as the "Transylvanian culture", which is in reality a regional diversity of the West-oriented Hungarian culture. The Rumanian culture is Balkan-oriented, and specifically Rumanian, based on the history of the Vlach migration from Italy across to Albania, and from there up to Wallachia and Moldavia. It was brought forth by Balkan influences, just as the Rumanian language itself, which is composed, according to the Rumanian linguist Cihac, "of 45.7% Slavic, 31.52 Latin, 8.4% Turkish, 7% Greek, 6% Hungarian and 0.6% Albanian words."

Even today, the Rumanian culture as such, has no roots in Transylvania. It is being "imported" constantly and purposefully from Bucharest into the Transylvanian province in order to crowd out and replace the traditional Hungarian culture of this conquered and subjugated land.

POPULATION

From the 11th to the 16th centuries every available datum indicates that the population of Transylvania was relatively dense in the river valleys and in the central basin, while quite sparse in the mountain regions. Descriptions of early Byzantine travelers and visiting Vatican priests from the 10th to 13th centuries, as well as those written by French, English, Dutch, Italian and German authors during the 14th, 15th, and 16th centuries, furnish sufficient proof that except the cities of the German settlers in the South-East, all Transylvanian towns and cities were populated by Hungarians, economically affluent and culturally abreast with the West. The small farming communities in the river valleys were inhabited by Hungarians also. These lands were owned partly by Hungarian nobility, worked by Hungarian cotters and serfs, and partly by free Hungarian peasants, as in the Székely districts.

Vlach herdsmen, migrating back and forth between the high mountain pastures and their winter quarters, are mentioned for the first time in the 13th century in Southern regions, later, during the 14th and 15th centuries in the Bihar district, Máramos and Naszód.

The first serious census in Transylvania was taken in 1440-41. According to these documents, kept in Nagyvárad /today Oradea/ there were 87 Hungarian towns at that time in Transylvania with over 1,000 "smokes" /meaning households/ and 817 Hungarian villages with over 20 smokes, as compared to 8 German towns and 22 German villages, and 37 Vlach villages. In 1505 a Vatican document estimated the total population of the Hungarian Kingdom to be "about four million Christian souls" of which 76% were Hungarian speaking, while the rest spoke the German, Croatian, Slovak, Serbian and Vlach tongues.

The next known census was taken again by the Jesuits in 1658, during the most turbulent times of Hungarian history, after the Hungarian population of Central Transylvania and the Szamos valley was almost completely eradicated by Turks, Tatars and ravaging Habsburg armies, and the Vlach immigration from across the Carpathians was in full swing. According to these figures the total population of Transylvania /the Banat, and part of the Great Hungarian Plane, which now comprise a good part of Transylvania, not included/ number about 860,000 souls, of which 240,000 spoke the Vlach language, 80,000 the German, and 520,000 the Hungarian, while 20,000 were listed as "others".

In 1794 Emperor Francis I ordered the first administrative census, performed by provincial administrators, not by priests. This politically motivated and anti-Hungarian census came up with the following figures, again concerning the Province of Transylvania alone:

Total population: 1,362,456; Germans, 118,782; Vlach, 512,988;

Hungarians, 687,244; and others, 43,442. According to contemporaty letters, kept in the archives of the Kolozsvár library, most of those "others" were in reality Hungarians with Slovak, Polish or other foreign-sounding names.

The last census taken before World War I, in 1910, shows a considerable increase in the population of Transylvania, this time including all the territories which were occupied by Rumania nine years later:

Total population 5,265,444. Hungarian speaking 1,704,851, German speaking 559,824, Rumanian 2,800,073. The remaining 200,696 were registered as Serbians, Slovaks, Ruthenians, Jews and others.

From 1910 to 1919 we must use the given figures of "natural increase percentage", which was, for the entire country, 13.4%. Using this figure we can assume that the Hungarian population of today's Transylvania must have been somewhere around 1,871,375 in 1919, at the time of the Rumanian take-over.

From this point on we must proceed very carefully in order to come as close as possible to the truth concerning the population figures. As it is documented in the Appendix / Testimonies 2 and 6/ the Rumanian census was politically motivated from the very beginning, therefore the figures presented by the 1930, 1948, 1956 and 1966 Rumanian statistics can not be regarded as accurate, due to the following reasons:

1./ Name-analysis was used as a principle to determine the nationality. Names ending with -an, -as were automatically registered as Rumanian, while German-sounding names were registered as Germans, Slovak-sounding names as Slovaks, etc.

2./ Religious affiliation also determined ethnic status in Rumanian census practices. All Lutherans were registered as Germans, while all Greek Catholics as Rumanians. After the Greek Catholic Church was abolished by law, and absorbed into the Greek Orthodox Church, all Hungarians who were previously members of the Greek Catholic congregations automatically became listed as belonging to the Greek Orthodox Church, therefore Rumanians.

3./ Intimidation. Census-takers, going from house to house in the villages, escorted by the local police, asking questions such as "Are you a good Rumanian or not?" They go through factories side by side with the personnel director asking the Hungarian laborers "Are you grateful to Rumania for your job? Are you a good Rumanian?" Those who insist on being registered as Hungarians lose their jobs or get beaten up by the police.

4./ Those Hungarians who were deported or relocated, and reside today outside of Transylvania in any one of the old Rumanian provinces, are automatically counted as Rumanians, based on the assumption that there are no "foreigners" in those provinces. The number of these

Hungarians is close to 350,000.

To compensate for these deliberate "errors" on the Rumanian census, we must again avail ourselves of the method already used previously. Namely the application of the "natural increase percentage", listed each year by the Rumanian government itself.

These figures, taken from reliable sources /Transylvania, a Cura Della Societa Stórica Ungarese, 1940 - Handbuch der Europaischen Volksgruppen, 1974 - and Demographical Statistics of the Socialist Republic of Rumania, 1976/ average out to 10,5% yearly population increase from 1919 to 1976. According to these figures, after taking into consideration the loss of more than one half-million Hungarians to executions, labor camps, emigration, etc., the total Hungarian population of Transylvania in 1976 should have been 2,816,555.

If we compare the above figure with those of Prof. Satmarescu /East Central Europe, University of Colorado, January 1975/ who estimated the number of *unreported* Hungarians at 900,000, bringing up the total figure of the Hungarian population in Rumania to approximately 2.5 million, and with the figures published in 1974 by the European Union movement in the "Handbuch Europaischer Volksgruppen" which put the number of Hungarians in Transylvania alone to 2.4 million, we are satisfied that our calculations are as close to the truth as is humanly possible in the given circumstances.

Dr. Jonel Popescu, who did special research in 1976 on "Churches in Rumania" claims the following figures: Calvinists 1.2 million, Roman Catholics 1 million, Unitarians 280,000, Hungarian Lutherans 20,000 and Hungarian former Greek Catholics 200,000. All together 2.7 million Hungarians.

According to the last Rumanian census the total population of Rumania is supposed to be 19,103,163. /See: "The Hungarian Nationality in Rumania", published by the Institute of Political Science of the Socialist Republic of Rumania, 1976, page 8./

According to the German language publication of the Rumanian Government "The Mitwohnenden Nationalitaten in Rumania, Statistische Dokumentation" 2% of the total population is German, and 1.8% are others /other than Germans or Hungarians/, 3.8% of the above total population makes 725,920. Adding to this the 2,816,555 Hungarians, we arrive at the figure of 3,542,478 as the total number of minorities in Rumania, leaving the number of Rumanians at 15,560,685, thus making the Rumanians 81% of the entire country's population, while the Hungarians 15%. However, if we relocate the Hungarians into Transylvania, where they belong, we see a different picture, especially if at the same time we relocate, back to their old homeland, those 600,000 Rumanians who were moved into Transylvania by the Rumanian government with the sole purpose of "diluting" the Hungarian population.

In this case we would have in Transylvania, 3.1 million Rumanians, 2.8 million Hungarians and 0.5 million Germans and "others", with a non-Rumanian population of 51.6%.

Adding to these figures the 200,000 Hungarians, called "csango's" located in the province of Moldova, the total number of Hungarians in the Socialist Republic of Rumania exceeds 3 million.

HISTORY

440 B.C.
Herodotus described the SCYTHIANS, inhabiting the "lands East and North of the Danube river". "Scythian" is the collective name of a group of TURANIAN people, supposedly descendants of the SUMERIANS, but certainly carriers and preservers of the Sumerian culture. To the family of Scythian nations belonged the "Dacs" of ancient Dacians, the Huns, the Avars, the Bulgarians and the Magyars or Hungarians.

300 B.C.
Roman historians mentioned the THRACIANS moving Northward across the flatlands of the lower Danube and across the high mountain ranges, into a land surrounded by mountains.

200 B.C.
Greek historians referred to "Upper Thracia" as a beautiful country North of the Danube, and surrounded by mountains "like a natural fortress". These Greek chronicles furnish us with the first geographic description of the CARPATHIAN BASIN.

118 B.C.
Roman historians described the same land as "Dacia", homeland of "The Scythians who call themselves Dacs."

85 A.D.
The expanding Roman Empire began the invasion of Dacia.

107 A.D.
The war for Dacia ended under the Emperor Trajan. According to Roman historians, the fierce Dac people put up an astonishing fight. Not even women and children were willing to surrender to the conquering legions, and had to be exterminated one by one.

117 A.D.
Emperor Adrianus ordered most of his troops out of the "completely devastated" Dacia into Asia Minor, leaving only two "legions of the Barbarians" in this North-Eastern outpost of his empire. The term "Legion of the Barbarians" meant army units recruited from the North-Western territories, inhabited by Germanic tribes.

271 A.D.
Yielding to the pressure of the invading GOTHS, Emperor Aurelian withdrew the last remaining legions from Dacia, under strict order to destroy buildings, food supplies, and completely evacuate the land before the oncoming "Barbarians". The Goths were a Teutonic people, referred to by Romans as "Barbarians".

433 A.D.
The HUNS entered the Carpathian Basin by crossing the North-Eastern Carpathians. According to contemporary historians, during the rule of Attila, Transylvania was still partly inhabited by Goths, and it was marked

as GOTHIA on the maps. Goth warriors of Transylvania participated in the Western adventures of Attila.

454 A.D.

After the death of Attila the Hun empire collapsed.

480 A.D.

The Western part of the former province of Dacia was under the rule of the GEPIDS while the Eastern part was still inhabited by a surviving tribe of the Huns, who later joined the new BULGARIAN-TURK tribal federation across the Eastern Carpathians. /Today's Moldova./

560 A.D.

The AVARS, a nation having the same language as the Huns according to contemporary Greek chronicles, crossed the Carpathians and occupied the entire Carpathian Basin, including Transylvania.

562 A.D.

Byzantine chroniclers observed the Avar envoy appearing before the emperor Justinian spoke the same language as the Hun-Bulgarian interpreter of the court.

796 A.D.

The Avar empire collapsed.

805 A.D.

Khan Krum "the terrible" created a strong Bulgarian empire on both sides of the Danube, including Transylvania. /Haleczky: Borderlands of Western Civilization. Ronald Press N.Y. 1952, Page 23./

892-894 A.D.

Vatican, Byzantine and Russian /Kiev/ chronicles described in detail the appearance of the Hungarians /Magyars/ in the Carpathian Basin and the lower Danube region.

896 A.D.

The Hungarians defeated the Bulgarians and took possession of Transylvania.

938 A.D.

Byzantine historians gave detailed account of CSANÁD and GYULA-FEHÉRVÁR /today Alba Julia/ as strong Hungarian forts and prosperous cities in Transylvania. The name "Gyulafehérvár" was even translated into Greek by one of the authors as "The White Fort of Gyula", explaining that Gyula was the name of the "Eastern Chief" of the Hungarian tribes.

946 A.D.

Byzantine documents mentioned for the first time the presence of the SZÉKELYS in the Eastern most tip of Transylvania, describing them as one of the Hungarian tribes settled there as border guards, within well organized military districts called "Szék" - chair or bench, referring to complete administrative and judicial power vested into their own chiefs. These privileges of the Székelys were recognized later by the Hungarian kings also.

952 A.D.

By compiling all available data, Greek historians gave the first account of the migration of the Magyars /Hungarians/ into the Carpathian Basin. According to this account, the Hungarians followed the trail of their brother-nations, the Huns and the Avars, moving first from the Volga region into Etelköz, then expanding slowly in a Westerly and south-westerly direction as far as today's Moldova, and finally crossing the Carpathians through three different routes, while a fourth unit, in alliance with the Byzantine forces, attacked the Bulgarians at the lower Danube, took possession of the fertile lands between the Danube river and the Southern Carpathians or Transylvanian Alps, and joined the rest of the nation at the Iron Gate: a gorge cut by the Danube through the mountains, south of the Great Hungarian Plain.

976 A.D.

Greek chronicles /Kedrenos II. 435 Ed. Bonn./ mentioned for the first time the name VLACH, describing a people of primitive herdsmen located between Kastoria and Prespa, near today's Albanian border, who centuries later became the ancestors of the Rumanians. The name RUMANIAN was created only after the unification of Vlachia /or Wallachia/ with the principality of Moldova in 1878.

978 A.D.

Vatican missionaries establish a church in the fort of Várad. later called Nagy-Várad, today Oradea. Reports sent back to Rome by the same missionaries described the small tribe of the JAZIG, who spoke "almost the same language" as the Hungarians, and was supposed to be living in the same region long before the Hungarians arrived. The descendants of the Jazig, called today "Jász", can still be found on the Great Hungarian Plain, west of Nagyvárad. They are the only recorded inhabitants found by the Hungarian settlers in the Carpathian Basin, including Transylvania, except a few scattered fragments of SLAVS, who became assimilated within a few decades, and completely disappeared, leaving behind nothing more than a very few and widely scattered geographical names.

982 A.D.

Byzantine traders reported "rich Hungarian towns" in Transylvania where "good wine, raw gold, hides and various carved tools and art objects" could be purchased in exchange for silk and jewelry. They described the inhabitants as "proud Christians" and the country as "lively towns, cultivated valleys, surrounded by uninhabited mountain ranges and dense forests." Since the wife of chief Gyula, residing in Gyulafehérvár was a Byzantine Princess, there was a lively exchange between the Eastern part of Hungary, called ERDŐELVE /Transylvania/

and the Byzantine empire. Thus, Christianity entered the Carpathian Basin at the same time from the West and from the East.

1002

King Stephen the Saint, first king of Hungary, defeating his uncle, the Gyula of Transylvania, established Western Christianity as official religion, and introduced the Western Feudalistic System by force. In spite of the defeat, Transylvania served for a long time as a refuge to all those Hungarians who either chose the Byzantine Christianity or held on to the ancient Hungarian faith of HADUR, the Lord of Hosts, also called UR, a monotheist religion dating back to UR of SUMER.

1038.

In a special letter sent by a Frater Anselmus to the Doge of Venice, Transylvania, called "the Easternmost corner of the Hungarian Kingdom" was mentioned as the main source of salt for the Carpathian Basin. The salt mine of Désakna, near the fort of Dés, was referred to as "the royal salt mine of Dés'.

1064.

László of the House of Árpád received from his father the title "Prince of Transylvania". From this date on, during the rule of the House of Árpád /1000-1301/ every crown-prince carried this title, with the obligation to reside in Transylvania, either in Nagyvárad, Kolozsvár or Gyulafehérvár, and to take care of certain administrative, judicial and military duties.

1097.

Emperor Alexios Komnenos of Byzantium ordered the relocation of the Vlachs from the Chalkidiké peninsula to Pelopponesos. With this, the northward migration of the Vlachs, ancestors of the Rumanians, began.

1166

Manuel Komnenus of Byzantium assembled a large number of Vlachs south of the Danube river /today's Bulgaria/ in order to launch an attack against the Hungarian fortifications along the left bank of the river, and to take the rich Hungarian settlement of Hosszumező, known today as Campulung. /Translated from the Hungarian, meaning "long field"./

1167.

Though the invading forces were defeated, and the land between the Danube and the Southern Carpathians remained officially until the invasion of the Turks / end of the 15th century/ a territory of the Hungarian Kingdom, migrating Vlach herdsmen received permission to cross the Danube in search of pasture-lands. They settled first the Southern slopes of the Transylvanian Alps /Southern Carpathians/ under their own tribal rulers, thus slowly establishing their claim to the land which was later called VLACHIA or WALLACHIA, and was declared in 1878 the "Kingdom of Rumania".

1168.

The first German settlers from the Moselle region were brought in by King Géza II in order to fortify some "empty lands" in the South-East of Transylvania. These new settlers established themselves near the royal fort of Brassó.

1220.

King András II invited several other groups of German settlers into Transylvania, settling them in autonomous districts. The royal charter granting these lands to the German settlers stated that they were settled "on the frontier of Transylvania, facing CUMANIA, a land without inhabitants".

This Cumania, land without inhabitants, was the same land between the lower Danube and the Southern Carpathians, into which migrating Vlach herdsmen were previously allowed to settle. However, the Vlachs, being nomadic people, kept on roaming with their herds back and forth across the mountains. The CUMANS, another Scythian tribe, also related to the Hungarians, after not being able to invade the Carpathian Basin, established their country East of the Carpathians and ruled over Moldova and Vlachia until the invasion of the TARTARS /1250/.

1222.

King András II gave the "Golden Bull", the first constitution, to the people of the Hungarian Kingdom, establishing the autonomous district system in "all the countries of the Holy Crown", and thereby granting self-government in Transylvania for the Magyar, German and the special Székely districts. The Székelys, though they were also Magyars or Hungarians, enjoyed very special privileges as "border guards" since their early settling in the 10th century. The new royal decree only upheld and re-affirmed these privileges.

1234.

Pope Gregory IX sent a letter to Béla, Prince of Transylvania /later King Béla IV / asking him "in the name of God" to grant asylum to "those poor Vlach refugees" who wished to escape the harsh rule of the Cumans. The asylum was granted, and the first three groups of Vlach immigrants entered Transylvania from the South, and were settled, under their own chieftains, in the Forgaras, Hunyad and Bánság districts, on specially designated mountain-pastures called in the royal documents as "Silva Vlachorum", Forest of the Vlachs. These Vlach immigrants, who received asylum within the Hungarian Kingdom, and others who followed later, became the ancestors of the Transylvanian Rumanians. Officially they were called VLACHS, from which the Hungarian name OLÁH and the German name Wallach derived, in contradistinction to the Rumelians and later Rumanians who did not enter the Western culture-circle but stayed East and South of the Carpathians under Byzantine and later Slavic influence, finally evolving at the end of the nineteenth century into Rumania.

1241.

The Tartar invasion, led by Batu Khan, swept through Hungary. King Béla IV lost the battle of Mohi, and fled to Austria. After the Tartars left, the king returned in 1242, and began to rebuild the devastated country. Several districts, especially on the Great Hungarian Plain, were left without population, making it possible for Serbians, Vlachs and Slovaks to seep into some of these empty lands, and establish a few scattered settlements.

1247.

New Vlach refugees gained permission to enter the Hátszeg and the Mármaros districts in Transylvania.

1253.

Guillaume Rubruquis, French envoy to Bulgaria, described the empire of Zar Michael Aszen as "reaching from the Danube river to Konstantinopel, including Vlachia in the lower Balkan Mountains." Vlachia therefore still existed at that time on the Balkan, under Bulgarian domination, while those Vlachs who tried to move Northward by crossing the Danube, fell under the rule of the Cumans.

1290.

Three Hungarian landowners in the Transylvanian districts of Hunyad and Fehér received permission from King András III to bring in some Vlach laborers "from South of the mountains."

1291.

The Assembly of Gyulafehérvár recognized the Transylvanian Vlachs as a "nation", with rights equal to other member nations under the Holy Crown.

1314.

After the downfall of Cumania, the Hungarian king Charles Robert incorporated two Vlach principalities /voievodines/ "across the mountains" into the "lands of the Holy Crown". The two new principalities were named MOLDOVA and WALLACHIA.

1358.

Mark, royal archivist wrote in his chronicles concerning Transylvania: "It is the richest part of the Hungarian Kingdom" where "Hungarian and Saxon /German/ cities bloom with industry and commerce, while the fertile lands of Hungarian farmers produce good wine, fat cattle, and plenty of grain for bread. High upon the mountains Vlach herdsmen tend to their sheep, and bring down good tasting cheese to the market places."

1385.

A new influx of Vlach immigrants was settled into the Szilágy district, establishing ten villages on the royal estate of Aranyosmedgyes.

1443.

Under the leadership of János Hunyadi, Duke of Transylvania, the combined armies of Hungarian, Polish, Bosnian and Serbian Crusaders defeated the invading Turks, and Serbia was freed. A.B. Yolland writes in his book "History of Hungary" Chapter X, page 64: "Hungary was indeed fighting the battles of Christendom, and the admiration of the Christian World was lavished on her soldiers." /See Bibliography./

1456.

János Hunyadi won a second victory over the Turks at Nándorfehérvár /today known as Belgrade/. In order to commemorate this decisive victory of Christianity over the Pagans, the Pope decreed that all church bells were to be rung from then on each day at noon, throughout the Christian world.

1458.

Mathias Corvinus, son of János Hunyadi, was elected king of Hungary. Under his rule Hungary again became one of the great powers of Europe. His birth-house in Kolozsvár /today Cluj/ was honored as a national shrine until the Rumanian occupation of Transylvania in 1919.

1471.

The first book in the Hungarian language was printed by a Transylvanian Hungarian printer.

1505.

Vatican census estimated the total population of Hungary to be about four million souls, of which 77% were Hungarians, and the rest Germans, Croatians, Slovaks, Serbians and Vlach. /At the same time the total population of England was four million also, while that of the Austrian Empire, including Bohemia and Silezia, five million, and that of France eight million./

1516.

The first Protestant /Calvinist/ congregation was established in Nagyenyed. /Today the Rumanians call it Aiud./ From here on Protestantism spread rapidly throughout Transylvania.

1526.

The invading Turks defeated the army of King Louis II in the tragic battle of Mohács, where the king himself fell. Hungary was split up into three parts. While the central part was occupied by the Turks for 150 years, the Western section and the Northern section of the country fell into the hands of the Habsburgs, who claimed their right to the Holy Crown or Stephen's Crown on the female line, but refused to uphold the constitution for which the Crown was the symbol. Only the Eastern part, including Transylvania carried on the traditions of an independent Hungary, under freely elected Dukes, until 1690. Many historians refer to this era as the "Independent Transylvania", forgetting that in reality Transylvania was the only free part left of Hungary, a last fortress between the Habsburgs and the Turks, where the elected Dukes, exercising the office of the king, kept the peace by wisely balancing their diplomatic relations with both sides, according to the demands of necessity.

1545.

Gáspár Heltai published the complete Hungarian translation of the Bible in the city of Kolozsvár, which not only served as the Hungarian capital but also as the new cultural center. A few years later Tinódi Lantos Sebestyén published his famous "Chronicles in Verses."

1556.

The Hungarian Congress of Torda /today called Turda by the Rumanians declared freedom of religion, stating in the new law that "everyone may follow the religion of his choice, and no one may interfere with persons professing any other faith". It was the first such law in the world.

1561.

The four Gospels of the New Testament were translated into the Vlach tongue, and published at the expense of the Hungarian landowner Miklós Forró of Brassó, thereby marking the birth of the Vlach /Rumanian/ literature.

1568.

The Reverend Ferenc Dávid established the Unitarian Church in Transylvania. Even today, though the Unitarian religion is widely spread all over the world, the center of the church is still in Transylvania, where the Unitarian Bishop resides as the successor of the founder of the church, Ferenc Dávid.

1570.

The duke Kristóf Báthory established in Gyulafehérvár the first Vlach printing shop in order that "culture may spread among those poor mountain-dwellers."

1576.

The Transylvanian duke Stephen Báthory became king of Poland, creating a Polish-Hungarian alliance against the Habsburg empire.

1582.

The Hungarian nobleman Ferenc Geszthy financed the translation and publication of the Old Testament in the Vlach /Rumanian/ language.

1586.

There were 18 Transylvanian Hungarian students enrolled at the Wittenberg University, and by 1640 more than 500 Transylvanians received diplomas from Wittenberg and Lynden. In the same time several world-famous scientists were teaching in Transylvanian colleges, such as Martin Opitz from Germany, John Alsted from England, Henry Bisterfeld and Isaac Basire from France.

1598.

There were 44 printing establishments working in Transylvania, producing up to this date 380 books of which 18 were in German, 6 in Latin, 4 in Vlach, and the rest in the Hungarian language.

1600.

Michael, voievod of Wallachia, invaded Transylvania from the South, ravaging Hungarian towns and villages, until General Basta, commander of the Imperial forces of Rudolf Habsburg, defeated him. This was the first terrifying encounter of the defenseless Hungarian population with the cruel Vlach /Rumanian/ savagery, of which they had to endure so much in later centuries.

1603.

Under Habsburg auspices, the military terrorism of General Basta devastated a large part of Transylvania by massacring entire villages in order to "exterminate all the Protestants."

1604.

Radu, Vlach voievod, received permission from Rudolf Habsburg to enter the country with his entire tribe and take possession of the devastated lands. However, the same year Duke István Bocskay and his famous Székely cavalry freed Transylvania as well as the Northern part of Hungary from the marauding Habsburg forces. Radu was ordered out of the country. Nevertheless, some of his people were allowed to remain, and build new Vlach /Rumanian/ villages in the central region of Transylvania.

1658.

Census taken by the Jesuit Fathers showed the total population of Transylvania as 860,000 souls, of which about 240,000 were Vlachs.

1659.

A Tartar invasion from the East devastated the main Szamos valley.

1664.

A new influx of Vlach /Rumanian/ immigrants entered from Moldova, brought in by Hungarian landowners to settle on the empty lands of the Szamos valley.

1690.

Emperor Luitpold Habsburg of Austria conquered Transylvania, abolished the Hungarian constitution, and turned the country into a province of Austria. The persecution of the Protestants began anew. Clergymen and schoolteachers were killed or tortured and sent to the galleys in the Mediterranean, where they died as slaves. With this, the last stronghold of the constitutional Hungarian Kindgom, Transylvania, fell into the clutches of Habsburg absolutism. All constitutional rights of the established nationalities as well as the established Protestant churches were revoked. One year later, Emperor Luitpold I officially terminated the Transylvanian principality and incorporated it as a province into the Austrian empire.

1698.

The Greek Catholic Church, known as "Uniate Church" was created through mutual agreement of Emperor and Pope. All Greek Orthodox congregations throughout the Empire were requested to join. Those who refused to join were deprived of all contacts with their mother-church across the borders.

Prof. Haraszti writes in his book "The Ethnic History of Transylvania" /Danubian Press, 1971/ on page 87: "The appearance of the Uniate Church, which was actually a handshake between Catholicism and Byzanthinism at the expense of Protestantism, represented an alliance between the Imperial conquerors and the Wallachian subjects against the Protestant Magyars. The 'Divide et Impera' policy, which became a very typical Habsburg tactic in the nineteenth century, appeared for the first time in the eighteenth century in Transylvania, with this classic example."

J. Slavici, Rumanian historian writes in his book "Ardealul, Studiu Istoric", published in 1893: "The only cultural institution of the Rumanians ..." /meaning the Vlachs or Wallachians, since in the 17th and 18th centuries the word "Rumanian" had not yet been created/ "... was the Greek Orthodox Church, which stood under complete Balkan-Slavic influence. Even its official language was the Slavic. Thus the era of national consciousness began only when half of the Transylvanian Vlachs converted into the Greek Catholic religion, and our priests were able to study in Rome and Vienna." /pages 95-96/ Eugene M. Osterhaven writes on the same subject in his book "Transylvania, The Pathos of a Reformation Tradition" /Western Theological Seminary, Holland, Michigan, 1968/ on page 18: "However, two thirds of the Transylvanian Rumanians resumed Orthodoxy by the mid-eighteenth century in spite of Habsburg attempts to keep them in the Roman fold."

C.A. Macartney states in "Hungary and Her Successors" /Oxford University Press, 1937/ page 261: "The Wallachian mass lived with one foot in Hungary. Most of them were shepherds, whose periodical migration on the high mountains took them regularly across the frontiers. Most of the Transylvanian Wallachians saw Wallachia and Moldova as their real homeland, and even the agriculturalists decamped readily across the Carpathians if times were hard - just as they immigrated, as casually, when conditions were severe in Wallachia or Moldova."

1703.

Under the Duke Ferenc Rákóczi II the Hungarian people revolted against Habsburg oppression. During this famous liberty war which lasted for eight years, many of the Vlach settlements, intigated by Habsburg agents, turned against their Hungarian hosts and neighbors, looting, burning, and massacring defenseless women and children.

1711.

The liberty war against the Habsburgs ended in defeat. Thousands of Hungarians who fought for liberty were executed, imprisoned or deported to forced labor. Those who proved to be loyal to the Habsburg throne were rewarded by royal grants to the properties of those who were found in treason. Considerable landholdings were given this way, mostly in the central parts of Transylvania, to Vlachs /Rumanians/ who led the bloody raids against defenseless Hungarian towns and villages.

1718.
The last strip of Hungary, the Banat, was freed from the Turks. According to contemporary reports, in the entire territory, which supports today nearly one-million people, there were no more than about 700 persons to be found alive.

1719.
From Vlachia /or Wallachia/ still under Turk domination, a steady stream of refugees began to migrate into the empty land of the Banat, as well as into other parts of Transylvania, where they were settled by special "Imperial decree" of the Emperor Charles III on lands confiscated from Hungarians for their participation in the liberty war.

1729.
Inocentius Micu Klein, Greek Catholic bishop, demanded for the Transylvanian Vlachs equal rights with other nationalities under the Crown. Emperor Charles III refused the demand on the grounds that "the Crown recognizes only subjects of different tongues and different religious denominations, not nationalities." Bishop Micu Klein was the first to use the word "RUMUN" instead of Vlach, and to claim LATIN origin. Until then the popular concept accepted the Slavic origin of the Vlachs, based on the use of the Slavic language in the Greek Orthodox Church as well as on the fact, established by several linguists /including Prof. Cihac, Rumanian linguist of the XX century/ that 48% of the Rumanian language consisted of Slavic words and only 31% of the Latin.

1766.
Empress Maria Therezia, following the advice of her Transylvanian governor, extended the system of "Military Frontier Privileges", enjoyed previously only by the Skékely districts, to three Vlach districts also. This enabled Peter Áron, Bishop of the Greek Catholic Church, to establish from public funds the first Vlach highschool, and the first Vlach seminary.

1784.
The Transylvanian Hungarian Assembly in Kolozsvár petitioned Emperor Joseph II to recognize the Vlachs as a "nation". Instead, the Emperor abolished even the rest of the Transylvanian constitution, dissolving the "three nation" concept. Two months later the "Vlach rebellion", led by Horia, Closka and Crisan, ignited the Central Mountain districts and the lower Maros valley.

Hugh Seton-Watson writes about it in his book "Eastern Europe" /Archon Books, England, 1962/ on pages 59-60: "Rumanian historians are inclined today to treat this as a nationalist rising. But the movement was essentially a social revolt of the peasant masses against the structure of the feudalistic Monarchy. The rebellion brought unprecedented horror to Hungarian towns and villages. Drunk Vlachs ruthlessly tortured, maimed and murdered thousands of men, women and children. Well informed sources claimed that Horia, the master-mind of the rebellion, received instructions in Vienna from the Emperor himself, who wanted to punish the 'rebellious Hungarians' for demanding the re-establishment of the Constitution and the Congress. Though the leaders of the rebellion were finally executed by the Austrian troops, the villages where the Hungarian population was wiped out were donated by special decree to the same Vlachs who did the killing. Another example of the Habsburg methods of playing one nationality group against the other."

1815.

The spirit of the French revolution penetrated the borders. The Hungarian National Assembly, finally granted by a reluctant Emperor Francis I demanded among others the re-unification with Transylvania. The Emperor rejected the demand. C. A. Macartney writes of this era in his book "Hungary" /Edinburgh, University Press, 1962/ on page 103: "The system of government in all of the Habsburg provinces was autocratic. The Transylvanian Diet was indeed convoked regularly, but it was so tightly packed with ex-officio members as to forfeit any claim to represent the people. The military administration was purely authoritarian. The democratic evolution of the Transylvanian Principality could not continue under Habsburg domination."

1822.

According to the official /anti-Hungarian/ census, conducted by Austrian administrative officials the total population of Transylvania proper was 1,500,000 of which 250,000 were registered as Germans, 700,000 as Rumanians and 550,000 as Hungarians. A later research, conducted by the newly established Hungarian Academy of Sciences in 1947, proved that about 100,000 Hungarians who admitted mastering the German or the Rumanian languages also, were registered as Germans or Rumanians.

1847.

Both Houses of the Hungarian National Assembly passed unanimously the decision to reincorporate Transylvania into Hungary. However, negotiations with the Imperial Government on this subject became deadlocked.

1848.

The Hungarian Liberty War erupted under the leadership of Louis Kossuth. The Hungarian National Assembly proclaimed the Republic. Transylvania was re-united with the Mother-land. The Transylvanian Assembly in Kolozsvár voted in favour of equal rights for the Vlachs /Rumanians/. /See: M. Ghyka "A Documented Chronology of Rumanian

History" Blackwell, Oxford, 1941./

In spite of this, the Transylvanian Vlachs again launched a well organized attack against Hungarian towns and villages, in support of the Habsburg forces. "These Wallachians committed such dreadful crimes against the elderly, women and children," wrote Mme. Lebergere, an eyewitness, whose memoirs were later published in Paris, "that even the Austrians were ashamed at what was going on under their authority. The password was: total extermination of the Magyars!"

T. Karsa writes in "Remarks on the Daco-Roman theory", Toronto, 1964 page 4: "The Wallachian peasants totally exterminated the Hungarian population of Nagyenyed, Abrudbánya and Zalatna. They annihilated one half of the Hungarian population in the district of Hunyad."

1849.

In spite of all the odds the heroic armies of the Hungarian Republic won every battle against the Imperial forces, until the new Emperor, the 16 years old Franz Joseph I called upon the Czar of Russia for aid. One hundred thousand Russian troops stormed into the Carpathian Basin, and the Liberty War was crushed. On October 6, thirteen Hungarian generals were executed in Arad. Thousands of others were imprisoned. An era of brutal terror and oppression descended upon the country, called the "Bach Age", referring to Baron Alexander Bach, Imperial Minister of Internal Affairs.

1858.

In the conference of Paris the powers of Europe decided to establish the "United Principalities of Moldavia and Wallachia" under separate but identical administrations.

These two territories were under Turk domination, ruled by Sultan-appointed "hospodars", until 1829, when Russia received full control over them through the Treaty of Adrianople. The Czar became the Head of the Greek Orthodox Church and thereby the "Father of all Wallachians". However in 1854 Russia was forced to evacuate the two provinces and Austrian forces took over, until the "United Principalities of Moldavia and Wallachia" were established at the Paris Conference.

1862.

Sultan Abdul Aziz allowed the fusion of the two Vlach or Wallach administrative bodies. The union of the two provinces became recognized under the new name of RUMELIA - later changed into RUMANIA.

1866.

With the approval of France and Germany /Napoleon III and Bismarck/ the German Prince Charles of Hohenzollern-Siegmaringen was proclaimed king of Rumania, and a new independent country was born between Central Europe and the Balkan Peninsula.

1867.

Due to diplomatic pressure from without and the unique statesmanship of Ferenc Deák from within, emperor Franz Joseph I made peace with Hungary. Austria and Hungary became "equal partners" within the frame-work of the Austro-Hungarian dual monarchy. Constitutional parliamentary system was re-established. Transylvania again became re-united with Hungary. All "special national privileges were abolished, and the equality of all citizens proclaimed, irrespective of race, creed or language." /C.A. Macartney: Hungary and Her Successors, page 262./ The Constitution of Dec. 21, 1867 was the masterpiece of liberal ideologists. It contained the complete catalogue of the *basic human rights*, limited the power of the government, introduced the responsibility of the cabinet, and contained directives concerning the equality of all nationalities. /Haraszti: Ethnic History of Transylvania, page 114./ The well known Rumanian scholar, Onisifor Ghibu writes in his book "Viata si organizatea bisericeasca si scolari in Transylvania" /1915/: "As an autonomous body, the Rumanian Greek Oriental Church in Hungary and Transylvania, by virtue of the rights ensured in 1868, administers, directs and manages independently its own ecclesiastical and educational affairs and trust funds in every respect ... school-inspectors have no authority over our schools ... parents are free to send their children to the school of their choice. In all Rumanian schools in Hungary and Transylvania the language of instruction is exclusively Rumanian."

1883.

Fearing Russia, the Kingdom of Rumania enters into alliance with the Austro-Hungarian Monarchy.

1907.

Peasants in Moldavia rebel against the cruel treatment they have to endure from Rumanian officials. The insurrection was put down by military force and martial law proclaimed throughout the Rumanian kingdom.

1913.

Rumania declared war on Bulgaria, and took Northern Dobrudja by force.

1914.

World War I erupted. In spite of the "Triple Alliance" /Germany, Austria-Hungary and Rumania/ Rumania proclaimed neutrality.

1916.

Based on promises to receive Transylvania, the Banat, and Southern Bukovina as booty, Rumania declared war on Austria-Hungary, and swept into Transylvania in a surprise attack. Within a few days the attack was repelled. Rumania was occupied by German forces and defeated.

1918.

March 5, Rumania signed the "Treaty of Bucharest", returning Dobrudja to Bulgaria, and giving up all claims to the Transylvanian passes. In October the Austro-Hungarian Monarchy collapsed. Rumania invaded Transylvania, and on Dec. 1 in a mass-meeting of 25,000 Rumanians in Gyulafehérvár /Alba Julia/ declared the "Union of Rumania with Transylvania" in the name of more than five million people who did not even know of the meeting.

Though the Hungarian and the German population strongly objected, the Rumanian army, instigated by the French, marched into Kolozsvár on Christmas Eve, in defiance of the Armistice, which stipulated that all military lines should freeze at their locations until further deliberations and agreements.

1919.

On January 19, Rumanian troops opened fire into a crowd of more than 30,000 unarmed Hungarians who gathered on the Mathias-Plaza in Kolozsvár to ask the representative of the Entente forces, the French general Berthelot, lodged in the hotel at the corner of the plaza, to order the Rumanians out of the city and back to the demarcation line, which was the Maros river. More than one hundred Hungarian demonstrators were killed, and more than a thousand wounded. In punishment for the demonstration Rumanian troops looted and ransacked the city.

Peter Pastor writes in "The Vix Mission in Hungary, 1918-1919, a Reexamination" /Slavic Review XXIX, No. 3 1970/ and in "Franco-Rumanian Intervention in Russia and the Vix Ultimatum: Background to Hungary's Loss of Transylvania" /1974/:

"The Vix Ultimatum, delivered to the Hungarians on March 20, 1919 by the head of the French Military Mission in Hungary, Lt. Colonel Ferdinand Vix, seemed to legitimize Rumanian occupation of Transylvania. The opening of the archives of the French Ministry of Foreign Affairs for 1918 and 1919 in the summer of 1972 shed new and startling light on the affair.... It is now evident that the ultimatum was prompted by a sudden crisis in southern Russia where Allied troops under French command were being defeated by the Red Army. To obtain quick reinforcements from neighbouring Rumania, the French Premier and Minister of War G. Clemenceau had to pay off the Rumanians at once with the Transylvanian territory they coveted..."

The documents of the French Ministry of Foreign Affairs make it quite clear now that Transylvania, as well as part of the Banat and part of the Great Hungarian Plain were given to Rumania by the French alone, in four separate chunks, with complete disregard of the Wilsonian doctrine of self determination, and without the knowledge and approval of the Governments of the United States and Great Britain in order to buy Rumanian support against Russia.

Already on January 27, 1919, the Peace Conference in Paris had adopted President Wilson's resolution against the use of armed force "to gain possession of territory, the rightful claim to which the Peace Conference is to be asked to determine." /Spector: Rumania at the Paris Peace Conference, page 80./Pastor writes in "Franco-Rumanian Intervention in Russia and the Vix Ultimatum: Background to Hungary's Loss of Transylvania", page 17: The Supreme Council referred Rumania's territorial claims to a 'Commission for the Study of Territorial Questions Relating to Rumania.' The eight-member panel of French, British, Italian and American experts was to examine Rumania's claims on its four neighbors - Russia, Serbia, Bulgaria and Hungary. *But the Rumanians disregarded both: Wilson's call for peace and the new commission. They continued to advance into Hungarian territory."* Thus, long before any decisions were made by the Peace Conference in regard of Rumania's territorial claim in Transylvania, Rumania with French encouragement took possession of Transylvania, the Banat and part of the Great Hungarian Plain. *Occupying lands with not one Rumanian inhabitant, whatsoever. Thereby deceiving the Governments of the United States, Great Britain and Italy, motivated by its own greed and by French desire to gain Rumanian military aid against Russia.*

1920.

By March 1920 all markers, street-signs, village-signs, railroad-signs etc. were torn down in the entire Rumanian-occupied territory and replaced by new signs in Rumanian language. Rumanian names were created for towns and villages with no Rumanian inhabitants. When the International Peace Commission came to inspect the new border-line proposed by France and Rumania, they were given the impression that not one single Hungarian inhabited the land.

On June 4, the Hungarian Government was compelled to sign the TREATY of TRIANON, by which the thousand year old Hungary was shorn of almost three-fourths of its territory, and two-thirds of its inhabitants.

However, on the insistence of the Allied Powers article 47 was included in the treaty, stipulating that Rumania pledge itself *to protect the interest of those citizens who differ from the majority of the population in respect of race, language or religion.*

However, by then more that 150,000 Hungarians mostly civil servants and teachers, were expelled from their native country and the "forced Rumanization of Transylvania began." /See: E. Osterhaven "Transylvania ..." page 19./

As a result of the Trianon Dictum from the 20,886,487 population of Hungary 13,271,370 were placed under the domination of other countries. Hugh Seton-Watson writes in "Eastern Europe Between the Wars" /Archon Books, 1962/ on page 300-301: *"The Hungarians became second class citizens in Transylvania*... Rumanian officials from across the mountains flooded the province..."

1923.

The Rumanian government executed a special land reform in Transylvania only, aimed against the Hungarians. A total of 2,718,146 acres of land was taken from Hungarians, mostly small landowners, and handed over to the Rumanian population and the Rumanian churches. /According to Rumanian statistics, prior to this land reform of the 5,461,200 acres of agricultural land in Transylvania only 1,904,635 acres were owned by farmers possessing more than 100 acres./

1924.

Discrimination against Hungarians increased. Prof. C. A. Macartney writes in his book "Hungary and Her Successors" page 322: Taxation has undoubtedly been discriminatory. Certain taxes exist which affect minorities almost exclusively. Hungarian shopkeepers, Hungarian professionals have to pay extra taxes for various reasons..."

Parallel with the economic persecution, the Rumanian government undertook an all-out offensive against Hungarian schooling. Hungarian, as a language of instruction, was abolished and its use strictly forbidden in all public schools. In many cases children were cruelly beaten for using their native tongue, even among themselves during the recess.

1925.

Protestant as well as Catholic parochial schools, some of them established in the 15th and 16th centuries, were closed down. The American Committee for the Rights of Religious Minorities reported: "The administrative oppression, the violent enforcing of the Rumanian language, the aggressive hostility... all these are aimed for the total destruction of the minority school system. The laws of 1925 serve as oppressive political and nationalistic tools against the minorities." /Religious Minorities in Transylvania, The Bacon Press, Boston, 1925./ While in 1911, under Hungarian rule, there were 2,813 public schools, in Transylvania in which Rumanian was the language of instruction, by 1925, five years after the Rumanian take-over, there was none left at all for the use of the Hungarian language. Transylvania's biggest Hungarian-language daily newspaper, the BRASSÓI LAPOK reported on December 14, 1925 from Csikjenőfalva, a 100% Hungarian community: "The new teacher, Mr. Clements Tratiu, who was sent recently by the government to teach in the purely Hungarian village of Csikjenőfalva, in his efforts to enforce the new language regulations handed out such beatings to his pupils that on the first day parents had to carry home twenty-four badly beaten children from the schoolhouse who were unable to walk."

1926.

The rigid censorship, instituted in 1919 toward all publications in Hungarian language was reinforced by two new laws. One of them required that even prayer-books and hymnals carry the stamp of approval of the State Censor before they could be printed, while the other prohibited the "import" of newspapers, magazines and other printed materials from Hungary, either by mail or otherwise.

1928.

A special delegation of Transylvanian Hungarians presented in Geneva to the League of Nations a 280 pages long list of grievances proving the breach of treaty on the part of the Rumanian government against the Hungarian people of Transylvania in 166 well documented cases. Rumania was reprimanded, and the Rumanian delegate promised redress. However, nothing happened. Members of the Hungarian delegation were taken off the train as soon as they crossed the border, detained, harassed under false pretenses, and their passports revoked.

1936.

The "Iron Guard", an extreme right-wing organization, secretly encouraged by Hitler's Germany, staged the first anti-Semitic and anti-Hungarian riots in Brassó /Brasov/, Nagyenyed /Aiud/ and Kolozsvár /Cluj/.

1939.

King Carol of Rumania declared full co-operation with the German Reich.

1940.

Rumania was forced to yield to the demands of the Soviet Union and evacuate Bessarabia as well as Northern Bukovina. Southern Dobrudja had to be returned to Bulgaria. In August of the same year the Axis powers at the request of the Rumanian government, and in order to avoid a Hungarian Rumanian military conflict, ordered the return of Northern Transylvania to Hungary, reuniting 1,200,000 Hungarians with their Motherland, while still leaving about 600,000 under Rumanian domination.

On August 19 of the same year there was a secret deliberation taking place between Dr. Jonel Pop, representing the Transylvanian Rumanians and Count Andor Teleki, representing the Hungarian government. Dr. Pop stated the propositions of the Rumanians in Transylvania in the following four possibilities:

1. Part of Transylvania to be returned to Hungary, followed by a population exchange.

2. The creation of an autonomous Transylvania, ruled by the three inhabiting nationalities, as part of the Rumanian Kingdom.

3. An independent Transylvania.

4. A Hungarian-Rumanian Federation under one king and composed of

three independent administrative units: Hungary, Transylvania and Rumania.

Dr. Jonel Pop, the aide of the ailing J. Maniu, declared that for the sake of a permanent solution the great majority of the Rumanians would accept any one of the above possibilities. Further deliberations were postponed until after the end of the war.

1941.

The German-Italian Officer's Commission, established for the supervision of the implications and applications of the provisions of the "Vienna Treaty" concerning the treatment of minorities, examined 387 complaints of abuses in Southern Transylvania committed by Rumanian authorities against the Hungarian population, and 26 complaints of Hungarian abuses against the Rumanians in Northern Transylvania.

1942.

Rumanian atrocities against Hungarians in Southern Transylvania reached the number of 1,372, while registered Rumanian complaints in Northern Transylvania numbered only 87. Cases examined by the Commission in Southern Transylvania included 273 murders, 687 severe beatings by the Rumanian police, the arrests of 48 Hungarian Clergymen, 6 newsmen and 317 professionals.

All Hungarian men in Southern Transylvania, between the ages of 17 to 45 were called into service by the Rumanian army, and sent under deplorable conditions into the labour camps of Bessarabia and Bukovina.

1943.

Though Rumania entered the war on June 22, 1941 as full-fledged ally of Germany, and recaptured with German aid Bessarabia and Bukovina from the Russians, after the German disaster at Stalingrad the Rumanian leaders engaged themselves in secret negotiations with the Allies.

At the same time the Hungarian Government attempted to make a separate peace with the West. However, the Teheran Conference /Nov. 28 1943 - Jan. 12, 1944/ brought about the unfortunate decision that Eastern and East-Central Europe, including Rumania, Hungary, Czechoslovakia and Poland constituted the "special sphere of regional interest" of the Soviet Union, therefore negotiations concerning these countries had to be pursued exclusively with the Soviet Union.

1944.

March 21. German forces occupied Hungary.

August 24, Rumania surrendered to and joined forces with the invading Russians. Together with Russian army regular Rumanian troops as well as guerilla-bands entered Transylvania, creating the most ferocious bloodbath in history. Thousands and thousands of Hungarians were killed, tortured, imprisoned and deported into forced labour camps.

According to eyewitness reports, from the city of Kolozsvár /Cluj/ alone, more than 24,000 Hungarians were herded together, beaten, tortured and deported. Within three months an estimated 200,000 Hungarians were moved out in this way from Transylvania, and placed into labour camps, mostly in the swamps of Dobrudja.

1945.

The Soviet Military Administration of Northern Transylvania was replaced by Rumanian administration. Mr. Zathureczky writes in his book "Transylvania, Citadel of the West" /Danubian Press, 1964/ page 52: "Stalin gave back Northern Transylvania to the Rumanians *under the condition that they would respect the rights of the ethnic groups.* With this step he introduced into Transylvania the Stalinist national policy. This policy consisted of the recognition of ethnic autonomies, and it was based on a federation of these autonomies. These autonomies are nationalistic in form, and socialistic in substance."

One of the conditions, under which the Russian Military Government returned the full administration of Transylvania to the Rumanians was *the setting up of two or more Autonomous Hungarian Districts* in order to secure complete self-administration to the Hungarian population of Transylvania.

This condition as well as many others pertaining to the basic rights of the Hungarians in Transylvania was never fulfilled by the Rumanian government.

1947.

On February 10 the Rumanian Peace Treaty was signed in Paris, officially declaring the return of Northern Transylvania to Rumania - in spite of American protest. Rumania again guaranteed the rights of the minorities.

On April 13 the Rumanian People's Republic was proclaimed.

On August 7 a new constitution was adopted, which again proclaimed equal rights and self administration to the national minorities. However, all religious and cultural organizations were subjected to State control. Roman Catholic opposition led to the arrest of the remaining bishops and to dissolution of all Roman Catholic organizations.

1949.

Lay leaders, priests, ministers of the Roman Catholic, Calvinist, Lutheran and Uniterian churches were imprisoned or sent to forced labour camps. *The Greek Catholic Church was liquidated by law.* The congregations of these parishes were automatically "returned into the Greek Orthodox Church and listed on census-sheets as "Rumanians" no matter to which ethnic group they belonged.

1950.

Under Soviet pressure the Rumanian government agreed to create an Autonomous Hungarian Region on the Territory inhabited by a compact Hungarian /Skékely/ population with the capital of Marosvásárhely -

Targu Mures. In this "autonomous" region, however, the official language remained the Rumanian, the top administrative offices were held by Rumanians, sent there directly from Bucharest, and the police force was kept 100% Rumanian. Those Hungarians who dared to object, were deported into the ill-famed labour camps in the Danube delta.

1956.

Following the uprising in Hungary, the Rumanian Government availed itself of the opportunity to order new mass-arrests throughout Transylvania. Though only seventeen Hungarians were executed - besides Imre Nagy, premier of Hungary for those few glorious days of freedom and his entourage who were handed over by the Russians for "safekeeping" - more that 200 died from the beatings during the interrogation, and about six thousand received heavy prison sentences in Kolozsvár /Cluj/ alone. George Bailey, American journalist, described the situation in THE REPORTER on November 1964: "After the Hungarian revolution thousands of Hungarians were arrested in Transylvania, perhaps hundreds put to death. In one trial alone in Cluj thirteen out of fifty-seven accused were executed. This year /1964/ some eight thousand political prisoners were released with considerable fanfare by the Government in a general amnesty."

M. Eugene Osterhaven /The Present Situation of Hungarians in Transylvania, Western Theological Seminary, Holland, Michigan, 1968, page 34/ adds to this: "... but as far as I could ascertain / in 1968/ in my recent travels through Transylvania, not one of the Hungarians arrested during the revolt has yet been released."

1959.

The Hungarian University of Kolozsvár /Cluj/ and the Hungarian high schools all over Transylvania became absorbed by their Rumanian counterparts. Thus Hungarian higher education was abolished in Transylvania. Several members of the Hungarian faculty were driven to suicide. /See: "Der Spiegel" No. 45, October 31, 1966. Also: "National Minority Problems" by George Hay in Kurt, London, ed. of Eastern Europe in Transition, The John Hopkins Press, Baltimore, 1966, page 133. Also: The New York Times, June 10. 1959./

The Hungarian Institute of Medicine and Pharmacy, located in Marosvásárhely /Targu Mures/ lost its autonomy. /See: Robert R. King "Minorities Under Communism", Harvard University Press, Cambridge, 1973, pages 153-154./

1960.

The Rumanian Government removed two districts from the Autonomous Hungarian Province, both with 92% Hungarian population, and attached them to a Rumanian populated district, while adding to it in exchange another large area with 88% Rumanian population, thus trying to weaken the Hungarian majority of the Hungarian province. The name was also changed from "Autonomous Hungarian Province" to "Autonomous Hungarian-Mures Territory."

1963.

Edward Crankshaw reported in his article "Hungarian Minority Fears Rumanian Axe" /The New York Herald Tribune, Apr. 15, 1963./ that Hungarian families are being deported in mass from purely Hungarian districts of Transylvania into other parts of Rumania, mostly to the Danube delta, into huge labour camps, where they die by the hundreds due to lack of food and medical care.

It is being noted also, that those deported or "re-settled" under the pretense of job opportunities - already more than 200,000 people - are immediately stricken from the official records in Transylvania, while in their new locations they are listed by the census takers as Rumanians. The Rumanization of Transylvania was so successful, that in September 1963, when Mr. Georghiu-Dej, party-boss and prime minister visited the so-called "Autonomous Hungarian Territory" and the Rumanian newspapers reported the names of the officials of the territory - there was not one single Hungarian name among them!

1964.

The International Commission of Jurists examined the Transylvanian minority problem, and published a report entitled "The Hungarian Minority Problem in Rumania". In this report the Commission stated among others that "Rumania ignores the political clauses of the Peace Treaty, and its own constitution, Art. 82, which clearly provides that 'all national groups are entitled to use their respective languages and to have at all levels establishments of public education in which instruction is given in their mother tongue, and further that the spoken and written language used by administrative and judicial authorities in districts where a national group other than Rumanian is in the majority should be the language of this national group. Civil servants in such areas should be appointed from among the members of this majority group...' This commission found that Rumanian administrative measures, and discrimination in the cultural field, *is actually leading to the final genocide of minorities in Transylvania."*

On July 4, the same year, the LE MONDE in Paris, France reported of a new wave of deportations from the Hungarian districts in Transylvania to the Danube delta. The same paper estimated the number of Hungarians forced to live in Bucharest alone to 250,000, *a figure not included in the official data of any census.*

On August 8: "Due to the de-Magyarization policy of the Rumanian government of forcibly removing Hungarian families from their native districts and deporting them or forcing them to locate in Moldavia, Dobrudja, even

Bucharest or any one of the former Vlach provinces, it seems that 35 to 50 percent of the Transylvanian Hungarians are no longer living in their native land. The vacated houses of the deported or removed Hungarian families are filled with Rumanian families imported from across the Carpathians in order to change the ethnic balance of the purely Hungarian districts. According to Government orders wherever there are two pupils in a Hungarian language school who do not speak that language, the language of the entire school must be changed into Rumanian. Thus, with the settling of these newcomers, all Hungarian language grade-, middle-, and high-schools are being abolished, one by one..." CONGRESSIONAL RECORD, August 8, 1964./

On November 1964 George Bailey wrote in THE REPORTER: "Rumanian has effectively replaced Hungarian at every level as the language of official and public life... Hungarians are intimidated, they are scared to use their native tongue. The Rumanian authorities have adopted a wide variety of measures to isolate the Hungarian population from contact with the homeland. Foreign tourists in Rumania are allowed the run of the country, unless they happen to be Hungarian citizens..."

Robert R. King wrote in "Minorities Under Communism" /Harvard University Press, Cambridge, 1973/ pages 156-157: "The 1964 redistricting of the Magyar Autonomous Region into Mures-Magyar Region increased the Rumanian population of the district from 146,830 /20%/ to 266,403 /35%/ while decreasing the number of Hungarians from 565,510 /77%/ to 473,154 /62%/."

1966.

CARE Packages and other aids sent by American, Canadian, Australian or West European church organizations, charitable institutions or private individuals to starving Hungarian families in Transylvania, or to Transylvanian Hungarian Churches were confiscated by Rumanian authorities.

1967.

On October 12 the Mures-Magyar Autonomous Region became liquidated. The previous 16 regions were rearranged nto 40 districts and 2,706 communes. The aim was to mix as many Rumanian inhabited regions with Hungarian regions as geographically possible, thus lowering the percentage rate of Hungarians within the administrative units. *"The chauvinistic policy of Rumania ... disregards all human rights and international obligations solemnly agreed upon and promised in peace treaties..."* /Osterhaven: Transylvania, page 40/

On December 3, 1967. the NEUE ZÜRCHER ZEITUNG, Switzerland, reported that in the "Hungarian populated areas of Transylvania the presence of the secret police is still strong. Political opponents /of Mr. Ceaucescu/ and troublesome intellectuals are put behind bars without delay..."

1974.

The "Handbuch Europaischer Volksgruppen" /Reference Book on European Ethnic Groups/ estimated the Hungarian population of Transylvania as two millions.

On November 2, 1974, Act 63 of the Socialist Republic of Rumania amended Law 472/1971, ordering the "nationalization of all documents, books, letters, pictures, art objects, etc, in possession of religious and cultural institutions or private citizens."

This amendment of the law was another decisive step toward the complete Rumanization of Transylvania by eliminating all traces of a Hungarian past, and thus clearing the way for a new, falsified history, already in the making.

1975.

On February 1, the NEUE ZÜRCHER ZEITUNG, Switzerland, reported under the title "Bureaucratic Chicanery Against the Churches in Rumania" that "The intent behind the nationalization of the ecclesiastical archives is to sever the religious communities from their historical roots. A church without a past /tradition/ has no future, especially one which represents a religious and national minority at the same time ... *the Rumanian government has openly embarked on an escalated campaign against the Church and the Hungarian minority.*" "The above mentioned outrages form a part of a systematic effort to re-write Rumanian history ..." /Human Rights Violations against the Hungarian Minority in Rumania, a Committee for Human Rights publication, 1976./

At the same time THE FINANCIAL TIMES reported: "A favourite device is to 'facelift' the tombs and crypts of famous Hungarian families in the Medieval Házsongárd cemetery in Cluj /Kolozsvár/ by allotting them to recently dead Rumanians. In this way the ethnic composition of the former population, now dead, is restructured favourably..."

Also The Financial Times reported on Apr. 2 1975 under the title "Transylvania's Ethnic Strains" that at least 25 students are required to set up a minority class in any school, while a Rumanian class has to be set up as soon as there are two Rumanian speaking students. This report refers to Law 278/1973 which calls for the merger of classes with insufficient numbers of students, and provides that every community with Rumanian speaking students, no matter how few, must establish a Rumanian section. Since most rural villages in Transylvania have only 500 to 1,000 inhabitants, there may very possibly not be enough Hungarian students for a separate class /25/. As a result of this law the merger necessarily occurs at the expense of the Hungarian section, even if the population of that village is 90% Hungarian.

Protests concerning the oppression of and the gross discrimination against the Hungarian minority in Rumania reached the United Nations

Division of Human Rights Office to be submitted to the Commission on Human Rights and to the Sub-Commission on Prevention of Discrimination and Protection of Minorities, in Geneva.

Thirty-eight members of the U.S. Congress condemned the treatment of the Hungarian Minority by the Rumanian Government, and asked President Ford to discuss with President Ceaucescu "the abridgement of human and civil rights of the ethnic and religious minorities in Rumania." /See: Congressional Record, May and June 1975. Also: "Documents on the Human Rights Violations Against the Hungarian Minority in Rumania Before the United Nations Human Rights Commission, The World Council of Churches and the United States Congress and Government" published by the American Hungarian Federation, Washington, D.C. 1975./

Prof. G. Satmarescu, Rumanian author and scholar, repudiated the published figures of the Rumanian census by estimating the number of Hungarians in Transylvania at 2.5 million. ("The Changing Demographical Structure of the Population of Transylvania", East European Quarterly, University of Colorado, 1975.)

1976.

In Rumania, the "Law on National Cultural Patrimony" nationalized all "documents, official and private correspondence, memoirs, manuscripts, maps, etc. that are more than 30 years old" regardless of ownership. Thus, the archives of all Hungarian and German schools, churches and cultural institutions were confiscated and methodically destroyed. (See: Foreign Report, 1976, published by the Economist Newspaper Ltd., London, England.)

In June 1976 a joint Memorandum of the American Hungarian Federation and the Transylvanian World Federation was presented to the United States Congress, asking for the withdrawal of the "Preferred Nation" status granted to Rumania previously, until that government fulfilled its obligations toward the minorities as outlined in the peace treaties as well as the Constitution of the Socialist Republic of Rumania. (See: Congressional Record, June 1976.)

In July protests against the blatant oppression of minority churches and ethnic groups in Rumania were entered to the United Nations, and the World Council of Churches Assembly at Nairobi, Africa, by Bishop Dr. Zoltán Béky, representing the American Hungarian Federation and the Transylvanian World Federation.

The Committee for Human Rights in Rumania demonstrated repeatedly against the Rumanian government in New York and Washington, D.C., demanding the investigation of minority grievances in Rumania.

In October 1976, the United States Government asked the Government of the Socialist Republic of Rumania to grant permission, in accordance with the Helsinki Agreement to a special investigating committee to enter Rumania and investigate the alleged human rights violations and discriminations against minorities. **The Rumanian government refused to grant the permission.**

1977.

From the 32 high schools, 626 seven-year basic schools and 1,256 four-year basic schools relying on the Hungarian language in Transylvania not one single institute was left in operation. Those who objected to the closing of the Hungarian schools suffered extreme cruel treatment by the hands of the Rumanian police for "resisting the trend of Rumanization" and "agitating against the interest of the Rumanian people". During the year, 67 Hungarian educators and 117 students were arrested and beaten to death or driven to suicide.

On September 10, 1977, Karoly Király, prominent member of the Hungarian minority in Transylvania, member of the Central Committee of the Rumanian Communist Party, wrote three letters accusing the Ceaucescu government with breach of the Constitution and acts against the principles of Socialism in the treatment of the Hungarian minority. These letters became public, Mr. Kiraly was arrested, disciplined and banished, without any legal procedure, to another part of the country. (See: The Times, The Guardian, and the Frankfurter Allgemeine Zeitung of Jan. 24, 1978, Le Monde, Jan. 25, 1978, and The New York Times of Feb. 1, 1978. Also: Amnesty International and Financial Times.)

In October 1977, the last of the Hungarian speaking Roman Catholic priests serving the Hungarian minority settlement in the province of Moldova, known as the "CSANGO", was forcibly removed, and all Hungarian churches in the region shut down. In spite of the official policy of the Kádár regime of avoiding controversies within the Communist Block, the forced Rumanization of the 200-250,000 Hungarians in Moldova was strongly criticized by Gyula Illyes, prominent Hungarian writer in Budapest.

During the 1977 earthquake some 80 Hungarian churches, some of them dating back into the 15th and 16th centuries, located in an overwhelmingly Protestant district of Transylvania were seriously damaged. News about these damages were suppressed by the Rumanian authorities. When Hungarian church groups in Western Europe, the United States, Canada and Australia were alerted, and substantial financial aid sent for the repair of the damaged churches, all donations were confiscated by the Rumanian government, and used for the repair of Rumanian buildings.

1978.

The propaganda-campaign, aimed to create the illusion of a homogeneous Rumanian population and a continuous Rumanian presence in Transylvania for two thousand years, increased in proportions within

Rumania as well as abroad. New books were published by the Rumanian government in Rumanian as well as in foreign languages in which the entire history of East-Central Europe, focusing on Transylvania, is re-written in order to serve Rumanian political interest, namely to underscore Rumania's claim to Transylvania.

Minority children are taught in the Rumanian schools that the cultural riches of Transylvania are the sole result of Rumanian creativity, and the "foreign intruders" - meaning the Hungarians and Germans - only destroyed ancient Roman cultural treasures, did not contribute anything. The aim is to make minority children ashamed of their nationality. Reference made by Hungarian teachers or parents to Hungarian cultural achievements of the past, result in arrest, torture and imprisonment. (See: "The Kunszabo Report" farther in this book.)

Paul Goma, Rumanian dissident author, now living in France (not of Hungarian descent) testified at an international press conference on human rights held in Frankfurt, Germany, that "interrogation, threat and torture can be expected in Rumania today by those who give the smallest sign of being Hungarian."

1979.

February: 250 French writers and scholars, among them **Aaron Raymond,** the well known historian and sociologist; **Pierre Daix,** outstanding member of the French Communist Party ; **Paul Thibaud,** editor-in-chief of the review "Esprit"; Jean-Marie Domenach, Andrei Bukovski, Natalia Gorbanevszlaia and many others presented a memorandum to the French President **Giscard d'Estaing,** in which they denounced the "inhuman and deplorable treatment" of Europe's largest and most oppressed minority, the Hungarians of Transylvania. They implored the President to send a protest note to the Rumanian government and demand that the "national rights of the Transylvanian Hungarians" be respected. The memorandum states that the "forced Rumanization program" of the Ceausescu regime has hundreds of Hungarian victims already, who did not survive the beatings, and there are several thousand imprisoned for refusing to give up their Hungarian heritage.

II. RESEARCH

THE EARLY HISTORY OF TRANSYLVANIA

by Eugene Horváth Ph.D.

/Reprinted from the book "Transylvania and the History of the Rumanians" with the permission of the publisher. Dr. Horváth served as professor of history at different Universities in Hungary, Germany and France before World War I./

I. Transylvania before the Magyars.

According to the evidence of prehistoric remains, Transylvania in very early times, was an inhabited region. The Greek historian, Herodotus, states that the first people known in Transylvania, the Agathyrs, dwelt along the river Maros. Later they were absorbed by the powerful Dacians, a race of Celtic origin, which was conquered by the Emperor Trajan sometime between A.D. 101 and A.D. 107. Thus Transylvania became a Roman Imperial province (*Dacia provincia Augusti*). In their battles against the Dacians the Romans approached the line of the river Maros from the south, and they therefore chose Sarmizegethusa, the centre of Dacian power, as the capital of the new province. The rest of Transylvania did not surrender until a later time when it was divided into three parts (*Dacia Apulensis, Malvensis, and Porolissensis*). The new province was, on the one hand, a rampart of the Roman Empire projected far out towards the south-east and, on the other, a valuable asset to the Empire because of its rich gold mines. These obviously, were the considerations which led the Roman authorities to exploit the treasures of the distant province with all speed and, at the same time, to restrain the population of Italy from venturing into a country wedged in among unknown lands and barbarian peoples. When fierce attacks from the East began to assail the Empire the Emperor Aurelian evacuated the province and, surrendering it, withdrew (271-75) to a more easily defended line. From that time forward Dacia ceased to signify Transylvania and became the line of the Lower Danube (*Dacia Ripensis and Mediterranea*).

It is upon this Roman rule of a mere century and a half[2] that the Rumanian inhabitants of Transylvania base their claim to unrestricted possession of that territory. Here it is not unimportant to remember that

2. The importance of Transylvania's history was the subject of a book by Count Anthony Széchen: As erdélyi történetirás jelentősége, Budapest 1887, and comprehensive histories of Transylvania were written by *Ladislaus Kóváry:* Erdély története, 6 vols. Pest and Kolozsvár, 1859-66. *Alexander Szilágyi:* Erdélyország története, 2 vols. Pest. 1866 and *Benedict Jancsó.* The latest work is that of *Professor Henry Marczali:* Erdély története. Budapest, 1935. No bibliography of Transylvanian history has yet been published, nor have the documents relating to it been compiled. *Teutsch and Firnhaber's* collection, Urkundenbuch zur Geschichte Siebenbürgens. Vienna, 1858, extends only to 1301 and is incomplete.

their claim was made before the scientific investigation of the question of *incolatus* was begun. Innocent Klein, Bishop of the Rumanian Greek Catholic Church, at a meeting of the Transylvanian Parliament in 1735, stated that it had been definitely ascertained that "We Rumanians have been autochthonous inhabitants since the days of Trajan."[3] He offered, however, no proofs to substantiate his statement. The dispute, therefore, may be traced back to that date (1735). Its history would fill a large volume, but hitherto, it has never been scientifically summarized or classified.

From the very beginning the Latin spoken by the Rumanians appeared in the same form as the Latin spoken in Italy in the sixth century, and it was marked by the same characteristics. This has lately been admitted by Rumanian historians, and their admission is a tactit endorsement of investigations which prove that it was not Transylvania, but Italy, whence the Rumanians came when first they appeared on the pastures of the Balkan Peninsula. The Greek inhabitants of that region gave them the name of herdsmen (Greek: *blachos, vlachos*). This name could scarcely have been given to Dacian Romans, for it had never been heard in Transylvania until the coming ot the Rumanians. Dacia was the happy hunting-ground of migrating barbarian races, and the last place-names which survived before the Magyars took possession can be proved to have been given by the Bulgars. On the other hand, the Rumanians of the Balkan Peninsula had no knowledge of the Latin and Roman names of Transylvania, for in the first thousand years of their sojourn in the Balkans they called themselves *Vlachs* and their country *Vlachia*, or *Valachia*. It was only later that the Rumanians discarded the name of *Vlach* and began to call themselves Rumanians and their country Rumania. In using the Hungarian name *Erdély* (Ardeal) for Transylvania, and Transylvania for Dacia, they were adopting the names given to the "lands beyond the forest" by the Hungarian State which had grown up in the territory bordering upon the rivers Danube and Tisza. It is therefore clear that the Rumanians must have entered Transylvania only after the

3. Books on the Roman rule. *Paul Király*, Dacia Provincia Augusti, 2 vols. Nagybecskerek, 1893 — 94., V. *Parvan*, Dacia. Recherches et découvertes archéologiques en Roumanie, 2 vols. Bucarest, 1924 — 25., Dacia. An outline of the early civilizations of the Carpatho-Danubian countries. Cambridge, 1928., V. *Vaschide*, Histoire de la conquête romaine de la Dacie et des corps d'armée qui y ont pris part. Paris, 1903.

Magyars had settled there.[4.]

In the period that elapsed between the Romans and the rule of the Magyars (275-895), i.e. in the early middle ages,[5.] the territory was overrun by Goths, Huns, Gepids, Longobards, Avars and Bulgars in turn. In Gothia, however (which was called Kaukaland), Hunnia, Gepidia, Longobardia, Avaria, and Bulgaria, no traces of Roman or Rumanian remains were left, the only vestiges being some belonging to the period of the migration of the peoples. The theories supporting the assumption that the Romans of Transylvania mingling with these barbarian races survived, may be set aside as arguments coined at a later date to prove Rumanian *incolatus*.[6.] Professor Seton-Watson argues that as no documents are forthcoming concerning the history of Transylvania between the time of the Roman Empire and the XIII century, there is no written evidence of Magyar occupation. This in no proof that from 895 onwards Transylvania was not part and parcel of the Hungarian State in the Danube Basin.[7.]

4. There is proof that the dispute regarding the origin of the Rumanians was begun by the statement of Bishop Klein in 1735. His pronouncement was based on a study of theology in Rome, which was made possible by the fact that, the Orthodox Greek Rumanians united with the Church of Rome in 1700. Bishop Klein's statement was the basis of the Rumanian political demands made in 1790 (*Supplex libellus Valachorum Transylvaniae*). These demands were hotly contested by contemporary historians (Bolla, Eder, Engel, Schlözer, etc.) and even more violently by the Slavs, e.g. Kopitar and Tökölyi, as well as by the Saxons of Transylvania; for in the pretext of Roman origin the Rumanians laid claim to estates belonging to Magyars and Serbs but more especially to the estates of the Saxons. It is a striking fact that the Bulgarians contest the Roman origin of the Rumanians on the grounds that when the former took possession of the reaches of the Lower Danube they found no inhabitants of Roman or Italian race there. On the contrary, the Rumanians of the Lower Danube were converted to the Daco-Roman theory by propaganda originating in Transylvania, after the union of the Churches had led to a campaign of Latinizing and Rumanizing there. The theory propounded by two Transylvanians George Sinkai and Peter Major was carried to Wallachia by Transylvanians, Trebonianu Laurianu and his disciple, Hilarion Pap, whose Rumanian history published in the fifties of the last century was refuted by *Robert Roesler*, Romänische Studien, Leipzig, 1871. The Hungarian school, which was represented by historians of such outstanding merit as *Paul Hunfalvy, Ladislaus Réthy* and *Benedict Jancsó*, followed in Roesler's footsteps.

5. A scientific history of medieval Transylvania has yet to be written. See *J. Deér's* essay. A középkori Erdély, Magyar Szemle XXII, pp. 194-205. Budapest, 1934.

6. The migration of the peoples. See *A. Alföldi*, A gót mozgalom és Dacia feladása. Budapest, 1930., Magyarország népei és a római birodalom, Budapest, 1934., *L. Homo*, Étude sur le règne de l'empereur Aurélien, Paris, 1904., *P. Horovitz*, Le problème de l'évacuation de la Dacie transdanubienne, Revue historique, CXLIX, pp. 82-90, Paris 1932., *G. Téglás*, Dácia megdőlésének története, Budapest, 1913. - For the Goths see *B. Rappaport*, Die Einfälle der Gothen in das Römischen Reich, Leipzig, 1898., *L. Schmidt*, Geschichte der deutschen Stämme bis zum Ausgang der Völkerwanderung. Die Ostgermanen, pp. 195-249, München, 1934. - For the Gepids see *C. C. Diculescu*, Die Gepiden. Forschungen zur Geschichte Daziens im früheren Mittelalter und zur Vorgeschichte des rumänischen Volkes, vol. I, Halle, 1922., Die Wandalen und die Goten in Ungarn und Rumänien, Leipzig, 1923., *Schmidt* op, cit. pp. 529-46. - For the Bulgars see *G. Tzenoff*, Die Abstammung der Bulgaren und die Urheimat der Slaven, Berlin, 1930.

7. "Veiled in impenetrable darkness for a thousand years." op. cit., p. 11 - The first Transylvanian document is dated 1165.

II. Transylvania at the time of the Árpáds. A.D. 895-1301.

Some historians hold the view that the Magyars invaded Transylvania from the east, but it is more highly probable that they entered the country by way of the Plain of the Tisza.[8.] This opinion is supported by evidence that the line of fortified earthworks serving as a defence was, in course of time, advanced in an easterly direction, and by the fact that the western parts of Transylvania were organized in a county system pointing to Hungarian administration, while the population of the eastern regions was chosen by the administration with a view to frontier defence.

Our sources of information indicate that the Magyars found no races other than the Bulgars in the river-valleys. The Bulgars retreated before them, and after the Magyars had established their kingdom, settled down on the right banks of the Danube and Save. They were accompanied by the Bulgar priests who had joined the Greek Church, and the place of the Orthodox Greek religion was taken by the Latin Church, a Latin bishopric being created by St. Stephen at Alba Julia, where Gyula, a Magyar leader, had established his headquarters on the ruins of a Roman settlement.

The peaceful possession of Transylvania was threatened in the Xth century by the approach of Bulgars - nomadic Petchenegs and Kuns - from the east. When finally their attacks were repulsed by St. Ladislas, the work of gradual colonization of their frontier districts and advancing the lines of earthworks was begun. Progressing from the north in a southerly direction the Germans of Beszterce and Naszód settled along the Transylvanian borders; to the south of them the land, as far as Brassó, was occupied by the Székelys. In the district of Bárca there were the Teutonic knights; to the west of the crown lands, at Fogaras, were Germans from the district of Szeben, and to the right of the latter, in the region of Szörény, the Knights of St. John formed settlements. In return for undertaking to defend the borders, the Székelys and Saxons were granted extensive privileges. This led to a system of administration different from that employed in the counties.[9.] Both races settled down in tribes, or groups, forming "seats"; but the word sedes, as they used it, changed its original meaning and signified a tribal settlement the word "seat" and settlement in this case being synonymous. These settlements for the defence of the borders, with their extensive autonomies, had access to the monarch through their leaders, the comes, who were royal officials. While the seven Transylvanian counties in the west possessed separate comes, in the east there were only two - one for the Székelys (comes Siculorum) and one for the Saxons (comes Saxonum). Thus the comes of the Székely and Saxon territories held dominion over wider areas than the comes of the counties, and their sphere of jurisdiction was also more exten-

8. For details see J. Karácsonyi, A honfoglalás és Erdély, Budapest. 1896., K. Tagány, A hogfoglalás és Erdély. Ethnographia. Budapest, 1890. - Compare with F. Maurer, Die Besitzergreifung Siebenbürgens durch die das Land jetzt, bewohnenden Nationen.

sive. As, however, the territory of the Magyar counties had been formerly a border-land, a border *voivode* was set over the counts of the seven counties. He was the same sort of royal official as the *comes* of the Székelys and the Saxons. In the histories of the Székelys[10] and the Saxons[11] we perceive an interesting development in the evolution of law[12] out of which, at a time when a Transylvania, ravaged by the Tartar invasion, was in course of reconstruction, there arose, by a process of natural evolution, the constitutions of the three Transylvanian "nations".[12.] It should be noted that "nation" in this case has a political, not a racial, significance. Racially the Székelys were Magyars, but politically they constituted a separate "nation". Statements to the contrary made by Rumanian writers must be regarded as attempts to create political conflict.

A separate paragraph must be devoted to the question of the two orders of chivalry - the Teutonic Knights, whose headquarters at that time were in the Holy Land, and the Knights of St. John (Hospitallers, Knights of Rhodes, and afterwards Knights of Malta). The Teutonic Knights received the district of Bárca from Andrew II in 1211, while the Knights of St. John received that of Szörény from Andrew's son, Béla IV in 1247. According to the royal charters,[14.] by which they were granted extensive rights similar to those enjoyed by the Székelys and Saxons, their settlement in those districts was designed to ensure a more effective frontier defence. When that purpose was no longer served, all their rights to these territories were lost. Such was the case with the Teutonic Knights in the district of Bárca, who began to exercise royal prerogatives on the estates received from the king. This circumstance, being contrary to Hungarian law, led to their expulsion in 1225, and resulted in a protracted lawsuit. The Knights, under the leadership of their Grand Master, Hermann Salza, withdrew to the Baltic territories where, undisturbed by the laws of the feudal German system, they were able to create a separate state. The state established by the knights was the beginning of what is now known as Prussia.

10. The documents relating to the history of the Székelys were compiled by *Charles Szabó, Louis Szádeczky,* and *Samuel Barabás:* Szekely oklevéltár. vols. I-VIII, 1211-1750, Kolozsvár, Budapest, 1872-1934. Their history was written by L. Szádeczky: A Székely nemzet történelme és alkotmánya, Budapest, 1927.

11. The documents relating to the history of the Saxons were published by *Zimmermann* and *Werner:* Urkundenbuch zur Geschichte der Deutschen in Siebenbürgen. vols. I-III, 1191-1415, Nagyszeben, 1892-1902. The history of the Transylvanian Saxons was written by *George Daniel Teutsch* and his son, *Frederick Teutsch* - both Lutheran bishops: Geschichte der Siebenbürger Sachsen. 6 vols. Brassó, 1852-58, 4th edition Nagyszeben, 1925-26.

12. The history of the evolution of law in Transylvania was written by *Schuler von Libloy:* Siebenbürgische Rechtsgeschichte, 2 editions 3 vols, Nagyszeben, 1827-68.

13. The rights of the Székelys were codified by the assemblies at Udvarhely in 1505 and Agyagfalu in 1506. The rights of the Saxons were determined by a royal charter (Andreanum), the renewal and recognition of which the Saxons were careful to obtain at later dates (1317, 1366, 1387, 1486, 1493, 1552, 1583, 1627).

14. L. Szentpétery, Az árpádházi királyok okleveleinek kritikai jegyzéke, vol. I, 1211: nos. 261, p. 84, 1224; 413, p. 135, 1247; 853, p. 257, Budapest, 1923.

The two settlements of Knights possessed in common a feature lacking in the other settlements. Their estates extended across the Carpathians into the Lower Danube territories which had been abandoned by the Bulgars. The Teutonic Knights of Bárca, for instance, crossed the mountains and on the southern slopes, built feudal castles, which still exist. After the knights had left the Saxons and Magyars spread in the same southerly direction. They created new settlements on the land on the Cumans, built towns and founded Latin churches there. In this way arose - beyond the Alps - (Transaplina), in the land of the Cumans (Cumania), Hosszúmező (German: Langfeld, Rumanian: Campolung), and thus began the Dominican missions[15.] and the gradual absorption of the Lower Danube territories into the sphere of interests of the Hungarian State. It was not without reason, therefore, that the king of Hungary in 1235 styled himself King of Cumania (Rex Cumaniae), or that he called Cumania his transapline kingdom. In 1235 the kingdom of Hungary actually extended to the Black Sea, the coasts of which then were in the possession of Genoese merchants.[16.]

The theory of Rumanian incolatus is disproved by a statement in the royal charter granted to the Saxons in 1224, according to which the Saxons who had settled down on the frontier of Transylvania facing Wallachia were given an unpopulated region (desertum). The royal charter makes no mention of any inhabitants whatsoever in those parts. The charter granted to the Knights of Bárca in 1211 states that the king gave the deserted Bárca territory to the Knights and the whole uninhabited region as far as the Danube (terra Borza desertata et inhabitata usque ad Danubiam). The Rumanian Kenezes referred to in the charter granted to the Knights of St. John in 1247 lived on the southern sloped of the Carpathians and not on Transylvanian soil. Those three royal charters there prove that at the time they were framed no Rumanian inhabitants whatsoever existed in the parts of Transyvlania minutely described in them. The assertion of Rumanian historians that Fogaras and Omlás were Rumanian principalities during the reign of the Árpáds is untenable as Hungarian political law did not recognize any sore of ducatus as representing feudal relations within the state, and because not only Magyar and Saxon, but also Rumanian witnesses testified in 1291 before the courts of justice (according to contemporary records) that Fogaras had always belonged to the Maygar family of Ugrim. Omlás was made over to the king by its Magyar owners in 1322.

There is proof that the origin of the Rumanians is not to be sought in

15. B. Altaner, Die Dominikanermissionen des XIII. Jahrhunderts, Breslau, 1924., K. Auner, A romániai magyar telepek történeti vázlata, Budapest., N. Pfeiffer, Die ungarische Dominikanerprovinz 1221-42, Zürich, 1917.

16. G. Bratianu: Recherches sur le commerce génois de la Mer Noire au XIII-e siècle, Paris, 1929.

Transylvania, but in the Balkan Peninsula, where, from the sixth century onwards they lived as emigrant Latin herdsmen from Italy, wandering gradually north, first to escape Greek, and later Bulgar, oppression. So insignificant were their numbers at the period when the King of Hungary took possession of Cumania, that little or no mention of their presence in the transalpine kingdom (regnum nostrum ultra Alpes) is made in contemporary documents.[17.]

This migration into Transylvania began in the year 1180 with the dissolution of the Eastern Roman Empire. After the death of the Emperor Emmanuel the Great the Byzantine Empire became the theatre of widespread internecine warfare. In consequence, the Bulgars and Serbs threw off the Greek yoke, under which they had hitherto been living, and created Bulgarian and Serb national Churches. They also formed Bulgarian and Serb national governments, which, in a spirit of natural reaction, turned against Greek influence. Thus it happened that the Rumanians, or as they were then called, Wallachians, who had migrated from Macedonia into Bulgaria to escape the rigours of Greek oppression, now began to move to the plains of the Lower Danube which the Cumans had deserted, in order to be free from the severity of Bulgarian national rule. They appeared on the left bank of the Danube as refugees who had lived under Greco-Slav influences, using the Greek alphabet and speaking the ancient Slav language. Having broken away from the Bulgarian national Church, they accepted the jurisdiction of the Ochrida Greek Church which allowed them wider liberties. Their names were Greek and Slav; the name "Dacia" was unknown to them. On reaching Cumania they either took service with the few Cumanians, Tartars, Saxons and Magyars they found there, or wandered on towards the north where, for the first time, they came upon a new factor in their experience - an organized state. Here they learned and adopted, one by one, Hungarian words which later on were destined to form the foundation of Rumanian political organization. (Hungarian: város, Rumanian: oras, English: town; H.: biró, R.: birou, E.: judge; H.: pecsét, R.: pecet, E.: seal; H.: gazda, R.: gasda, E.: farmer; H.: mester, R.: mester, E.: master; H.: vám, R.: vama, E.: customs; H.: határ, R.: hatar, E.: frontier.) It was there they heard that the land beyond the mountains was called Erdély (Ardeal) where the money coined by the Bán of Szörény, which to this day is a Rumanian monetary

17. *Baron Eudoxie Hurmuzaki* published the documents relating to the history of the Rumanians: Documente privitoare la istoria Romanilor, 1199-1849, Bucarest, 1880. This was followed by a series of publications issued by the Rumanian Academy and dealing with the years from 1849 on: Acte si documente relative la istoria renascerei Romaniei, 1391-1859, 10 vols. Bucarest, 1884-1904.Recently *Endre Veres* published: Documente privitoare la istoria Ardealului, Moldovei si Tzarii-Romanesti, vols, I-VIII, 1527-1613, Bucarest, 1929-34. Summary works supporting the Daco-Roman theory were written by Professor *A.D. Xenopol*: Istoria Romanilor din Dacia Trajana, vols. I-VI, up to 1859. Jassy, 1888. 2 nd edition Bucarest, 1914. A compendium of this work was published in Paris, 1896: Histoire des Roumains de la dacie Traiane. 2 vols. Professor *Nicolaus Jorga*, Geschichte des rumänischen Volkes. 2 vols. Bucarest, 1915 and Histoire des Roumains et leur civilisation. Bucarest, 1920. Also in English, German, and Italian translations.

unit (ban), was in circulation. Until that time they had experienced Greek and Slav influences only, and in church matters they retained unchanged the Greco-Slav nomenclature (Bulgarian: *krestin*, Rumanian: *crestin*, Greek: *basilika*, Rumanian: *biserica*). By degrees the number of Rumanian refugees in Cumania became so great that the name was actually changed to *Vlachia, Valachia*, which later was to develop into Wallachian province of the King of Hungary *(Ungrovlachia)*. Since there was no rigid political or customs frontier between Cumania and Transylvania - both of which belonged to the Hungarian state - the landowners in Transylvania gladly welcomed the poor refugees, for their advent meant cheap labour. As the greatest landowner was the king himself, the Transylvanian Rumanians were to be found, primarily, in his service. As late as the close of the thirteenth century the king insisted that he alone should have Rumanian labourers, whom he gathered together from the whole of Transylvania for employment upon one of the royal estates. This affords proof that even after a hundred years, the Rumanian refugees in Transylvania did not exceed in number more souls than could be employed on one single estate.[18]

The existence of these documentary proofs should not be concealed by those who are writing the history of Rumanians. The supporters of the Daco-Roman theory, however, dislike hearing them quoted.[19] They declared instead that Moldavia and Wallachia were colonized by the Emperor Trajan's Roman settlers from Transylvania.[20] The fact is, however, that during the whole of the above period Rumanian refugees in Transylvania were merely a sporadic phenomenon.[21]

18. For details concerning the Knights of Bárca see *E.G. Müller*, die Ursache der Vertreibung des Deutschen Ordens dem Burzenlande und Kumanien in Jahre 1225. Korrespondenzblatt des Vereins für siebenbürgische Landeskunde, XLVIII. pp. 41-68, Nagyszeben. 1925., *F. Obert*, Hermann von Salza und Besiedlung des Burgenlandes, Vienna, 1905., *M. Perlbach*, Der Deutsche Orden in Siebenbürgen. Mitteilungen des Instituts für österreichische Geschichtsforschung, XXVI, pp. 30-415, Innsbruck, 1905., *E. Reissig*, A német lovagok a Bárcaságban, Századok XXXV, Budapest, 1901.

19. Rumanian historiography is adjusted to requirements of the Daco-Roman theory and propaganda and hesitates to accept evidence which proves the theory untenable. - Critical authoritative works are A. *Philip pide's* Originea Romanilor, 2 vols. Jassy, 1925-28, and the article under the heading "Vlach" in the 11th edition of the Encylcopaedia Britannica. Compare with L. *Tamás*, A román történtirás régi és új arca, Magyar Szemle XXII, pp. 256-276, L. *Treml*, A románság öshazája és a kontinuitás, Jancsó Benedek Emlékköny, pp 81-96, Budapest, 1931. - for the wanderings of the Rumanians see O. *Lecca*, Formation ét developpement des pays et des États soumains, Paris, 1929., O. *Onciul*, Romanii in Dacia traiana pana la intermerile principatelor, Bucarest, 1902., A.D. *Xenopol*, Une énigme historique. Les Roumains au moyen age, Paris, 1885. - On Transylvania and the evolution of the Rumanians. J. *Horváth*, Erdély és a románság kialakulása. Történelmi Tanulmányok, Budapest, 1935.

20. L. *Kropf* on the Daco-Roman theory: Radu Negru, a honalapitó, Századok XXXI, p. 707. Budapest.

21. Between 1210 and 1294 only 16 documents make mention of the Rumanians. They have been enumerated separately in my work, Történelmi Tanulmányok, II. pp. 258-73, Budapest, 1935. - For the first document see L. *Szádeczky*, Az oláh telepités legelső okleveles emléke. Századok, XXXII. pp. 577 and 938. Budapest, 1908.

ORIGIN OF THE RUMANIANS

(Vlach Origin, Migration and Infiltration to Transylvania.)

by
Andrew Haraszti

Prof. Andrew Haraszti /Hamilton, Canada/ is a recognized specialist in East-Central European history. /For biography see "Men of Achievement", Cambridge/ His Master Thesis: "Hetumoger, the Origin and Migration of the Medieval Magyars", published in 1971, was recognized as the most outstanding research work on the subject and brought him the Gold Medal Award of the Árpád Academy in Cleveland./

Library of Congress Catalog Card No. 77-89426
ISBN: 0-87934-017-7.

C 1977, Danubian Press, Inc. Astor, Florida, 32002.

Printed by Patria Publishing Co. Toronto

Table of Contents

List of Maps

I
INTRODUCTION

A "ROMANTIC" IMAGINATION:
THE "DAKO-ROMAN" EXISTENCE.

One of the unsolved questions of the European Historiography is the problem of the Rumanian origin.

Some indubitable traces seem to prove that the origin of the Vlach (Wallachian) people was actually the southern part of the Balkans. It seems that some groups of "Romanized" Balkan shepherds survived the historical storms that followed the fall of the Roman Empire. These groups migrated gradually from the south towards the north, and arriving first to the Bulgarian then to the Munthenian area (*1), with a natural increase in the population the density increased to such an extent that then appeared the basis of a genuine nationality.

The modern Rumanian political interest sharply opposed to the facts of the historical migration and the evolution of the Vlachs. Rumanian "romantic-minded" nationalists presented a theory which connected the descendants of the Wallachians directly to the Romans; especially to the Roman conquest in Dacia. This romantic imagination became a myth, and gradually also became a political propaganda. Influenced by this newly recovered myth, western historians (even those who previously adopted the documented migration of the south-Balkanic Vlachs) became confused. They were affected by the romantic idea that the modern representatives of "Urbs Eterna" were still in existence in Eastern Europe! Having actually two theories of Wallachian origin from now on (the northwardly Vlach migration and the newly discovered Dako-Roman theory), most of the historians faced this problem as one of the unsolved questions of European history.

Realistic Rumanian politicians were never really sure that the romantic myth of Dako-Roman origin had anything to do with historical reality. They realized, however, that this myth was useful to serve another dream which was the dream of "Greater Rumania". They found that young nationalists need historic national myths and if a young nation does not have such a myth, one should be created. Therefore, even without real historical evidence, Rumanian imperialists used the myth of "Dako-Roman continuity" as a great incentive for the "re-conquest" of those territories which were "lost" by their "Dak" and "Roman" forefathers".

Byzantine, Bulgarian, Slav, and other historical sources have mentioned various Vlach nomadic elements, which came to the historical surface from the chaotic Balkan situation following the great Goth, Hun,

---

1. Munthenia, or Muntenia is an area which is situated between the Carpathian Alps and the Lower Danube.

Avar migrations and their temporary settlements. These nomadic shepherds did not seem to have too much connection to the ancient and disintegrated Roman Empire. These mountain people did not reveal the proud, and sophisticated characteristics which were so typical of the legionaries and citizens of "Urbs Eterna". Then all of a sudden in the annals of Balkan history, Wallachia appeared at the end of the XIIIth century, north of the Lower Danube. First it was a semi-independent, later as an independent Principality. It was united with Moldavia in 1859, and with the disintegration of the Austro-Hungarian Monarchy after World War I an opportunity occurred for the Wallachians (already called "Rumanians" at this time) to claim Hungarian Transylvania as a former "Roman province"! (*2)

Since Transylvania was an essential part of the Hungarian national sphere, continuously since the IXth century, Rumanian imperialists realized that a selfcreated myth of "Dako-Roman continuity" was needed. Pointing out again that they were originated from a historical intermarriage between the Roman colonizers and the ancient inhabitants of Dacia, they claimed it was "obvious" that they have had every legal right to "reconquer" the area, which was part of the great Roman Empire in the Age of Antiquity. (*3).

The so-called "Dako-Roman continuity" (*4) could not confuse many historians, who reconstructed the history of the ancient and Medieval Ages, with original documents and archaeological findings as bases of their works. There were, however, as it was mentioned before, some others, who were rather naive, more easily influenced, or not so well educated, who could not help but to be affected by the romantic imagination of the Dako-Roman intermarriage. They forgot that the "Dako-Roman intermarriage" or the "Dako-Roman continuity" was not supported by any archaeological findings or by any Roman, Byzantine, Slav or Bulgarian sources either. It is quite clear that a certain part of the Wallachian vocabulary showed Latin elements, however, there does not exist any historical evidence, which seems to show that the Balkan-originating Vlachs have had any ancient connections with Dak tribes, or with the Roman colonizers of ancient Dacia.

2: Lacia was an eastern region of the Roman Empire, conquered by Emperor Trajan in about 107 A.D. and abandoned by Emperor Aurelian in 271 A.D. It was a Roman Province for 164 years. Iis territory superficially indentical with Transylvania, which became part of the Hungarian Kingdom following the Hungarian Conquest of the Carpathian Basin in 896 A.D. Between 1540 and 1690, Transylvania was an independent, sometimes semi-independent Hungarian Principality, under the leadership of Hungarian sovereigns. After this, up to 1920, Transylvania was part of the Hungarian Kingdom and (as such) part of the Austro-Hungarian Empire again.

3: According to evidence presented in this essay, the Wallachians have had nothing to do with Dacian colonizers or with the colonized. Hypothesizing the non-existent Dako-Roman connection, however, the Rumanians have had about the same " right" for Transylvania, that Italians would nave for Noricum (Austria), Gallia (France), or Britannia (England).

4: This theory, of course, bases itself on pure speculation without any evidence. One example of the typical Rumanian "historical" phraseology: "... the historical sources, it is true, do not mention, hence, it must have been a slow but steady infiltration that turned into a Roman population, speaking the vulgar Latin tongue, the Illyrians and Thracians." N. Jorga: A history of Roumania. p. 24.

At this point it also should be mentioned that the first decades of the XXth century proved to be a very suitable socio-political atmosphere for extreme, chauvinistic and even imperialistic political propaganda. It was used much more frequently instead of objective historiography. In this era of extreme and noisy nationalism many highly educated historians (who attempted to be objective and apolitical) were pushed aside. Their logical, clear, but quiet voices were surpassed by those who really did not wish to serve Clio, Muse of History, but who served Mars, the god of war. These political propagandists, acting as "historians", have had mainly political interests, which motivated them to rewrite history in their own particular way, serving their own, new political view. As I mentioned, some of them were simply naive, but many of them falsified history deliberately to fulfill the "national interest" which seemed to be so "sacred" that the "great national interest" seemed to justify even dishonest methods.

Following World War I, France desired to paralyze the destroyed German State, and wished to frustrate the possible resurrection of the disintegrated Austro-Hungarian Monarchy. President G. Clemenceau created several, artificial, multinational states in East-Central Europe. (*5). He was assisted by several selfish and Machiavellian politicians, and by those whose knowledge of East-Central European history was spare. They created a "new Europe", but the dictated "peace" which enforced the new situation of artificial frontiers and new multinational states was actually nothing else but the germs for several future wars to come.

The statesmen who redrew the map of Europe welcomed the "Dako-Roman theory" and accepted it as true history. Now the Rumanians could "legally" become "Romans", or "Daks", or "Dako-Romans". They could become anything and anybody whenever they wished, because their claim could be well adjusted to the ideas, and plans of French revenge, and of Russian-oriented Panslavism. The Wallachian administration received the "green light" from the Entente so the descendants of Vlach shepherds were able to march into Hungarian Transylvania.

Of course, anyone could say at this time, that the lamentation of the harshly treated Hungary was a seemingly biased voice. The voice of a nation which is losing one of her thousand-year-old parts is similar to the sound of a person who is losing one of his arms or legs. This seemingly biased cry, however, coincided with the voices of objective historians, but their writings did not reach the ears of the Great Powers. It became fashionable that victorious countries were "right", losers were always "wrong".

5. George Clemenceau (1841-1929) was premier of France (1906-9, 1917-19), called "the Tiger". He opposed the honest, peace-minded USA President W. Wilson in Versailles and Trianon, using the post-war conferences as opportunities for chauvinistic revenge.

Objective historians of the world were astonished. There were no sources, nor historical maps anywhere (except in Rumania) which ever showed Transylvania as a Wallachian province before 1920. Nobody could show any documents, chronicles, archaeological findings, which could prove any Rumanian right to Transylvania. In spite of this, however, Transylvania remained a Rumanian province not only after the First War, but also following the Second Great War. Politicians of this World recognized, accepted with considerable cynicism, that not only History creates nations, but sometimes nations are re-creating their actual history. These new historical interpretations were poor as far as historical evidence is concerned, but since "might was right", powerful armies "guaranteed" their "rightful" existence.

Since then, Rumanian historians were desperately trying to find some real evidence of the "Dako-Roman origin and continuity", which would justify the Rumanian conquest in Transylvania. They remained unsuccessful. They were able to produce generalizations which seemed to prove that ancient Vlachs adopted many cultural customs from Roman colonizers, but they still could not find evidences which would aid the myth of Dako-Roman origin in Dacia. Let us quote from some of these typical compositions.

> Rumanian is derived directly from the low Latin spoken in the Imperial era. In syntax and grammar it reproduces Latin forms of striking purity. Words dealing with agricultural pursuits, however, are generally of Slavic origin...(*6).

> It is still customary in any Rumanian village to attach a small coin to the finger of the dead after an ancient Roman custom of providing the soul with its fare across the Styx ... Rumania's national dance, the Calausare, commemorates the rape of the Sabines to this day.(*7).

> The mountains saved the Latin character of Rumanian speech.(*8).

It is really not necessary to argue with these points above. The Vlachs as pastoral subjects of Roman landholders in Epirus, Macedonia, perhaps in Dalmatia, obviously adopted some sort of vulgarized Latin from their masters, and adopted several Roman customs as well. It was probably also truth that by hiding in the mountainous regions they were able to preserve these linguistic and cultural characteristics for several centuries. All of this, however, does not seem to prove that these Vlachs originated from Roman Dacia, where the Roman legions in comparison to other provinces colonized the land the least. Thus informations about adopted vocabulary and customs are not adequate evidence to recreate history in lines with the Rumanian myth of the Dako-Roman theory.

> There is much argument about the priority of the Rumanians in Transylvania. Rumanians claim that they are the descendants of the

6. Leon Dominian: The Frontiers of Language and Nationality in Europe. p. 166.
7. Ibid. p. 161.
8. Ibid. p. 162.

Romanized Dacians of the emperor Trajan's day, who have lived uninterruptedly in Transylvania since Roman times. Many historians point out, however, that according to all available evidence, the Romans completely evacuated their Dacian settlements, and that from the third century to the twelfth, during the course of nearly a thousand years, not a single trace of the Dacians may be found in Transylvania - even if the Rumanians were their descendants. On the other hand there are chronological data concerning the Rumanians' gradual immigration into Transylvania from the twelfth century onward.(*9).

One of the well known Rumanian historians, Prof. Giurescu often used to say, that "historians should not be employed by extreme nationalistic forces". Let us mention something about this Rumanian scholar, honoured by his own nation. His way of writing actually proves that Rumanian nationalism that incorporates the Dako-Roman myth as some sort of springboard for further, more extended dreams, is really ready to re-write the history of the whole European Continent.

On the same page on which Professor Giurescu ostracizes exaggerated patriotism, he says that the history of the Rumanians is based on four positive and unassailable facts: (1) that the Rumanians are one of the oldest peoples in Europe, (2) that the Dacians were an elite people of the ancient world; (3) that the Rumanians are the oldest Christian peoples of south-eastern Europe; and (4) that they are the only people in these regions who can boast of an uninterrupted political continuity. (*10).

It is not the purpose of this essay to argue "how old" the Rumanians really were, or "how elite" the Dacians were under Roman colonization or before the Roman conquest. We don't really think that it would be sensible to investigate which south-eastern peoples were the "oldest Christians". If the distinguished professor, mentioned above, and his fellow Rumanian "scholars" believed and attempted to force the belief, that they were the "oldest", the "most elite", or the "oldest Christian" people, I feel we should let them enjoy their unbased belief and happiness. The false proposition about the "national continuity" in Transylvania represents, however, a deliberate historical falsification, with serious political consequences. This attempt must be criticized and internationally corrected.

This essay does not wish to deal with the "Dako-Roman political continuity", "myth", or "theory" in detail. The real purpose of this essay is to re-introduce the history of the Vlach migration on the Balkans from Byzantine Epirus and Macedonia to medieval Bulgaria, from Bulgaria to Wallachia, and from Wallachia to Moldavia and Transylvania. Before

9. Dominic G. Kosary - S.B. Vardy: History of the Hungarian Nation. P. 20.

10. Zsombor Szász: Rumanian History. (The Hungarian Quarterly. 1941. pp. 198-99.)

doing it, however, we will outline the tragedy of the heroic and unfortunate Dak people. Following this, this essay will deal with the real history of the medieval Rumanians.

II

THE TRAGIC DEFEAT AND EXTERMINATION
OF THE DAK PEOPLE

The racial and linguistic origin of the Dak people (the Dacians) is an example of the unsolved problems in the history of Ancient Europe. We really do not know what sort of people they were and what part of the Eurasian Continent they came from before settling in the eastern portion of the Carpathian Basin. This area was called Dacia by the Romans, in the 1st century A.D., after the name of the inhabitants.

Some historians believe that the Daks actually belonged to the northern subgroups of the Thracians. (*11). Herodotus, the "Father of historical writing", visited Dacia around 480 B.C. and he named the people there as "Getae". There is every probability that these "Getae" were identical with the Daks. Another assumption was that these people were the most western element of the Scythian people. (*12). According to Herodotus and other ancient authors, the inhabitants of Dacia were living in the framework of four or five tribes and they built their tribal culture under Greek and Celtic influence. They build strong rock fortresses, they formed highly disciplined clans with militaristic social character, but they practised agriculture and animal breeding. They were also experienced miners, and they sold their gold, silver, iron and salt to the Greeks, using Greek coins in their commercial affairs.

Their connection with Hellas was mainly peaceful, but occasionally some of their tribes were probably victimized by Greek expansionism. In the 4th century B.C., for instance, slaves of Getae origin (assumably war-prisoners) appeared on the Athenian slave market. In about the same time they were ruled by the female-dominated "Agathyrs" people, but not much later the Daks with a larger population absorbed the conquerors.

In about 280 B.C. Celtic tribes penetrated into the Carpathian Basin probably from the north and they dominated the Daks for a short time. (*13). Beginning with the 2nd century B.C., however, Dak tribes (called 'Davi" and sometimes "Daii" by the Romans) became a strong force in Dacia. They sent troops against the Balkanic colonies of the Romans, to prevent the encroachment of Roman imperialism into their country.(*14). One of their greatest kings was Burebista (70-44 B.C.), who established his capital, called Sarmisegethusa, in the Southern Carpathians, and extended his power from the River Tisza (German: Theiss)

11. Early Thracians populated the area of the East-Balkans from the mouth of the Ister (Danube) down to the Bosphorus. They absorbed Hellenic culture only to a limited extent. In c. 1300 B.C. they occupied probably much larger areas, but in the 5th century B.C. they were pushed to the Black Sea area by Illyrians and Macedonians. Beginning with the 1st century B.C. Thracian rulers were vassals of Rome.

12. The Scythians were nomadic horsemen, who inhabited E. Europe and W. Asia. They were probably Turanian (by some historians: Indo-Iranian) in origin. They traded with the Greeks and sometimes acted as Greek mercenaries.

13. The very same Celtic invasion ravaged Macedonia in 279 B.C., defeating the Greeks in Thermopylae, and reaching even Delphi. They ruled Thrace until 210 B.C.

14. The Dak campaigns threatened Moesia, Dalmatia and Thrace in 112, 109, and 75 B.C.

to the Pontus Euxinus (Black Sea). His political and military power was recognized by the Roman Empire. (*15).

In the age of the early (Julian-Claudian) emperors, Dacia was already under the shadow of the Roman eagle. When Moesia (*16) and Pannonia (*17) appeared as new Roman strongholds, it became clear that Dacia would be the next step. In 10B.C. the Dak forces withdrew to the northern side of the Danube, forming a defensive line in the Carpathian Alps.

A new, and final renewal of the Dak power appeared in A.D. 85, when King Durosdak resigned and King Decebal took over the leadership of Dacia. (85-106). He was ambitious and warlike, and he decided to defend Dacia against Roman colonizing tendencies. He proved to be a successful military leader against the legions of Emperor Domitian (81-96), when his Daks invaded Moesia from the north (85), and when he was able to secure his position even when various German tribal fragments (Quads and Marcomans) threatened Northern Dacia. Domitian made a quite humiliating peace with Decebal, who retained his independence. The king of the Daks also defeated the nordic German invaders, and crushed the Sarmatian Iazyg horsemen, nomads, who populated the area between the Danube and the Tisza Rivers at this time.

The final tragedy of the heroic but unfortunate Daks came about with Emperor Trajan (98-117), who was a brilliant and ambitious soldier. His name and activity coincide with the final page of Dak history. He was responsible for the invasion and complete annihilation of the Daks, and also for the colonization of Dacia.

> Nurtured on war, the Emperor was a frank imperialist who preferred order to liberty and power to peace. Hardly a year after his arrival in Rome he set out for the conquest of Dacia... Its annexation would give Rome control of the road that ran down the Save to the Danube and thence to Byzantium - an invaluable land route to the East. Besides, Dacia had gold mines, In a campaign brilliantly planned and swiftly executed, Trajan led his legions through all obstacles and resistance to the Dacian capital, Sarmisegethusa, and forced its surrender.(*18).

The emperor reinstated Decebal as a client king and returned to Rome in 102. Decebal, however, did not like his new and very humiliating role, and soon broke the agreement, resuming his independent rule. Trajan marched his legions back to Dacia (105) where he bridged the Danube, and stormed Sarmisegethusa again.

The Daks defended their country with enthusiasm and with blood-

---

15. King Burebista influenced even the internal affairs of Rome when he was allied with Pompey against Julius Caesar. (Between 49-46 B.C.)

16. Became a Roman province in the time of Octavianus (Augustus) in 29 B.C.

17. Around the time of the birth of Christ, the legions of Augustus advanced the frontiers of the "Imperium" to the Danube. The Romans, however, considered Pannonia as a Province already in 10 B.C., when Roman forces of Noricum (today's Austria) extended their domination east from the Alps.

18. Will Durant: *Caesar and Christ*. (In the series of *The Story of Civilization*. Vol. III. pp. 409-410.)

thirsty hatred against the Roman invaders. This fact was recognized even by those Rumanian historians, who later supported chauvinists to create or popularize the myth of Dako-Roman intermarriage.

The Dacians resisted in the mountains "with an incomparable fury, in which all the people shared. Even the women joined in". (*19).

Sarmisegethusa was burned to the ground at this time. The Dacian chiefs had drunk poison at a final banquet, and assumably, most of the soldiers and their families followed the heroic example of the Dacian leaders. Following this almost unprecedented collective suicide, the legions, full of bloodthirsty revenge because of the great loss in human resources on the Roman side too, almost completely exterminated the entire population of Dacia. The unfortunate country became one burning bloody slaughter. Some survivors were forced to leave their destroyed home-country, in chains as slaves. In about 110, the victorious emperor raised in Rome a triumphal column (by Apollodorus), which aimed to proclaim the victory and a serious warning to the world: all those who resist will follow the Dacian example and, if necessary, populations of whole countries will be annihilated.

In the 2,000 figures of the 124 spiral panels we follow the conquest of Dacia step by step: the Roman cohorts issuing from their Stations in full armor; the crossing of the Danube on a pontoon bridge; the pitching of a Roman camp in the enemy's land; the confused conflict of spears, arrows, sickles, and stones; a Dacian village set to the torch with women and children begging Trajan for mercy; Dacian women torturing Roman prisoners: solders displaying before the Emperor the heads of slain enemies; surgeons treating the wounded; the Dacian princes drinking one after another the cup of poison; the head of Decebalus brought as a trophy to Trajan, the long file of captive men, women, and children snatched from their homes into foreign settlements or Roman slavery - this and more the dark column tells in the most masterly narrative relief in sculptural history.(*20).

Trajan's column in the Roman forum is actually one of the best historical evidences of the complete destruction of Dacia indeed, which produces a considerable addition to the contemporary historical documents (of Dio Cassius, Dio Chrysostomus, Plinius, Iuvenalis, Marcus Aurelius, etc.), which were describing, stating or indicating the fact that the Romans actually succeeded in almost completely exterminating the nation of the Daks. Trajan's Dacian War was extended into a genocide (*21). It is interesting however, that the "Dako-Roman theoreticians"

19. N. Jorga. *The History of Roumania.* p. 27. (Note: let us mention at this point that we are using the spelling: "Rumania" in this essay, however, we are bound to use spellings as "Romania" our "Roumania" in quotation).

20. Will Durant: *Caesar and Christ.* p. 412.

21. The modern term "genocide" was used mainly in modern history (it was made an international crime by a UN convention, adopted in 1948, and took effect only in 1950), but we have used this word as a very characteristic one, because this case was really a prototype of it.

were using even Trajan's column as some sort of strange "evidence" supporting the Dako-Roman myth, "recognizing" that the Dacians (on the column) used to wear a cap, which was "very similar" to the skin-cap of the Rumanian peasants of today. (*22).

Let us also mention in connection with Trajan's Dacian war, that Apollodorus, the emperor's great architect, built a bridge across the Danube at Dierna (Orsova). The Romans built several military camps and roads. In Apulum (Hung: Gyulafehérvár, Rum: Alba Julia) a Pannon legion, in Potaissara (Torda) a Macedonian legion guarded the province. Near to the destroyed Sarmisegethusa, a new military town was built, called Ulpia Traiana. Only the officers were pure Romans of Italy, while the legionaires were recruited from Asia Minor, Syria, Greece, Iberia, even from Berber-Africa. The soldiers were isolated by living in their fortresses (castellum), from the almost completely depopulated country. We have to assume that no elements of any human life ever appeared around the brutal conquerors, but the military command realized the possible dangers of these hostile mountains, so military orders protected these soldiers from any connections with natives. Dacia became the Land of Death, but the careful Roman administration wished to isolate the legions from even visiting those ghost towns and deserted forests. Mining was mainly a military duty because Roman civilians did not dare to appear in this dangerous far-east province, and natives were not available either. (It was really amazing that modern political interest was actually able to fabricate the myth that the "Dako-Roman population" was made upon a "happy intermarriage" between the Romans and Daks ...)

In 270 A.D. Dacia became the very first province which Roma abandoned. The Marcoman tribes invaded the area since about 180, and in 250, the Roman administration began the evacuation of Dacia. In the winter of 270-271, Emperor Aurelian ordered the legions to leave Dacia and to march to Moesia, which became "Dacia Aureliana" from now on. The Danube represented the borderline against the possible barbarian invasions coming from the north. Carpathian Dacia became a German territory for a while.

Let us take a final look at the Carpathian and Balkanic provinces of the Roman Empire. Let us compare Dacia with the other East-European territories, with possibility of Romanization in mind:

Province	Year of Conquest	Year of Evacuation	Years of Colonization
Illyricum & Dalmatia	168 B.C.	476 A.D.	644
Epirus & Achaea	168 B.C.	395 A.D.	563

22. The brimless felt hats (appearing on the column) were generally worn by Scythians, Thracians, and all peoples of the Carpathian Mountains both in ancient and modern times, however N. Jorga, the famous Rumanian historian mentioned that the cap of Dacian nobles was identical with the skin-cap of Rumanian peasants of today, and used this observation as evidence. (N. Jorga: A History of Roumania, p. 27.)

Macedonia	146 B.C.	395 A.D.	541
Thracia	46 B.C.	395 A.D.	441
Moesia	44 B.C.	395 A.D.	439
Pannonia	10 B.C.	408 A.D.	418
Dacia	107 A.D.	271 A.D.	164 (!)

In the Dalmatian coast, in Epirus, in Macedonia, in Thracia and in Moesia, even in Pannonia, many hundreds of years provided the opportunity of Romanization. In the depopulated mountains of Dacia only a relatively limited period was associated with the Roman conquest. The mountainous regions of the Balkans, however, preserved some fragments of Romanized, rural peoples, which were called later as Vlachs.

Romanization of the Balkans was stopped when Emperor Flavius died (395), and the Empire was divided between his sons: Arcadius and Honorius. Arcadius received the eastern part of the Empire including the Balkans. His rule marks the beginning of Re-Hellenization. This revival of Greek culture was, of course, very slow in the 5th century because of the Roman traditions and of the Goth, Hun, etc. invasions, but later became quite aggressive, when the civilian bureaucrats were supported by military forces. "Dacia Aureliana", which existed for 124 years (271-395) as a Roman province, became also a Byzantine territory. Illyricum and Dalmatia remained Latin for a longer time, thus "Romanization" could have its effect there most intensively. The most western parts of the Balkans became part of the Eastern Empire only when Rome itself finished its long history. (476 A.D.)

The Roumanians were not descendants of Roman colonists of Dacia left behind in East Hungary and Transylvania ... After the removal and withdrawal of the Roman colonists, Dacia, for untold centuries, was the arena of the wildest international struggles known to history, and these could not have been outlived by any nomad people remaining there. To be sure, some express the opinion that the Roumanian nomad herdsmen fled into the Transylvanian mountains at each new invasion (by the Huns, Bulgarians, Avars, Magyars, Patzinaks, Cumans successively) and subsequently always returned. But the nomad can support himself in the mountains only during summer, and he must descend to pass the winter. On the other hand each of these new invading nomad hordes needed these mountains for summer grazing for their own herds. Thus the Roumanians could not have escaped, and their alleged game of hide-and-seek would have been in vain.(*23).

In the westernmost parts of the Balkans (Dalmatia and W.

23. T. Peisker: Origin of the Roumanians. (The Cambridge Medieval History. 1911. Vol. 1. p. 357.)

Macedonia), along the Adriatic coast and the mountainous background, the Romanized pastoral societies could hide themselves much easier. These former slaves of Italian patricians, whose language still preserved some vulgar elements of their previous masters, survived both the nomad invasions and the disturbances of Byzantine tax-collectors.

> During the summer they grazed on most of the mountains of the Balkan peninsula and took up their winter quarters on the seacoasts among a peasant population speaking a different language. Thence they gradually spread, unnoticed by the chroniclers along all the mountain ranges.(*24).

While the heroic and unfortunate Dak people disappeared from the stage of History, those Romanized rural peoples of the Western Balkans who were more familiar with the hidden forests and roads that the uninvited nomads and Greeks, could gradually take the opportunity to migrate, step-by-step, to new, northern pastures. The descendants of these Romanized Balkan shepherds became inventive enough to claim that they were actually descendants of the so-called "Dako-Romans".

24. T. Peisker: *Origin of the Roumanians. (The Cambridge Medieval History*, 1911. Vol. 1. p. 356.)

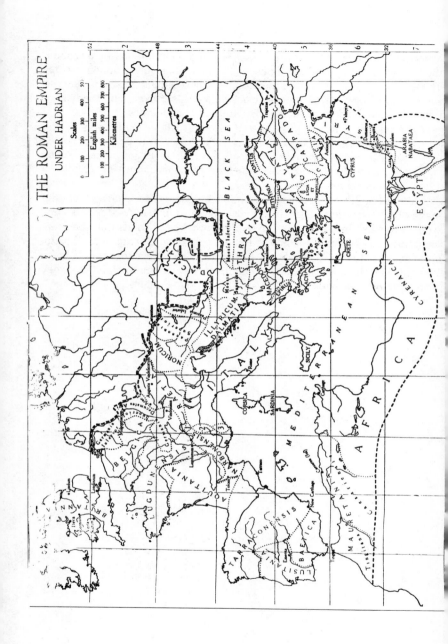

THE ROMAN EMPIRE
UNDER HADRIAN

Scales

English miles
0 100 200 300 400 500

Kilometres
0 100 200 300 400 500 600 700 800

BRITANNIA

BELGICA

LUGDUNENSIS

AQUITANIA

NARBONENSIS

TARRACONENSIS

LUSITANIA

BAETICA

MAURETANIA

A F R I C A

NUMIDIA

New Carthage

SARDINIA

CORSICA

SICILY

ITALY

Rome

NORICUM

ILLRICUM

DALMATIA

RAETIA

DACIA

Moesia Inferior

Moesia Superior

THRACIA

MACEDONIA

EPIRUS

ACHAIA

CRETE

M E D I T E R R A N E A N   S E A

B L A C K   S E A

BITHYNIA ET PONTUS

ASIA

GALATIA

CAPPADOCIA

LYCIA ET PAMPHYLIA

CILICIA

CYPRUS

SYRIA

Damascus

Jerusalem

ARABIA NABATAEA

EGYPT

Alexandria

CYRENAICA

CRENAICA

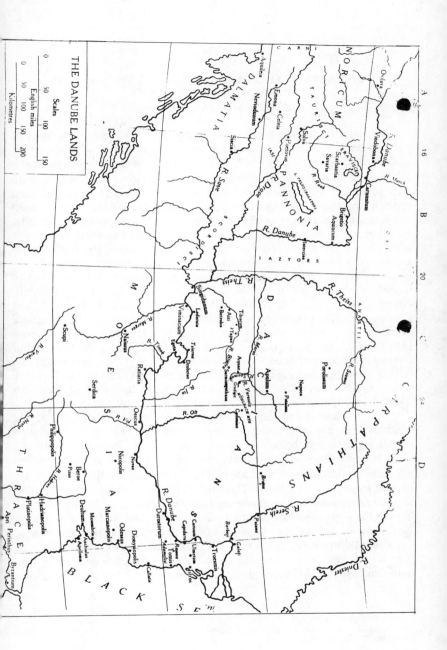

THE DANUBE LANDS

Scales

0   50   100   150
English miles

0   50   100   150   200
Kilometres

III

"ROMANIZED" SHEPHERD-SOCIETIES OF THE BALKANS IN THE STORMY CENTURIES OF THE MEDIEVAL MIGRATION

It would be almost impossible to estimate how many thousands of people remained in the mountains and in the hidden valleys, forests, caves of those Provinces which were abandoned by the Roman legions in the Balkans. No doubt that Illyricum, Thracia, Macedonia and Epirus were still populated by pastoral societies speaking some sort of degenerated Latin at the end of the 4th century. These peoples did not wish, or were not permitted to follow their lords or the evacuating legions back to Italy, and they faced (if they were aware of them at all) two sorts of dangers which came from two opposite directions: the Byzantine-Greek expansionism from the south and the barbaric invasions from the north.

The drama which created serious turmoil on the Balkans, actually began in the far-off north-east. Balamber, king of the Hun tribalorganization defeated the Alans and Heruls north of the Black Sea, and then destroyed the Ostrogothic Empire of King Hermanrich, thus pushing the Ostrogoths to the west. The Ostrogoths entered into Transylvania from the east, and for a couple of generations they lived in the Carpathian Basin as some sort of servant-people of the growing Hun power. The Huns, before crossing the Carpathians, defeated the Visigoths at the Dniester River, which caused the Visigoths, under King Athaneric to turn to the south, toward Moesia, and penetrated into the Balkans.(*25).

At this time (376) the Romans still attempted to stop the Great Migration so Emperor Valens (*26) intended to disarm the uninvited guests, and ordered them to settle in Lower Moesia. He failed to fulfill his plan, because the Visigoths, under the leadership of Fritigern, defeated and killed Valens near Adrianople (378). Following this, the Visigoths appeared even south of Thrace. Theodosius, Emperor of the East, was able to pacify the invaders by influencing the new, young king, Alaric, who was hoping for a position in Byzantium. Theodosius died in 395, and Alaric was disappointed because he realized that Arcadius, the new Emperor of the East, did not recognize him as a "Roman" authority. In a passion of fury he ravaged Thrace to the gates of Constantinople. Arcadius was quite helpless until his field marshal, Stilicho, a Vandal by blood, was able

---

25. The Visigoths were later also called as "Thervings"

26. Valens was the younger brother of Emp. Flavius Valentinianus I. (364-375.) The Roman Emperor appointed him "Co-Augustus in the East."

to push Alaric and his Visigoths away from Constantinople.(*27).

In 398-99, the Visigoths were wandering first to Achaea, then to Epirus and then they turned north-west to Illyricum. These areas, especially along the Adriatic coast, were still populated by various rural peoples, who were left behind by their Italian masters, and who still preserved some sort of deformed Latin in their languages and some Roman memories in their customs. These people, mostly shepherds, were hiding in their forests, swamps and caves, but some of them left their settlements far behind. Certain groups migrated to mountainous high-pasturages, many others took refuge to the north-east, and settled in the Balkan Mountains (mountain ranges in today's Bulgaria). Some of them were pushed to the northern coasts of Dalmatia by the Visigoths (Alaric arrived in northern Dalmatia in 400 and left the Balkans for Italy in 401).(*28).

The disturbed peoples of the Balkans now breathed more freely, but not for too long. The Hun power which ruled a large part of Europe from Gallia to the Caucasus (*29) realized the opportunity of extension in the Balkans down to Constantinople. The Hun horsemen crossed the Lower Danube several times, and they raided Moesia, Macedonia and Thessalia (446-47). At this time the Romanized pastoral peoples of the Balkans were obliged to tolerate the patronage of the Eastern Emperor, who represented the only security for them, however, many branches of them chose the high mountains and deep forests again rather than the support of the Greek bureaucracy. The mountains were cold and dangerous, but they were isolated and free.

It is obvious that the dangerous age of the Goth and Hun invasions was not too suitable for any northward migrations for the Romanized people of the Balkans. The adventure of the Visigoths stopped, paralyzed their movement for a while; most of them hid themselves on the higher pasturages of Illyricum, Macedonia and Epirus. Those, who already reached the Balkan Mountains, stopped and settled, because north of the Lower Danube, the Hun Empire seemed to be a very dangerous place to live in. Transylvania (the former Dacia) was still called as "Gothia" in King Attila's time (445-453), since the great king of the Huns placed many of the dominated German tribes in that area. (*30). the Carpathian

27. Stilicho actually avoided any battle with Alaric, who was forced to leave mostly by shrewdness of diplomacy. Stilicho himself betrayed Arcadius, and was appointed later as "magister milicium" of Illyricum by Honorius, Emperor of the West.

28. Stilicho, in service of Rome at this time, halted the Visigoths at Verona and Alaric withdrew to Epirus, but in 407-08, he left the Balkans forever, invaded Italy and, in 410, he sacked even Rome.

29. Following the rules of King Kharatom and King Uldin, the first representative of the Hun Golden Age was King Ruga (Rugilas). He fully occupied the Carpathian Basin, which became heart of the Hun Empire. Transylvania was populated by the Goth vassals, so it was called as "Gothia". After 409, he ravaged the Balkans and Theodosius II (408-50) was forced to pay tribute. In c. 440, Attila (his cousin) campaigned the Balkans, repeating the campaigns again in 446-47, making Singidunum (Belgrade), Naissos (Nis) and Sardica (Sofia) Hun military strongholds.

30. Even Rumanian historians recognized 5th century Transylvania as "Gothia" since they were unable to find any traces of Daks, Romans or Dako-Romans in the eastern part of the Carpathian Basin at this time.

Mountains were guarded by elite Hun troops. These forces were quite hostile against any movements which would appear from the south.(*31).

After the disintegration of the Hun Empire, (*32), Marcianus, Emperor of the East (450-57), continued the Hellenization of the Balkans. The Romanized pastoral-societies did not understand Greek and worried about the growing frequency of the appearing Greek military units and Greek-speaking tax-collectors. Their natural tendency was, of course, to continue their migration to the north, however, their movements were stopped, or slowed, once again by Hun patrols in the Balkans, Ostrogoths in Pannonia, and by Gepids in Gothia.(*33).

At the end of the 6th century, the Avar Empire (proud inheritors of the "Inheritance of Attila") (*34) extended from the Alps to the Caucasus. The people of Bajan khagan, which invaded the Balkans several times in the 7th century, threatened the gates of Constantinople. They seemed to be a new appearance of the Huns.

The new patrons of the Latin-fragments was surprisingly not Byzantium, but the Bugarians.

The Bulgarians, first mentioned by this name in 354 A.D. were members of the Turkish branch of the Turanian race. Their northern branch (the Volga-Bulgars) were populating the area between the Ural Mts. and the Central Volga River. The southern branch were organized in tribal and clan-system, and were ruled by the "Dulo" princes of Attila's Hun dynasty. Their first authenticated ruler was Kan Kurt (or Kubrat; 584-642), proud descendant of Attila, who dominated the steppes north of the Caucasus. In 619 he visited Constantinople to request aid against the Avar Khaganate. After his death Great Old Bulgaria was disrupted by simultaneous attacks of the Avars (from the west) and of the Khazars (from the east). Isperikh (or Asperuch; 643-701) son, or grandson of Kubrat, leader of one of the fragments moved to former Dacia Inferior (area between the Transylvanian Alps and the Lower Danube) with his people (after 650). In about 680, the Bulgars crossed the Lower Danube, moved to former Moesia, defeated the army of the Eastern Roman Empire, and established their capital at Pliska. At this time they dominated both sides of the Lower Danube, Moldavia and Bessarabia. Isperikh and his successors welcomed more and more Romanized refugees coming from the south, and they became the most important patrons of them.

Pushed by various Turanian (Ural-Altaic) tribe organizations (Huns, Avars, Bulgarians) a new type of race and language appeared on the Northern Balkans called the Slavs. This (eastern) branch of the Indo-European language family was already known by Greek and Roman writers of the

31. "We have even documentary evidence about the Skékelys as direct Hun descendants". 'Anonymous', the anonymous chronicler of Bela III, who represents one of the most authentic historical sources mentioned the Székelys as 'Populi Atthyle Regis'" (C.A. Macartney: *Studies of the Early Hungarian Sources.* p. 217). (Note: the descendants of those Székelys who were mentioned already by the medieval chroniclers as "siculi": frontier guards, are suppressed minorities in Greater Rumania today.)

32. After the battle of Nedao (454 A.D.).

33. Emp. Marcianus allowed the Ostrogoths to settle as "foederati" (military allies) in Pannonia.

34. The Avars were related to the Huns and ruled by kings of Hun origin.

1st and 2nd centuries as "Venedi" and in these early times they already inhabited the region beyond the River Vistula (in today's Poland). As a direct result of the Hun and Avar conquests, the Slavs were separated into northern (Poles, Czechs, Moravians, Slovaks), eastern (Russians, Ukrainians), and southern branches (Slovenians, Croatians, Serbians), however, the officials of Constantinople called them only by the simplified name of "Sclaveni".

They quickly populated the Balkan valleys and they became servant-peoples of Hun, Avar, and later, Bulgarian lords. After the fall of the Hun Empire, and in a later time, when the Avar Empire was already weakened by the growing Frankish power, the Slavs already outnumbered by population all other races of Illyricum-Dalmatia, Western Moesia and Northern Macedonia. Krum, one of the greatest Bulgarian rulers (808-814), a Pannonian Bulgar, was probably still Hun by origin, but when Boris I (852-89) converted his Bulgars to Greek-Orthodox Christianity, supposedly almost the whole Bulgarian population was actually Slavicized, and the blood-brotherhood of Attila was nothing else in Greek-Orthodox Bulgaria but a part of a foggy and heroic mythology.

In the 9th and 10th centuries, Greek-Orthodox and Slav Bulgaria (especially its central mountainous regions) was the best pastoral area for those fragments which still preserved certain elements of Latin in their language. These people (the Vlachs) were converted to Greek Orthodoxy by Greek missionaries, but they remained illiterate. They did not know anything about the fact of Roman disintegration or about the long time exterminated Dak people. Living in primitive circumstances among their sheep and goats, they did not even know that there is an old City, called Rome, somewhere in far off Italy. In other words: we have to assume that they did not have historical memories and they did not have geographical perspective either.

In the 10th century one of the largest portions of these degenerated "Romans" were living in the Pindos mountains, in Thessalia (Between Epirus and Macedonia). They were called by linguists as "Megleno-Rumuns". Another significant group, the so-called "Arumuny" (Arumuns) were already in the Balkan Mountains, populating the valleys from the Central Balkans to the Black Sea. The third, and a considerably large group, the "Istro-Rumuns", still populated the Adriatic Coast (Dalmatia and W. Macedonia) areas, which belonged to the old Roman Empire centuries earlier.(*35).

Just as the Bulgarians, the Wallachians were also Slavicized by intermarriages with Slav elements. The only difference was that the Bulgarians became Slavs almost completely, while the Wallachians still

35. Megleno-Rumuns, Arumuns and Istro-Rumuns; these expressions are clearly showing the fact that the Vlachs were actually peoples who were left by Roman colonizers in these areas. These names are also showing the fact that these fragments were the main starting points of a later unified people, which called itself: Rumania.

preserved as almost half of their vocabulary a sort of deformed Latin.(*36).

The immigration of the Slavs did not fail to influence the ancient Rumanians. That is clearly proved by many Slav features in the Rumanian ethnical development and by the richness of the Rumanian language in Slav elements, which goes so far that on this basis several earlier scholars numbered the Rumanians among the Slav peoples. (*37).

One could ask a question: were these shepherd societies really "Slavicized Romans", or were they rather "Romanized Slavs"?

Modern Rumanians are stressing the Roman connection, but minimizing the Slavic influence, in spite of the fact that the Rumanian language actually consists of more Slavic than Latin words.(*38). Let us admit, that since the Roman Empire disintegrated already in the 5th century, and because the first Slavic fragments appeared in the Balkans only around the 7th century, the shepherd-societies in question were probably Macedonians, Illyrians and other peoples of the Balkans, who were first Romanized by their Roman landlords and later Slavicized by the Slav newcomers, who were infiltrating from the north. It was quite obvious, however, that these pastoral clans, villages were not "pure" Romans.

The origins of the Rumanians point to many different components. This is not astonishing if we consider that all European nations have experienced a considerable mixture of blood so that in most cases the racial basis is no longer recognizable. This is naturally the case of the Rumanians, who lived at one of the most troubled points of the Continent and thus were exposed to many and varied foreign influences. (*39).

In light of historical evidence there is proof that these mixture-peoples migrated from south to north, and moved as clans, families or as individuals, but not as tribes. Of couse, this piece of historical evidence did not fit to the "Dako-Roman theory", and it certainly did not fit to the imagination of a "Dako-Roman continuity in Transylvania". Consequently, it seemed to be a national task for modern Rumanian politicians, and government-supported historians to prove that the Wallachian migration was actually not from the south to the north, but from the north to the south! For example, Ghyka was mentioning some "Romanized population" which was established by the Avars in Pannonia (A.D. 618), and he also explains the unquestionable existence of Vlachs in Northern

36. According to Cihac, a Rumanian linguist. even in the 20th century, the Rumanian language consisted 45.7% Slavic, 31.5% Latin, 8.4% Turkish, 7% Greek, 6% Hungarian, and 0.6% Albanian words.

37. L. Élekes: The Development of the Rumanian People. (The Hungarian Quarterly, Winter, 1941. p. 680).

38. The linguistic statistic mentioned in *36 was taken from I. Szakonyi: The first historical notes about the Wallachians and the historical bases of the Dako-Roman theory. (Kanadai Magyarsag, 1966).

39. L. Élekes: The Development of the Rumanian People. p. 678.

Bulgaria (A.D. 860) as "Dacian refugees from the north"(*40).

The traditional date of the Hungarian Conquest of the Carpathian Basin is 896. This was the year when Árpád the Conqueror led the Magyar tribes (*41) into the Carpathian Basin. Some of the latest researches, however, seem to suggest, that the so-called "Late Avars" which joined the Avar Khaganate in 670, were actually "Pre-Magyars". They were related both to Avars and the Magyars, and represented some sort of transitional tribe-organization between Avars and Magyars, both racially and linguistically. (*42). According to this newest theory, the Magyars of 896 were simply the final link in a Hun-Avar-Late Avar-Magyar chain. Each link was interrelated to the others, each of them included Mongol, and Turkish elements in a certain extent, each of them were led by Hun kings or chieftains and all of them consciously belonged to the great Turanian (Ural-Altaic) people.(*43).

From the point of view of the Transylvanian problem it did not really make any difference if the actual Hungarian Conquest took place at the end of the 9th century, or two hundred years earlier. The Late Avars did not find any traces of "Dako-Romans" in Transylvania, and the Magyars did not find them either. They certainly found, however, Hun and Avar fragments and Gepid, Goth, Hun, Avar cemeteries.

Simultaneously, the Vlach fragments were still to be found in various places of the Balkans at this time. Supposedly, most of them reached the Balkan Mountains, and several clans and families were slowly migrating northwards in Macedonia and the Dalmatian coast. The new, Orthodox Bulgaria seemed to be very attractive for them. The Bulgars of Boris (852-89), Vladimir (889-93), and Symeon (893-927) counteracted the aggressive Byzantine influence and consequently there appeared a natural base for all those who took refuge from Greek soldiers and tax-collectors. Both Bulgarians and the Romanized fragments were already Slavicized, consequently communication was relatively easy. Finally the mountains of Bulgaria offered excellent pasturages, well-separated dwellings for these welcomed shepherd-societies.

---

40. M. Gyka: A Documented Chronology of Roumanian History, P. 21-26.

41. Constituting seven tribes, they were called the "Hetumoger" (The Seven Magyars).

42. The westward movement of the Late Avars was somewhat associated with the migration of Isperikh's Bulgars to Moesia. This fact seems to indicate that perhaps both fragments were racially related, and both were directed by Hun chieftains. (The Late-Avar/Pre-Magyar Theory was introduced by Gyula László: A Kettős Honfoglalásról. (About the Double Conquest: Archaeological Ertesito, Budapest. 1970. p. 161-190).

43. Assuming the reality of this theory, the Székelys (who are traditionally Hun fragments) could be Late Avars by origin. The conscious interrelationship between Turanian (Ural-Altaic) tribe-organizations were suggested by several historians before G. Laszlo.

87

IV.

VLACHS IN THE "FIRST BULGARIAN EMPIRE" (VIII-XI CENTURIES).

In 867, the Schism between Byzantine and Roman Christianity was associated with the sharp controversy between the pro-Roman Ignatius and Patriarch Photius, who proved to be not only an enthusiastic Greek-Orthodox by faith, but an anti-Roman and pro-Greek by national feeling (*44). His patriarchate coincided with the rule of Basil I, founder of the Macedonian Dynasty (867-886), an Armenian, whose reign initiated what was probably the most glorious period of Byzantine history. Under his direction the Empire became a purely Greek Monarchy. In 867, Photius had been banished and Ignatius, the pro-Roman, was recalled for a while, to symbolize the peace with Rome on papal terms, (*45), but the conflict between Greeks and Latins became permanent. The emperor himself was only Armenian by extraction, but he was born in Macedonia, thus he concentrated on Balkanic affairs much more than his predecessors had done.

We could rightly assume that the reinforced re-Hellenization, and the increased bureaucratization of the Balkans disturbed the lives of all those rural fragments, which still communicated using some sort of deformed, vulgarized Latin, and did not wish to adopt Greek language and culture. These clans, families and individuals followed the ways of those who left Epirus, Thessalonica and Macedonia decades (perhaps even centuries) ago. This northward migration used the natural roadways of rivers (and their valleys) flowing into the Aegean Sea (Vardar, Strymon, Hebrus, etc.). They also moved along the Adriatic coast up to Dalmatia, where the direction of their movement turned to the east, and using the rivers (Drina, Morava, Sava) again, most of them reached the area south of the Lower Danube. In 877, this northward movement of these pastoral societies assumably became quicker, when the enthusiastically pro-Greek Photius was restored once more and he, in alliance with imperial troops, turned sharply against Roman customs and Latin-speaking groups everywhere in the Byzantine Empire. It was true that Leo VI (the "Wise"; 886-912) put Ignatius back in power again, but this time (c. 900) most of the Romanized inhabitants had already left the southern Balkans.

We must not think that the Romanized elements of the Balkans knew anything about the Greek-Latin controversy. Living in the mountains, or on the Adriatic coast, occupied with grazing their animals, they were separated from internal and international events not only by their permanent separation but by their illiterate characteristics too. They really

---

44. In the Council of Constantinople (867), Photius anathematized the pope, and rejected the idea of Rome's primacy.

45. The popes of this time were Nicholas I (the Saint: 858-67), and Adrian II (867-72).

did not know anything about political, social, religious, etc. reasons, but actually suffered under the circumstances of the growing Greek pressure.

The most attractive place of migration was (or seemed to be) Bulgaria, where Symeon, second son of Boris I, was ruler at this time (893-927). He was a proud, ambitious ruler, and the first of those Bulgarian kings, who assumed the title of "Tsar". (*46). He had been educated at Constantinople (as a monk), and he was deeply imbued with Hellenistic culture, but he also realized that his people were a mixture of many racial elements, and not any of these elements were Greek.(*47). Ambitious to be the only authority in the Balkans, he turned against Byzantium several times with force, and obviously he welcomed non-Greek refugees, especially those peaceful-looking shepherds, in his country.

The Balkan Mountains proved to be not only a good pastoral area for the newcomers, but it was a relatively peaceful place, quite far-away from wars of the north and of the south. (*48). As a result of these wars, Bulgaria lost its territories in Southern Transylvania, Munthenia and Moldavia.(*49). In the south, the Byzantine forces prevented Symeon from becomming ruler of Byzantium. However, this could not stop "the Tsar" from proclaiming himself "Emperor of the Romans and the Bulgars."(*50)

At the time, when various Romanized pastoral fragments were migrating (northwards) in the Balkans, and many of them found temporary security in the Balkan Mts. of the Bulgarians, it was also possible that some limited groups crossed already the Lower Danube, and even infiltrated to S. Transylvania, Anonymus, notary of King Béla III (or IV), mentioned "certain Vlach", named "Gelou", who ruled a small group of "Vlachs and Slavs" in Transylvania in the 10th century. Although Anonymus confused his own (political, social, ethnographic) age (which was the XII-XIII C.) with the age of the Hungarian Conquest (IX-X centuries), after all, it was not completely impossible that some few Vlach settlers already had infiltrated from the Balkans. (*51). Rumanian historians, however, welcomed "Gelou" as the "missing-and-found link" between the "Dako-Romans" and modern Rumanians of Transylvania,

46. "Tsar", or "Czar" was actually a shortened form for the Latin "Caesar".
47. The term "Bolgar" ("Bulgar") means "mixture" in Old Turkish language. This term is understandable, if we consider that Old-Bolgary (N. of the Black Sea) already combined elements of Hun, Turkish, Tatar, Mongol, etc. The Slavization of the Balkan Bulgars, who were still ruled by Hun aristocracy, represented newer elements of mixture. The majority of the Bulgars became Slavs. The adaption of the Romanized population from the south brought another racial and linguistic element into the country.
48. In the north, Symeon was allied with the Petchenegs against the Magyars, but finally, the Bulgarian Zalan was driven out from Maros valley (Transylvania). The Petchenegs stopped at the Carpathians, but conquered Moldavia and all areas N. of the Lower Danube. In the south the Bulgars defeated the Greeks in 894, peace was made three years later, but Symeon attacked Byzantium in 914 again, raiding into Macedonia, Thessaly, and Albania. Symeon also defeated the Serbs (926), but was unable to take Constantinople without a fleet.
49. The Petchenegs (Slav: Patzinaks, Hung: Besenyős) were Turko-Tatar nomads.
50. Constantinople considered itself as "the Second Rome", thus the title represents the claim to rule both Bulgars and Byzantines. Emp. Constantinos (Porphyrogenitos; 913-59) protested, but Pope John X (914-28) recognized his title.
51. We will return to this Anonymus-problem in our Chapter VI.

and they introduced Gelou as "Prince" of a "Wallachian Principality" in Transylvania in the 10th century.(*52).

The Magyars, arriving in the Carpathian Basin (considered as the "Inheritance of Attila") at the end of the 9th century, called Transylvania as "Erdőelve" ("Erdő: forest, "elve": principle, or - in this case - inland; later it became "Erdely", and Transylvanian Vlachs deformed it to "Ardeal"). In the 10th-11th centuries, the most powerful lord or Erdoelve was Gyula, a chieftain, whose daughter Saroldu (Sarolta) was educated in Constantinople and married to Prince Géza, who was later to become head of the Hungarian state (972-97). Saroldu became the mother of Vajk (christened as István), first king of Hungary (997-1038); canonized in 1083). (*53).

Although "Wallachian Principalities" did not exist in Hungarian Transylvania after the Hungarian conquest (or before it), one should not completely deny the possibility of the existence of small Vlach clans on both sides of the Lower Danube and even in the Transylvanian Alps. Most of them, of course, were victimized by bloodthirsty Petcheneg nomads, who ruled the outside semi-circle of the Carpathians at this time, or forced to assimilate. There is no evidence of any Vlach principality in Transylvania in the 10-11th centuries, and there is not any authentic historical map of the world which would show "Wallachians", or "Vlach principalities" on the map of Transylvania before the 13th century.

The Magyars assert when they entered it, Transylvania was still uninhabited, unless the Székelys were there, or a few Bulgars and Slavs. The Roumanians, they say, are of Balkan origin, and entered Transylvania only after the twelfth century as refugees, vagabonds, and wandering shepherds. The Roumanians claim with passion that their ancestors have, on the contrary, inhabited Transylvania, in unbroken continuity, since the days of Roman greatness ... I have no intention attempting to judge between these rival views ... Whether, in any case, there were no Roumanians in the tenth century, or one, or thousands: whether they constituted a quorum within the meaning of the act or no, they cannot have been either numerous or important, neither can they have possessed any ordered social or political society, for the organization which Hungary adopted for her new possession took small account of them; at most, perhaps, accepting the allegiance of certain mountain chieftains, who were, presumably, held responsible for the conduct ot their followers. They

52. Rumanian historians are mentioning also "Menumorut", and "Glad" as "Wallachian princes" in X Century Transylvania. According to Anonymous, "Mén-Ma-rot" was the grandson of Marót one of Árpád, the Conqueror's chieftains, who settled in the area of the Maros-Szamos rivers. (He became "Mén-marót", because he kept too many concubines. Hung "Mén": horse). Glad was probably a Bulgarian chief, living south of the Maros at this time.

53. The term "gyula" meant a high military position among the Magyars, based on the Turkish "jula". It became the name of a respected Transylvanian Magyar family in which the high position of the "gyula" was inherited from father to son throughout generations. Gyula's residence was Gyulafehérvár (Rum: Alba Julia). The Petcheneg tribal-system have had also a tribe, named "Gyula".

were not, however, granted any status as a "nation" nor do we find any record even of isolated groups possessing "privileges" in the interior of the country. (*54).

As we realize from this quotation, C.A. Macartney, the eminent British historian, a specialist of medieval East-Central European history, attempted to be as cautious and as objective as humanly possible. With the exception of Anonymous' (mentioned) "Gelou", he could not find any traces of Vlachs up to the 13th century in any of the (Byzantine, Bulgarian, Slav, or Hungarian) sources, but he assumes some slight possibility of some Vlach fragment even before it. He did not believe, however, that "Gelou", or any other Vlach existence in the country of the early Árpáds (*55) could represent any evidence of the "Dako-Roman continuity", only supposed that the pre-13th century Vlachs (if there were any) were the first forerunners of the Wallachian infiltration to Transylvania.

Unquestionably, Symeon's Bulgaria, which was forced to abandon the Northern side of the Lower Danube to the Petchenegs, still owned a stronghold at the point where the River Sava flows into the Danube. Its Byzantine name was Singidunum. Assumably, Tsar Symeon sent only trusted, reliable and warlike Bulgarians to guard this fortress - some of them could have been Vlach by origin.(*56).

Symeon died in 927, and his son and successor was Peter (927-69), a ruler, who was pious, well-intentioned, but rather weak. He made peace with Constantinople, and Leo (the Wise) recognized him as Bulgarian ruler, and he also acknowledged Bulgaria as a semi-independent Greek-Orthodox patriarchate. Bulgaria, during this period was preoccupied by the constant threat from the Magyars and the Petchenegs (or Patzinaks) (*57), who occasionally reached even the mountainous hiding places of the Vlachs. The Croatians and Serbians simultaneously established their small but independent nation-states, (*58), and gradually became quite hostile to Bulgaria. In the second half of the 10th century, Sviatoslav and his Kievan (Russian) Slavs invaded Bulgaria. In 967, King Peter was able to force Sviatoslav to withdraw, but his successor, Boris II (969-72) was able to defend Bulgaria only by the help of Byzantium. As a consequence the king of the Bulgars was obliged to abdicate, thus the Bulgarian patriarchate was abolished, and Bulgaria itself became a Byzantine vassal-state for a while.

These were black years for the Romanized shepherd societies of the

54. C.A. Macartney: *Hungary and Her Successors.* Oxford University Press, 1937. p. 256.

55. "The Árpáds' : kings of the Árpád dynasty, descendants and successors of Árpád the Conqueror.

56. Singidunum was called "Nándorfehérvár" by the Hungarians. (Nándor: north-Bulgars, - "Fehérvár": white fortress). The city is called "Belgrade" today, and it is the capital of Yugoslavia.

57. The tribes of Zsolt, Vaisz, and Taksony (successors of Árpád the Conqueror) raided Bulgaria in 934, 943, 958 and 962. The Petchenegs crossed the Lower Danube and raided Bulgaria in 944.

58. Tomislav became King of Croatia already in 924, accepting a crown from Pope John X (914-28), and turning his people towards Roman Christianity. The Serbians remained Byzantine-Orthodox, but under King Chaslav (960) they separated themselves both from Bulgaria and Byzantium.

Balkan Mountains. They were disturbed by the attacks of Magyars, Pet-chenegs, Kievan Slavs, and also by Byzantine bureaucracy which reached them once more again. Several of them abandoned their ancient occupations, such as sheep-breeding, and instead they became transport-carriers. As a matter of fact, probably so many of them adopted this new occupation, that the Bulgars and Serbians used them as "kjelators" (carriers, or transporters in medieval Slavic language). (*59).

The year of 976 was a significant year in Bulgaria both from the Bulgarian and a Wallachian point of view. In this year, Samuel, son of a Bulgarian governor of one of the western districts, which had been unaffected by the Russian invasion, set himself up as the new ruler of Bulgaria. (*60). In this very year, the Byzantine chronicler, named Ioannas Skylitses, noted that one of Samuel's brothers, named David, was murdered by some of the "kjelator-Vlachs", somewhere in the region of the Lakes Prepa and Kastoria. (*61). According to our best knowledge, this was the very first occasion when the word "Vlach" appeared in historical writing. The Byzantine chronicler obviously picked this expression up from the Slav-Bulgarian vocabulary, since the Bulgarians (and also the Serbians) called almost all peoples of the Balkan Mountains as "kjelator-Vlachs", or simply as "Vlachs" at this time. (Its linguistic variations are: "Vlahi", "Volochi"; its Greek versions are: "Vlachos", and "Vlachus".)

The first Bulgarian Empire (founded by Isperikh in the 7th century) disintegrated at the end of the 10th century. Already in 996, Emperor Basil II (who was called by Byzantines as "Bulgaroktonos", "Slayer of the Bulgarians"; 976-1025) proceeded to reduce one Bulgarian stronghold after another. Samuel was helpless, since officers defected from his army, and, remembering the tragedy of his brother, David, he saw the probability of betrayal by his Vlach subjects, too. His son, Gabriel Radomir (or "Romanus", was murdered (1016) by his own cousin, John Vladislav (1016-18), who (as successor of the Bulgarian throne) continued the war against the Byzantines. He was also killed in the battle near Dyrrhacium. Following this, Bulgaria was incorporated into the Byzantine Empire. The Bulgarian Patriarchate was once more abolished, only the Archbishop of Ochrid retained practical autonomy. Many members of the Bulgarian aristocracy settled in Constantinople and assimilated into the leading Byzantine families.

Some of the Vlach subjects were obviously trying to save themselves by betraying their Bulgarian lords to the Byzantines. Others, however, probably those on the northern slopes of the Balkan Mountains, attempted

59. "Calator" is a brother-word of "kjelator" in the modern Rumanian language. It still means: pastoral-, or carrier-Vlachs.

60. Samuel expanded his dominion to Sofia, re-established the Bulgarian partiarchate and after 986, extended his power to the Black Sea.

61. These lakes are at the area where the River Vistrica springs.

to leave dangerous Bulgaria, by migrating northwards. Many Vlach fragments crossed the Danube and appeared in Petcheneg-occupied Munthenia, offering their services to the Petchenegs. They chose life in the unknown, dangerous Petcheneg land, fearing the possible Byzantine persecution. In the first half of the 11th century, the gravity of the Vlachs was still in Northern Bulgaria, but more and more Vlachs moved one-step-northwards again.

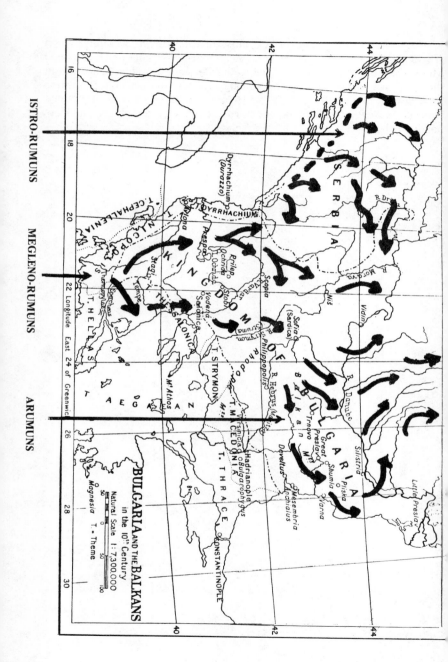

ISTRO-RUMUNS

MEGLENO-RUMUNS

ARUMUNS

BULGARIA AND THE BALKANS
in the 10th Century
Natural Scale 1:7,300,000

T = Theme

V.

VLACHS IN CUMANIA
AND IN THE SECOND BULGARIAN EMPIRE.

Following the collapse of the First Bulgarian Empire (1018), Bulgaria was, for 168 years, part of the Empire of Byzantium. Taxation was heavy in the newly occupied Bulgarian territory. Basil II, the "Slayer of the Bulgarians" cruelly suppressed all new subjects who survived. The Bulgarian Vlachs attempted to disappear among their rocky mountains, or they tried to confuse the Byzantine tax-collectors and other bureaucrats by their permanent migration. From 1020 still remained one of the "sigillions" (orders) of the emperor, which prescribed the duties, and responsibilities of the Archbishop of Ochrida. (*62). Detailing the bishoprics and listing all the duties, the sigillions notes, that the Archbishop should organize the wandering Vlachs somehow, and should attempt to collect the ecclesiastical tax. The Vlachs were forced to pay and to settle down, but many of the Vlach families hid themselves successfully again, or crossed the Lower Danube joining their fellow nationalities on the fields of the Petchenegs, because they chose danger and uncertainty rather than settlement, organization and tax-payment.

The Vlachs favoured peace and separation and they avoided fight at this time. They used every opportunity to escape from military service, but in some cases they were forced to serve their masters on the battlefields, whichever side they incidentally belonged. For example, when the Petchenegs invaded the Balkans in 1027 (in the time of Cons'antine VIII, the younger brother of Basil II; 1025-28), we may assume, that some Vlachs were recruited both on the Petcheneg and the Byzantine side.(*63). When Byzantium organized campaigns against the Sicilian Saracens, Vlachs were also in the mercenary army.(*64).

In 1028, a female ruler followed Constantine on the imperial throne. Her name was Zoe, and she was the third daughter of the late emperor. Though she was 48 years old, married three times, associating her husbands (and favourites) in the imperial office (1028-50). In the period of her rule Byzantium was involved mainly in the defense of its far-eastern frontiers against the Seljuk Turks, and it could not concentrate on the organization and supervision of its Bulgarian territories with the same strength. The Bulgarian-Wallachian combined forces used this opportunity to revolt under Peter Deljan, who was a descendant of Tsar Samuel, the son of Gabriel Radomir. Deljan was defeated in 1041, but in

63. Ochrida is in Macedonia (it belongs to Yugoslavia today). It was an important political and social center of Bulgaria in the X-XI centuries.

63. The Petchenegs (Patzinaks) were finally driven back over the Danube by the general Constantine Diogenes.

64. The Byzantine fleet attempted to clear the Mediterranean of Saracens (Moslem Arabs). Part of this campaign was a campaign to Sicily (1038).

1072 another Bulgarian, named George Voitech led an uprising against the Byzantine overlords in which he was also suppressed.

Bulgaria had to suffer under the repeated attacks of the Petchenegs during the same period. Their final raid came in 1048-54, but this invasion proved to be rather a sort of migration, under the pressure of the Cumans.(*65).

The Cumans were also nomadic horsemen of Turkish origin. (They were also called "Kipchaks", and "Polovtsi" by the Russians and "Kuns" by the Magyars.) They used the very same east-west road which was used by the Huns, Avars, Magyars, Petchenegs (tribe-organizations to which they were related) before them: the road of the Great Migrations north of the Caspian and Black Seas. They conquered South Russia, later the region between the Crimea and the Eastern Carpathians in the 11th century, and they appeared also north of the Southern Danube valley, destroying the Petcheneg Empire and threatening the Kingdom of Hungary. In 1064, they crossed the Danube, invading the Bulgarian-Wallachian settlements, and flooded the Balkans as far as Thessalonica. They were finally driven back by local forces, but they occupied Munthenia, the Sereth, Pruth, Dniester valleys, Crimea, the southern Dniepr, the Donets valleys east to the Ural Mountains, and the northern coast of the Caspian Sea. They took over all the servant-peoples of the Petchenegs who survived the turmoil, including the Wallachian settlements of Munthenia.

Unquestionably, several smaller Wallachian fragments were wandering in the Balkans at the same time. One of the well informed Byzantine officials was a man by the name of Kedrenos, who mentioned them as shepherds migrating all over the Balkans. Another chronicler was Kekaumenos, who was a chronicler of Romanos Diogenes (1067-71), emperor of Byzantium.

Kekaumenos, who was a man of Armenian origin, but a faithful servant of the Byzantine Imperial Court, wished to commemorate his uncle, who played some sort of positive role on the Byzantine side, when the Thessalian revolt broke out. This revolt was associated with the Cuman invasion when the Cumans attacked Thessaly, and when some portion of the local population used this opportunity to revolt against Constantinople. According to the description of the chronicler, the Wallachians of Thessaly undertook the role of the traitors immediately, attempting to instigate the Thessalian Greeks and other nationalities against Byzantium, and, possibly, for the support of the Cuman invaders. Kekaumenos details the life-style of the Vlachs, reminding the readers that the language of these pastoral peoples shows some traces of Latin. He also mentions that the illiterate society of these semi-nomads could be quite

65. Many of these settled down in northeastern Bulgaria and assimilated into the Bulgars. The era of Petcheneg domination was over. The Bulgars were forced to face the menace of the Cumans.

suspicious, wherever they appear, since they are notorious double-dealers. They are serving everybody and they are usually betraying anybody, whoever is their master. (*66). In one of his other works,(*67), Kekaumenos returns to this Thessalian rebellion again and mentions Nikulitsas, his uncle, and calls him "Prince of Hellas" at this time. He also makes some remarks about those "traitorous Vlachs" again. It seems that the Wallachian problem engaged the Byzantine public opinion quite a lot in these critical years, and probably the Imperial Court did not really mind the northwardly migration of these unreliable shepherds.(*68).

The Cumans realized the strength of Byzantium and attempted to invade Hungary in 1068 thus pursuing those Petcheneg refugee fragments, which were requesting asylum in the Hungarian Kingdom. (*69). The invaders penetrated into Hungary almost to the Tisza river, but finally they were defeated by King Solomon's cousins, Princes Géza and László at Cserhalom.(*70).

The Petchenegs were already partially annihilated by the Cumans at this time, but some surviving fragments still represented a considerable force, and they were pushed by the Cumans slightly westward in the Lower Danube valley. They probably mixed themselves with migratory Vlachs in 1071, when they conquered Sirmium (Hung: Szerem-ség), which happened to be a Hungarian dominion at this time. The Hungarian army crosssed the River Száva (Sava) and cleared Sirmium of the Petchenegs, who. as it was clarified at this time, were actually acting as frontier guards employed by Byzantium. This incident spoiled the relationship between Emperor Michael VII (1071-78) and Hungary, and the situation became even more serious when the ambitious King Solomon turned against Nicetas, the captain of Nándorfehérvár (which was a Byzantine stronghold at this time), to punish him as the person who started this Petcheneg adventure. Nicetas surrendered Nándorfehér-vár, and the Hungarians penetrated south into Byzantine territory down to Nis. There, Prince Géza, one of the leaders of the Magyar army, made peace with the Byzantine representatives, returning all the war prisoners. This gesture improved the Greek-Magyar relationship right away (*71), and it was important for both Byzantium and Hungary, which countries equally faced the problem of Cuman invasions at this time.

66. Interestingly enough, Kekaumenos mentions even Dacia Aureliana in his work in association with Romanized peoples on the Balkans. He proved to be very confused in this particular subtopic, since he puts even King Decebal into the IIIrd Century.

67. Kekaumenos' works were found by V. Vasiljevskij, a Russian Byzantologist in the Synodian Library of Moscow (1881). The overall title of the Codex, written in Greek, was "Strategikon" (Knowledge of Strategy).

68. The northward migration of the Vlachs permanently continued in these decades in two major areas: (a) from Epirus, Thessaly and Macedonia to the Balkan Mountains of Bulgaria and (b) from Bulgaria to the land of the Cumans.

69. These Petcheneg refugees were settled down by Solomon, King of Hungary (1063-74) in the Lake Fertő and River Vág area (1065).

70. Princes Géza and László (sons of King Béla I) both became rulers of Hungary in a later period. Prince Géza (as King Géza I: 1074-77), and his younger brother, ruled Hungary as László I (the Saint: 1077-95). According to the Hungary Chronicles, especially Prince László proved to be a hero in battles against the invading Cumans.

At this point, let us raise the question: just how much were those Cumans really "Cumans", or in what extent were rather a mixture of Cumans and Vlachs?

Unquestionably, a very large portion of the Balkan-Vlachs were already in Cuman service, since they amalgamated themselves with Cumans. This amalgamation was useful for the Cumans (because the Vlachs could be used not only as pastoral servants, but as guides on the hidden roads, and forests), and was good for the Vlachs (who were looking for military support against the Byzantines). The Vlachs, originally humble shepherds and refugees from the south, were proud to be associated with the powerful Cumans, whose country extended from the Lower Danube Valley to the Caspian and up to Russia.

"They were enriched by a new ruling class. That is why, in medieval Rumanian documents, most of the nobles have Turki names; ... they prove that a considerable part of the Rumanian leaders in the Middle Ages was of Turki origin, and for a long time remained faithful to Turki customs" (*72).

Another episode of Hungarian history in which Cumans were involved came in 1083, when Solomon, the former king, who was deposed by Geza I, in 1074, visited Cumania and suprisingly married one of the daughters of Kutesk, ruler of the South Danubian Cumans.(*73).

Solomon encouraged Kutesk to invade Hungary, but László I, the royal hero of Cuman wars defeated the invaders again. Then Solomon and Kutesk turned the Cuman forces against Byzantium (1087), but his attack was unsuccessful again. (*74).

A much more dangerous and memorable Cuman invasion threatened Constantinople in 1094, when Constantine Diogenes, a pretender to the throne of Alexius Comnenus, the ruling emperor (1081-1118), crossed the Danube with a large army of Cumans. He besieged Adrianople, but finally was defeated in the battle of Taurocomon. Anna Komnena, daughter of the emperor, and enthusiastic chronicler of the age, mentions the Wallachians again in connection with the Cumans. When the emperor led a campaign against the invaders (1095), he reached even the Balkan Mountains of Bulgaria, where he considered a decisive battle. Pursuing the already defeated Cumans, and being prepared for some other confron-

71. As a symbol of Byzantine gratitude, King Géza I received a crown from Michael Vii (Dukas) in about 1074-75. This crown became part of the Hungarian "Holy Crown". Géza also married Synadene, a Byzantine princess. For Byzantium this step was important because the Empire was endangered by the attacks of the Cumans (from the north), and of the Seljuk Turks (from Asia Minor) in the same time.

72. L. Élekes: *"The Development of the Rumanian People"*. p. 681.

(Note: The looks of most of the Rumanians are still Turkish. The ethnic customs are similar to the customs of Turkey Proper. The reason was not so much connected with the long Moslem domination of Wallachia, but with the fact of Cuman-Vlach intermarriage in the XI Century.)

73. Solomon became a bigamist, since he was already husband of Judith, d. of Emperor Henry III of Germany (1039-56).

74. The Cumans ravaged the entire eastern Balkan region as far as Constantinople, until Emperor Alexius bought them off, took them into imperial service and used them to annihilate the Petchenegs (Battle of Leburnon; 1091.)

tation with other Cuman forces, the Byzantine army arrived to Anchiales (a certain point on the northern slopes of the Balkan Mountains, not too far from the Danube, dominated by the Cumans at this particular time). Then, Pudolos, a Vlach advisor of the emperor, suggested that the Byzantine forces should approach the Danube, where the Cumans could be expected to appear. At the same time, other Vlachs (we do not know that they were co-operating with Pudolos or not), led the main force of Cumans and advanced in various hidden paths to surround the Greeks, and to attack them from behind. The Vlachs (both in Byzantine and in Cuman service) were more familiar with the Mountains than their masters. Anna Komnena could not really justify who were planned victims of this treachery, and whether the Vlachs in Cuman service and in Byzantine service were co-operating at all. Beside the possibility of co-operation it was also possible that the Cumanian Vlachs attempted to betray their cruel Cuman masters, while Byzantine Vlachs tried to betray the hated Greeks, so the Vlachs, coincidentally, betrayed each other. Whatever was the real case this incident (described by the imperial chronicler), it seemed to prove Kekaumenos' opinion about the Vlachs, whose history contains several very similar acts of treason, whoever was their ally.(*75)

While Vlach fragments amalgamated with the Cumans north of the Danube, a considerable number of other Vlachs remained among the Bulgars, who were dominated by Byzantium since 1018, and who attempted an unsuccessful rebellion against Constantinople in 1040 and also in 1072. Using the confusion of the Balkans caused by the Cuman invasions, the Bogomil heresy(*76), the marches of the First and Second Crusades (1096 and 1147), and also using the opportunity that Byzantium was weakened by the Seljuk Turks, a third attempt finally brought freedom for the Bulgars. In 1185, two Bulgarian lords, John and Peter Asen, (*77) collected a large force of embittered Bulgarians and Vlachs, and being supported by the Cumans, attacked the local imperial forces of Emperor Isaac Angelus (1185-95). The imperial army defeated them in the first battle, but the two Asens fled to the Cumans and returned again with a huge Cuman army. The combined Cuman-Bulgarian forces devastated the Central Balkans and even Thrace, annihilating the Greek population. The Greek commanders were unable to suppress the movement at this time, which resulted in the formation of a new Bulgarian State north of the Balkan Mountains (1188), called the Second Bulgarian Empire. It became a very powerful kingdom, and Trnovo became the new political and cultural centre for the two Asen brother, who were joint rulers of this

75. Byzantium learned from this bitter lesson; Constantinople did not need to use Vlach "advisors" or Vlach "alliance" anymore. (Emperor Alexius rather employed Cuman mercenaries attacking King László's Hungary - without success. Later, Emperor John Comnenus, 1118-43, also used Cuman forces defeating the last surviving fragment of the Petchenegs in 1122).

76. This religious movement flourished especially among Bulgars, advocating political independency and resentment of Byzantine culture.

77. The Asen brothers appeared from the vicinity of Trnovo (North-Central Bulgaria).

new Bulgaria.

The participation of the local Vlachs could have been very strong in this new kingdom. The founders, John and Peter Asen, were Vlachs themselves.

"The Bulgarians ... regained their independence and again created a powerful kingdom under the Asenids ... That dynasty was of 'Vlach' origin." (*78).

The Asens were supported, of course not only by their local Bulgarians and Vlachs, but by their northern neighbours, the Cumans and Turko-Wallachians. This alliance, however, did not seem to be strong enough facing the still powerful Byzantines. Then, in 1189, the Asens attempted to effect an alliance with Frederick Barbarossa, ruler of the Holy Roman Empire (1152-1190), when he took the Cross, and led the Third Crusade to the Holy Land (1189-1192). John Asen offered him a combined Bulgarian-Wallachian-Cuman army, if he would turn all his crusading forces not against the Seljuk Turks but against Byzantium. The German Emperor avoided friction and did not welcome the proposition.(*79.). The Bulgarians, however, resumed their raids into Thrace and even Macedonia, and they completely defeated the imperial army of Isaac Angelus near Berrhoe (1190) and at Arcadiopolis (1194).

In 1196, John Asen was murdered by boyar conspirators, and Peter Asen became the sole ruler, but one year later he himself became victim of his rivals. Their youngest brother, Kaloyan (Joanitsa) took over leadership (1197-1207) and the Asenid Dynasty ruled Bulgaria until 1258. The greatest ruler of the Asenids was John Asen II (1218-1241) (according to some sources: Ivan Asen). During his rule, Bulgaria became the strongest and largest state of the Balkans. After his rule, however, Bulgaria was victimized by the invasion of the Mongols (Tatars; 1241), and by the insurrection of Ivajlo, the "Tsar of shepherds" (1277-80), which was directed both against the Tatar invaders, and Bulgarian feudal lords. When the Turkish invasion began at the beginning of the 14th century, Bulgaria already had disintegrated into three small portions (Trnovo, Vidin and Dobrudja). Thus they became easy victims of Osman imperialism of Bayazid I (1389-1402).

Until this time, part of the Vlachs of Bulgaria assimilated to the Bulgars, the largest part, however, followed the roads of their relatives into Cumania and even to the Hungarian Kingdom.

---

78. Oscar Haleczki: *Borderlands of Western Civilization.* 66.
79. To the satisfaction of Barbarossa, Isaac Angelus did not oppose the crossing of the crusaders into Anatolia.

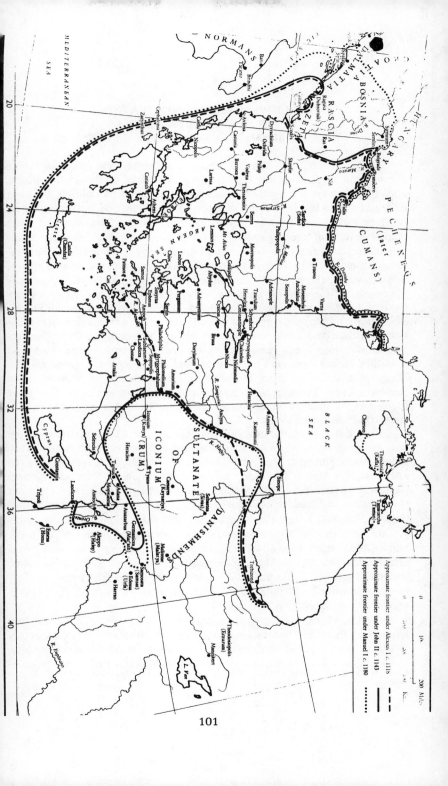

MEDITERRANEAN SEA

NORMANS

CROATIA
DALMATIA
BOSNIA
RASCIA
HUNGARY
PECHENEGS
(later CUMANS)

Bari
Taranto
Brindisi

Spalato
Sebenico
Ras
Sirmium
Semlin
Belgrade
Branicevo
Nish
Vidin

Ragusa (Dubrovnik)
Cattaro
Antivari
Scodra
Dyrrachium
Ochrida
Prilep
Skoplje
Velbuzd
Vodena
Berroea
Thessalonica
Serres
Sardica (Sofia)

Corfù
Nicopolis
Cephalonia
Zacynthus

Larissa
Mt Athos
Philippopolis
Trnovo
Varna

Corinth
Athens
Thebes
Aegina
Euboea

Serres
Lemnos
Adramyttium
Chios
Lesbos
Gallipoli
Mt Athos

AEGEAN SEA

Mesembria
Anchialus
Sozopolis
Adrianople
Heraclea
Selymbria
Traianupolis
Constantinople
Chrysopolis
Chalcedon
Nicomedia
Nicaea

Crete (Candia)

Patmos
Cos
Samos
Ephesus
Smyrna
Sardis
Pergamum
R. Maeander

Attalia

Philadelphia
Sublaeum
Laodicea
Choma
Doryiaeum
Philomelium
Myriocephalum
Sozopolis
Amorium

Brusa

R. Sangarius
Ancyra
Heraclea
Kastamuni
Amastris

Sinope

Trebizond

BLACK SEA

Cherson
Theodosia (Kaffa)
Tamatarcha (Taman)

SULTANATE OF ICONIUM (RUM)

Iconium (Konya)
Heraclea
Seleucia
R. Halys
Caesarea
Tyana

DANISHMENDS

Sebastea (Sivas)

Cyprus
Constantia

Tripoli

Laodicea

Orontes

Antioch
Mopsuestia
Tarsus
Anazarbus
Germanicea (Mar'ash)
Sozopetra
Samosata (Samsat)
Edessa (Urfa)
Harran

Emesa (Homs)

Melitene (Malatya)

Theodosiopolis (Erzurum)
Manzikert
L. Van

R. Euphrates

Approximate frontier under Alexius I c. 1118
Approximate frontier under John II c. 1143
Approximate frontier under Manuel I c. 1180

0   100   200 Miles
0   Km.

R. Strymon
R. Marica
R. Danube
Morava
Drin

101

VI.

EARLY WALLACHIAN INFILTRATION
TO THE HUNGARIAN KINGDOM.
(XII-XIII CENTURIES.)

Some groups of Vlachs from Munthenia and Oltenia (*80) crossed the Transylvanian Alps in the second half of the 12th century, and appeared on the northern slopes of these high mountains. It is not easy to assume the first years of their appearance, and it would also be hard to justify as to what exactly was the real racial and linguistic characteristic of those pastoral families, who sneaked into the Transylvanian Basin from the land of the Cumans, using the high and narrow mountain-passes, the valleys of the Olt, Csill, Jolomica and Bodza rivers, and especially the Focsáni Gate, which led to Fogaras county. Were they "Romanized" Cumans or were they "Turkicized" Vlachs? Since a large part of their vocabulary indicated that they were actually of Slavic, Bulgarian, or Serbian origin, since they used a considerable number of vulgarized Latin words, and since they entered from Cuman-Wallachia, their name remained Vlach even in Transylvania. This was how they called their own nationality, and following this expression, the Magyars also called them as "Olah". These newcomers seemed to be humble. They chose the high-mountainous no-mans-land for their dwellings, for their sheep and goats, and they seemed to be quite grateful for the permission of settlement.

They did not call the new land as "Dacia", or "Transylvania", since they never heard of these geographical terms. Since they did not have too much connection with Magyar officials, whose official language was the Latin at this time, they adapted the expressions of the local rural Hungarian population. Transylvania was not called Erdőelve at the turn of the 12th - 13th centuries, but as Erdely. The newcomers deformed this term to "Ardeal", and this word remained their expression for Transylvania up to the 20th century. They seemed to acknowledge with humility that they were admitted, and they could occupy certain limited areas, consequently the Hungarian word for "admission" - "befogadás" became "fagadui", and the other Hungarian word, which means "offering a shelter" - "szállasadás" was adapted as "salasdui" in their primitive communication.

For the Vlachs it seemed to be natural that they could not claim any leading cultural position in Hungary. First of all, they were completely illiterate, and without any desire or tendency for education. Secondly,

80. Oltenia and Munthenia are the main areas of the territory between the Transylvanian Alps and the Lower Danube. On the historical maps this area was marked as Wallachia beginning with the XII-XIII Centuries.

they did not wish to be part of the peasant society of Medieval Hungary since they isolated themselves to areas which were previously unpopulated. Thirdly, these newcomers had a tradition of being only humble servants, wherever they appeared in the course of their wanderings of many centuries. In Byzantium the Greeks, in Bulgaria the Bulgars, in Cumania the Cumans were the ruling class and

> "... the Serbian princes, for example, bought and sold the Rumanians living in their country like slaves." (*81).

The other - rather linguistic - observation was that

> "... the ancient neo-Latin element, the core of the Rumanians, was at the time latent, mostly hiding in the lower classes, but by its numerical majority it was gradually getting the upper hand and assimilating its leaders of ethnically foreign origin. This process was not a difficult one, because of the primitive social order, in which leaders did not come from a secluded group but mingled with the people in undifferentiated forms of small communities." (*82).

It was quite possible that in this early time of Wallachian migration, their chiefs, their leaders, heads of clans and families were not Vlachs at all, but Slavs or Turki-Cumans.

> "Thus, the Council of Ragusa once mentions 'Slav Vlachs', Pope Clement VI speaks of 'Rumanian Vlachs' "

- but this expression was born already in the middle of the 14th century (*83).

When in the year of 1150, Géza II (1141-1162) permitted a Saxon settlement (Germans from the Moselle region) in the Southern Transylvania regions, in the same period some Petcheneg and Cuman fragments were also permitted to settle in Eastern Hungary. Were these Turkish elements associated with Wallachians? There is no documentary evidence which concerns it, but after all, it is not completely impossible. The following years could be characterized partly as the years of Byzantine wars, and partly as the years of Byzantine influence. The opportunity of infiltration was very limited. The southern frontier-line was heavily guarded, and in times when Byzantium influenced the Hungarian internal affairs, Vlachs and Cumans probably did not feel to join a country where bureaucrats from Constantinople introduced customs and gave advice.

After the death of Béla III (1172-1196) who proved to be one of the greatest rulers of Medieval Hungary, and who was educated in Constantinople himself, troubled times came to Hungary. Béla's weak, unable successors between 1196 and 1235 did not have time or did not take time to look at what was really happening in Transylvania, or as a matter of fact in other parts of Hungary as well. This was the period when more and

81. L. Élekes: The Development of the Rumanian People, p. 680
82. Ibid. p. 681-682.
83. Ibid. p. 682.

more Vlachs poured into Southern Transylvania, especially into the un-populated areas of the Fogaras county. More and more shepherds of Balkanic origin appeared on the mountain pasturages.

On these mountains life was very simple. Even though starvation was part of the problem, these newcomers enjoyed the fact that the inhabitan-ts of Transylvania did not disturb them, and from then on the Tran-sylvanian Alps separated them and defended them from the south. Many of these shepherds probably escaped from their Cuman lords, taking the flock with them. Some of them perhaps were previously victimized by the severe domination of the Serbians, where (since 1168) the new Nemanyid Dynasty subdued them vigorously.The semi-nomad shepherds did not like order and organization, so they used the first opportunity to leave. In Bulgaria, Joanitsa Kaloyan, the youngest of the Asen brothers (1197-1207) began a series of wars against his neighbours and there were many Vlachs in Bulgaria who left this country (where their forefathers spent some generations), and joined their relatives in Cumania, or in Fogaras, where they were not forced to perform military duties. (In Hungary the Székelys were the traditional frontier-guards.) In the year 1204, Byzan-tium collapsed, Alexius V (Dukas) escaped and the Empire was divided between Latin and Greek states. This turmoil also gave opportunities for thousands of Vlachs to leave the Southern Balkans and to migrate north-wards, possibly up to Transylvania, where they could continue their hum-ble, simple life, but also where their future seemed to be secured.

Until the age of Béla III, chroniclers of Hungary did not mention Vlachs in Transylvania at all, simply because there were no Vlachs there in their times.

The "Gesta Ungarorum", which was written in the time of László the Saint (1091), reports about Transylvania several times, but this (unknown) author never heard about Vlachs. Bishop Miklos (official chronicler of Andrew I in the 11th century), and an unknown author from the court of István II (from about 1130) did not hear about Vlachs either. Some modern historians assume that Rumanians settled in Transylvania already in the 11th century, basing their theories, of course, on the "Dako-Roman con-tinuity", but without any produced evidences. The question could be raised: why would any chronicler of the 11th and of the early 12th cen-turies deny the existence of these settlements? These contemporary chroniclers describe the political, social and ethnographic circumstan-ces of Hungary, including Transylvania, which was an integral part of the Kingdom. These medieval historians performed these duties in the royal Court with a demonstrated responsibility and knowledge in detail. These chroniclers gave accounts about many non-Magyar elements, such as Jewish and Ismaelite tradesmen, Kievan Slavs (who came to the country with King Kalman's wife in c 1100), German, French, Italian crusaders

(1096, 1147, and 1189), Petchenegs and Cumans. There were documents about Saxons, who were invited in by Géza II in 1150 from the Moselle region and were settled down in Southern Transylvania, and on the northern frontiers. Why would these chroniclers completely ignore the presence of Vlachs if they were already in the country?

No doubt, these chroniclers were responsible to their feudal lords and to the king himself. The royal court had every right to know what was going on in the country. In the rigorous circumstances of the 11th-13th centuries, those chroniclers (usually monks), who were employed to note every notable thing in the country, and who ignored any facts, could be seriously punished and even executed. On this theory, we have every reason to believe that the Vlachs did not infiltrate into the Transylvanian Basin before 1200, and if few families hid themselves in the Forgaras Mountains, they were clever enough to disappear from the watchful eyes of the guarding Székely military force or of the local government.

The first chronicler who mentions Vlachs in Transylvania was "Master P.", or "Anonymous", the Paris-educated priest-historian of Béla III. His work was written in Latin, and it describes the assumed origin of the Magyars and their settlement in the Carpathian Basin. His "Gesta Hungarorum" mentions various events of the Conquest (of 896), but he confuses these events with the political, social, economic and ethnographic circumstances of his own age (the 12th-13th centuries). He put Chief Árpád into the focus of a late-medieval, chivalric Court, and the semi-nomad fellow chieftains appear in the Chronicle as baronial oligarchs. This enthusiastic but quite superficial chronicler also mentioned "a certain Vlach", named "Gelou", who, according to Anonymous, fought against the conquerors. (We touched this "Gelou" problem already in Ch. IV.) With Gelou, there appeared another Transylvanian chieftain, whose name was "Glad" and whose settlement (south of the River Maros) was supported by "his Cumans". Although we may assume some early Vlach infiltration to Transylvania, at this point we must express some scepticism again, since the Cumans were somewhere north of the Caspian in the 10th century, and they appeared in Transylvania only in the second half of the 11th century. Looking at this obvious mistake about the Cumans, we may conclude that perhaps this mysterious "Gelou", the Vlach chieftain also appeared in Transylvania only in Anonymous' own age.(*84).

It is possible that the war between the combined Cuman-Bulgarian

84. "Master P" or "Anonymous" was (by some sources) Peter, notary of King Béla III (1171-96), provost of Esztergom ("Anonymus Belae regis gloriosissimi notarius.") He completed his chronicle in c. 1200. As a result of a new research, however, Professor Karsai stated (1961) that Anonymous' identity was Bishop Posa, a Dominican, who was notary of King Béla IV (1235-70), and died c. 1272. This assumption makes even more probable Anonymous' knowledge about Vlach and Cuman settlers. (Note: Those "Dako-Roman theorists, who welcomed Anonymous' "Gelou" as the found "missing link" between the Daks and modern Rumanians made not only "Gelou", but also "Glad", and the Hungarian Menumorut as "Wallachian Princes" of 10th century Transylvania. Of course, these historians forget to mention that the same Anonymous also called the Magyars "The people of the great King Attila.")

forces against Byzantium (1185-89) was one of the major events which forced most of the Vlachs to move northwards and enter the Transylvanian Fogaras by the use of the Focsani Gate and other paths. Imre (Emerich; 1196-1204), and László (Ladislas III; 1204-05) were shadow kings and their successor, Andrew II (1205-35) represented the most disastrous reign in the Árpád period. He led a crusade to the Holy Land (1217) which required much money. He accomplished this by liquidating huge tracts of the royal domain, thus supporting the emergence of powerful oligarchs. (*85).

It was the second year of this rule that a document (the first in Hungarian history of this kind) mentioned the appearance of a few Vlach shepherds (1206). This document was followed by another one in 1222, when the privileges of the Transylvanian Saxons were set down. They received self-government, directly under the king of Hungary, and Andrew II in a document permitted the Saxons, when they were transporting salt in the areas of the Székelys and Vlachs ("per terram Balacorum") not to pay any toll. At this point, it is also important to mention that "Terra Balacorum" was often mentioned also as "Terra deserta et inhabitata" (deserted and uninhabited territory), which in fact seems to prove that only the uninhabited, unclaimed or neglected areas were yielded or ceded to the Vlachs, and these areas remained uninhabited to a large extent, because the Vlach population was still too small in the beginning of the 13th century to populate the mountainous regions, the pasturages and valleys of Fogaras.

In the same year another document mentions that the king gives the forest of the Vlachs and of the Petchenegs to the Saxons ("Silvam Balacorum et Bissenorum"), thus they had to leave certain areas in favour of the Saxons. We have to assume, however, that in the third and fourth decades of the 13th century, some of their fragments were already leaving Fogaras, and they even reached with their families and with their flocks some other areas of Transylvania, as far as the Bihar county by carefully remaining on the high pasturages.

They were not dissimilar to the other Slavs who were infiltrating to Hungary from the Balkans in these years. They did not show any characteristics of Roman origin. As we mentioned previously, they did not adopt the name of "Transylvania" from the Hungarians, whose official language was the Latin, (*86), but used the term "Ardeal", which was the deformed way to use the Magyar word "Erdely". A Latin-oriented people would probably welcome Latin terms very happily. The Vlachs did not seem to adopt any other Latin terms from the Hungarians, and, hating and escaping the educational attempts and efforts of the local governments,

85. In resistance against oligarchs the lesser nobility forced the king to declare the Golden Bull (1222) as a charter of feudal privilege (7 years after the Magna Charta).

86. Since Hungary adapted Roman Christianity already in the 11th century, ecclesiastical Latin became the official language of Government, Church and literature for many more centuries.

they remained illiterate. They came from a Byzantine-oriented Slav world, so they detested anything which was "Roman", "Latin, or "Western". They still belonged to the Old-Slavon Archbishopry of the Bulgarian Trnovo, and their priests (the "popas") who joined their Transylvanian settlements in growing number, did their very best to irritate them against the Latin-oriented, Roman-Christian Magyars and Saxons.

Considering the mentioned three small branches of Vlachs on the Balkans (*87), we may call those fragments which poured from Cumania to Transylvania the fourth branch.

*The fourth branch turned north-east and crossed the Lower Danube in the course of the tenth and eleventh centuries. In the thirteenth century we find them mentioned in the Banat, (*88), and in Southern Transylvania as subjects of the King of Hungary.(*89).*

Following this philosophy of grouping, it would be safe to say that in the 13th century there were not three or four, but actually five branches of Vlachs: (1) the "Megleno-Rumuns" on and around the Pindos Mountains, (2) the "Aurumuns" on and around the Balkan Mountains in Bulgaria, (3) the "Istro-Rumuns" on the Dalmatian Coast and to the east of the Adriatic on the mountains, (4) the "Turko-Wallachians in Cumania, in the area between the Transylvanian Alps and the Lower Danube, and (5) the infiltrated Vlach fragments in and around Fogaras and the Banat of Transylvania.

These branches represented the step-by-step migration of the Romanized pastoral fragments. The "Megleno-Rumuns" and the "Istro-Rumuns" became only quite small branches, and almost completely assimilated into the Macedonian and Dalmatian-Slav population. The Bulgarian "Aurumun" branch was still large in the 13th century, and it lost most of its Latin identity under the influence of the Turco-Slav Bulgarians. The population of Cumania was not Turko-Cuman and was not Wallachian anymore, but a mixture of the two. It became a society led by the Turko-Cumans, gradually absorbing the growing number of the Bulgaro-Slavo-Vlachs. Although the Transylvanian branch of the Vlachs in the 13th century was much smaller than the Cumanian, or Bulgarian branches, later it gradually became larger than the Bulgarian branch and approached the size of the Cumanian branch, because (1) circumstances for the Vlachs were much more favourable in Transylvania than in Cumania or Bulgaria, thus the Transylvanian Vlach population was growing faster both by natural increase, and further infiltration, and (2)

87. Megleno-Rumuns. Aurumuns, and Istro Rumuns.

88. The term "Banat" was originally used for several military frontier provinces of Hungary and Croatia. The governors had the titles of the "Bán". The Transylvania "Banat" was actually the "Banat of Temésvar", a fertile plain between the Danube, the Tisza, and the Maris rivers. Its largest city was Temesvár (Fort of Temes), which name was deformed in today's Rumanian Transylvania as "Timisoara". (Rumanian officials just could not find any suitable "Dak", "Roman" or Wallachian name for this old Hungarian city, so they simply re-wrote its original name using Wallachian dialect and spelling.)

89. Zsombor Szász; *"Rumanian History" (The Hungarian Quarterly*, 1941. p. 199).

because the Magyars did not intermarry with the newcomers, which the Cumans and Bulgarians did, so thus the Vlach identity especially in Bulgaria disappeared.

In this chapter I already mentioned two important points about the Transylvanian Vlachs: (1) they favoured the high mountainous no-mans-land, and (2) they made attempts to isolate themselves from the Latinized society of the Magyars, because they felt that they could preserve their old Slavonic culture by this isolation.

> "At all events, we find them occupying in compact masses the head waters of the Maros (Mures), the Aluta, and the Nagy Kukullo (Tarnava Mare) in the extreme east of Transylvania; and there we find their descendants to-day. They retain, indeed, a strong local and 'tribal' patriotism.[*90].

> "If you look at the country today where Magyars and Roumanians live together, you will still find the mountain portions, and especially the tops, settled by Roumanians, and the lowlands settled by Magyars, who also enter to mouths of the valleys; because the one has always been fond of the mountains and the other has always been fond of the plains.[*91].

Looking at the Wallachians, these people which jealously guarded its Slavonic culture from Western Christians, and which tried to isolate itself as much as possible on the high mountain regions, one could not help but to suspect that they favoured mountain-life not only because Alpine-pasturage was their traditional occupation, but because the mountains represented the best way for separation from the dominating Hungarians.

Going back to the edict of Andrew II, which was discussed previously in this chapter in association with the privileges of the Saxons, let us mention an aspect which belongs to this particular subtopic: the infiltration of members of another Wallachian branch - from the East:

> "The edict of King Andrew II of Hungary in 1222 for the establishment of the Teutonic Knights in Burzenland speaks of the land of the Brodnicii, east of the territory granted to the Teutonic Order. And a Papal Bull of the same year, repeating this passage of the royal edict, replaces 'ad terminos Brodnicorum' by 'ad terminos Blacorum' as if these two terms were interchangeable."[*92].

Yes, in the time of Andrew II, the actual Wallachian infiltration poured into Hungary not only from Cumania, but crossing the Eastern Carpathians, from the east as well. The "Brodnicii" were a Vlach-Slav mixture, between the Sereth and Dniester rivers, and having been molested by their Cuman overlords, they joined their fellow-Vlachs (coming from the south) in Transylvania. Obviously, since "Brodnicii" and

90. C.A. Macartney. "Hungary and Her Successors". p. 255.
91. Count Paul Teleki: The Evolution of Hungary and Its Place in European History. p. 39.
92. M. Ghyka: A Documented Chronology of Roumanian History." p. 40.

"Blacii" were actually the same people, these two terms became "interchangeable" in the land of the Hungarians.

In 1235, an interesting Hungarian political step gave opportunity for even more Wallachians to pour into Transylvania from Cumania:

"King Béla organized in 1235 a large Hungarian settlement ... for the protection of the Focsáni Gate. The autonomous settlement was called the 'Bánság of Szörény.' Even today, more than 200 town and village names remind us in this area of their Hungarian origin." (*93).

This "Bánság of Szörény" was south of the Transylvanian Alps, which cut off a considerable area from the land of the weakening Cumans. (The possible reason was probably not connected with the coming Mongol invasion, since the king received information about it only one year later). The reason was to protect Transylvania from the growing power of Ivan Asen II of Bulgaria, who broke with Rome in 1232, and allied himself with John Dukas Vatatzes, the powerful Greek emperor of Nicaea (1222-1254). This "Bansag of Szoreny" actually embraced an area with a large Wallachian population. From this new "Bánság" the Vlachs could quite easily pour into Southern Transylvania again but they did not have to cross an "international border" anymore, since both sides of the Carpathian Alps actually belonged to the same royal authority.

It is interesting that the modern Rumanian historiography writes about the Mongol (Tatar) invasion of 1241 with the same dramatic solemnity as that of Polish or Hungarian historians, in spite of the fact that Wallachians of Cumania or Transylvania certainly did not act as "defenders of European Christian culture ", as it was the case in Poland and in Hungary.

Béla IV (1235-70) was informed about the Mongol danger from Dominican Monks, who were investigating traces of Asiatic Magyars at the northern areas of the River Volga (1236-37). (*94). In 1223, the Mongols defeated a strong force of Russians and Cumans at the Kalka River, but after their victory they returned to Asia. In 1239, new and huge Mongol armies appeared under Batu and Sabutai and they defeated another Cuman force led by King Kutun (Kotony) at this time. Remainders of this army were asking permission from the King of Hungary to enter the country. Since they promised military co-operation against the Mongol invaders, Béla allowed some 40,000 families to settle between the Danube and Tisza rivers. (*95). The Mongols overran Hungary, Poland and even Bohemia with great speed. Previously, they easily conquered Cumania, south of the Transylvanian Alps, and those Wallachians who survived became slaves of the new conquerors, who willingly guided them throughout

93. Zathureczky: *Transylvania, Citadel of the West.* p. 39.

94. The Mongol chief, Temujon (1162-1227) proclaimed himself as "Chinjiz Khan" ("Very Mighty King") making the foundation of the Great Mongol empire. Father Julian brought information about them from "Great Hungary" at the Volga.

95. Interestingly enough, the Rumanian historian Ghyka puts a "Rumanian-Cuman duchy in Transylvania in the XIIth century." *(A Documented Chronology of Roumanian History.")*

109

the well-known paths into Transylvania. The Hungarian army was defeated at Muhi (beside River Tisza), and the Mongols devastated the country. Suddenly they gave up their conquests when news arrived of the death of the great Khan (Ogodai at this time).

When the Mongols left Munthenia and Oltenia the Wallachians came forth from their hiding places. From now on they represented an over-whelming majority between the Transylvanian Alps and the Lower Danube, since many of their former Cuman masters died in the Mongol-wars, or were permitted to settle in Hungary. Many Wallachians, however, used this opportunity that the king, returning to Hungary, plan-ned to rebuild the country and had a great need for more population. The Bánság of Szörény and Transylvania Proper received more Vlach im-migrants, and Béla IV accepted the foundation of a semi-independent "voivode", as part of the Bánság (1247).

This royal grant (which was associated with the simultaneous set-tlement of the Knights of St. John), (*96), was followed by another similar document of royal grant, dated on June 23, 1250. In this letter the king was obviously trying to attract various minorities, including Vlachs to come and settle in Hungary's depopulated areas. This royal letter indicates that faithfulness of some national minorities was already proven in 1210, when Székely, Saxons, Petchenegs and Vlachs were participating in an army, which was sent by Andrew II to Boril, King of Bulgaria (1207-18) against the Franks. (*97). Béla IV permitted new Wallachian settlements in the countries of Bihar (Rum: Bihor), Máramaros (Maramures), Hunyad (Hunedora), and new Wallachian waves poured into Fogaras (Fagaras). One of the active organizers was Voivode (Vajda) Lorincz, who personally invited Vlach shepherds and Cuman-Petcheneg families from Cumania. It was very possible that the number of Vlachs increased significantly in Transylvania both by natural increase and immigration between 1250 and 1260. Some Balkanic Vlachs moved first to the Duchy of Boszna-Mac-so (an area south of the Sava river, which had belonged to Hungary since 1210), and to the most northern part of Bulgaria (which became a sort of vassal territory of Béla IV, since Ratislaw, shadow-king of disin-tegrated Bulgaria became a permanent guest in the Hungarian royal court, in the year 1255). Later these Vlachs joined their fellow-nationalities in the southern counties of Transylvania. (*98). They did not mingle with the Hungarians but instead they isolated themselves on the mountainous regions under the leadership of their own (Cuman?) chiefs, and under their Greek-Orthodox priests. They did not participate in inter-

96. This Order grew out of a hospital (which was established in the XIth Century to care for pilgrims in the Holy Land. Later it was reconstituted as a Military Order.

97. This aid of the King of Hungary did not help Boril. He was defeated at this time by Henry I (1205-16), Latin emperor of Constantinople.

98. The number of the Vlachs was probably still very limited comparing them to the original inhabitants (the Magyars and Székelys) of Transylvania. The census of Nagyvárad (today's Rumanian name is Oradea) of 1256 did not show any Vlach names on the citizenship lists.

nal affairs, partly because they were still illiterate, and ignorant about the official Latin administration, and also because they did not seem to be nterested in Hungarian events. Consequently, one could understand why Master Akos (a chronicler working around 1270) did not mention them in nis chronicle, and why Simon Kézai, chronicler of László IV (1272-90), working around 1285, could not find anything remarkable about them.

It is necessary to record that a peculiar national hatred appears to have reigned between the Roumanians and the other nationalities of Transylvania. Old documents and literature abound in scathing and venomous references to the Vlach vagabonds, thieves, and whores. They were regarded as an alien element and, if in theory membership of the Hungarian "nation" was open to them as to every Hungarian subject, in practice the vast majority of them remained outcasts, an element deliberately excluded from the body politic. Nor did the Roumanians, on the whole, want assimilation. Notably unsedentary in their habits, and practically unencumbered by the ownership of things, they seem only to have lived with one foot in Hungary. (*99).

It would be hard to say to what extent the Vlachs participated in the rebellion of the Cumans in 1280 and if they did, they only followed orders of their Cuman chiefs, since they occupied always a secondary role in their relationships. When László IV (son of a Cuman woman) spent most of nis reckless life among his Cuman friends, assumably some Vlachs awned around his throne too. When the troops of Nogaj (Khan of the Dnyeper Tatars) appeared as the king's guests (1285), we do not hear about Vlachs, but when the Cumans finally murdered their royal "friend" 1290), chroniclers mentioned the quick Vlach reappearance. For the first time in their history, some of them began to dream about the foundation of an independent Wallachian state.

Some historical accounts suggested that Radu Negru (or Rudolf the Black), a Transylvanian Vlach escaped the religious persecutions of the Catholic Kings, (*100) and returned to Wallachia. We do not think that this was the reason. Stephen V (1270-72) was a weak ruler, who did not have time to deal with Transylvanian affairs during the course of his short rule. His successor, László (Ladislas) IV, was excommunicated from the Catholic Church himself and the Holy See declared a Christian Crusade against him, because of his Cuman friendship and anti-Christian attitude. Radu Negru, this courageous adventurer, simply used the opportunity offered by history, when Hungary was in chaos. László was dead, and his successor, Andrew III (1290-1301), last ruler of the Árpád Dynasty, spent most of his early "rule" as prisoner of the Austrians and his own oligarchs.

According to legend, Radu Negru, a voevod in Transylvania founded Wallachia in 1290. He settled near Fagarash and, according to Rumanian historians, began to plan a role analogous to that of Pied-

100: W. Miller: The Balkan States. (The Cambridge Medieval History. Vol. III, p. 540.)

*mont in creating Italian unity. Many nobles followed Radu Negru, and the result was a weakening of the Rumanian base in Transylvania.(*101).*

Radu Negru did not dare to touch Transylvania, because the Vlachs represented only a small minority there, and Radu did not know anything about the possibility of "Dak relationship". He declared himself as a true Wallachian, and considered Wallachia as the main homeland of the Vlachs. Returning to Wallachian, he established himself at Campulung and became one of the leading chieftains. He gave the essentially flat country of Wallachia the local name of "land of mountains", in memory of those mountains whence he came. At this time, the large majority of the Wallachian population were his fellow Vlachs, because the Cumans were killed by the Tatars, or they already had settled in Hungary. The Mongols (The Khanate of the Golden Horde of Kublai Khan) withdrew eastwards, since the Great Khan concentrated on Chinese affairs and he did not wish to disturb European countries for a while. When the weakened Hungarian Kingdom released the Bánság of Szörény, then the weak Balkanic nationalities concentrated their attention on the growing power of the Ottoman Empire, nobody stopped the Wallachian effort to the foundation of their own country. Radu Negru was able to secure leadership, and by his successors' time (the Basarab family) a new principality, Wallachia, appeared on the historical map of the Balkans.

Meanwhile, in Transylvania (as M. Ghyka, the Rumanian historian reports in his Chronology (*102), on March 11, 1291, the Assembly of Gyulafehérvár (Rum: Alba Julia) recognized the Vlachs of Transylvania as a nationality with equal rights to other member nationalities under the Hungarian Holy Crown. ("Cum universis nobilibus, Saxonibus, Syculis et Olachis".) Two years later

*Andrew III decreed in 1293 that "all Wallachians, whether to be found on noblemen's estates or on others' estates, should be settled on his own estate known as "Székes", the territory of which is estimated between 45,000 and 65,000 acres.(*103).*

The king did not have any choice but to take this step, since the Vlachs did not seem to give up their semi-nomad behaviours, and did not stop wandering from county to county, from village to village. The royal estate mentioned was relatively small, thus once more this indicates again that at that time the Vlachs comprised only a small percentage of Transylvania's population.

101. R. Ristelhueber: A History of the Balkan Peoples. p. 49.
102. M. Ghyka: A Documented Chronology of Roumanian History. p. 54
103. D.G. Kosary: History of the Hungarian Nation.p. 34

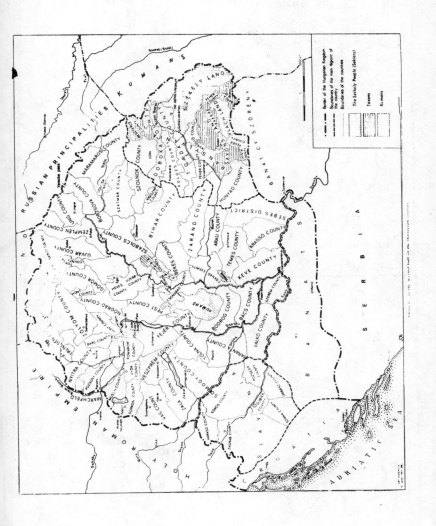

113

TRANSYLVANIA
PART OF HUNGARY SINCE THE END OF THE 9TH CENTURY

About 1100

About 1350

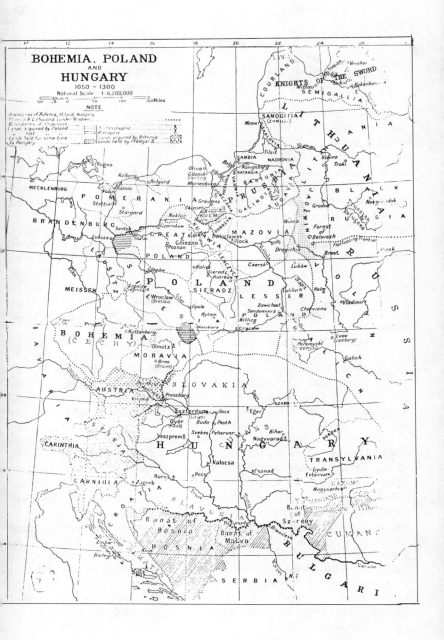

BOHEMIA, POLAND
AND
HUNGARY
1050 – 1300
Natural Scale 1:6,200,000

NOTE

Boundaries of Bohemia, Poland, Hungary,
Russia & Lithuania (under Mindovg)
Boundaries of Provinces
Lands acquired by Poland
Lost
Lands held for same time
by Hungary.

Archbishopric
Bishopric
Lands acquired by Bohemia
Lands held by Premysl II.

MECKLENBURG

Rügen

Kolberg

Belgard

Stettin

Stargard

POMERANIA

BRANDENBURG

Santok

Lubusz

Gdansk
(Danzig)

Oliva

Marienburg

Graudenz

KULM

Naklo

Czernkow

GREAT

Gniezno

Poznan

POLAND

Glogow

Lignica
(Legnitz)

Wroclaw
(Breslau)

MEISSEN

BOHEMIA
(CECHY)

Olmutz

MORAVIA

Brno
(Brünn)

AUSTRIA

Vienna

Pressburg

Kuttenberg

Prague

BRANDENBURG

Opole

Bytom

P O L A N D

Kalisz

Sieradz

Piotrkow

SIERADZ

Wloclawek

Plock

MAZOVIA

Drohicin

Czersk

Brest

Wizna

Grodno

Forest
of
Belovezh

Pinsk

R U S

Lukow

Lublin

Holm

Chervien

Vladimir

Zawichost

Sandomierz

Wisleg

Cracow

Peremyshl
(Przemysl)

Galich

Lvov
(Lemberg)

S I L E S I A

Kalocsa

SLOVAKIA

Esztergom
(Gran)

Gyor
(Raab)

Buda

Pesth

Vacs

Eger

Veszprem

Szekes Fehervar

Bihor

Nagyvarad

SZABO

C U M A N S

TRANSYLVANIA

Nagyszeben

H U N G A R Y

CARINTHIA

CARNIOLA

Zagreb

Borcs

Pecs

Csanad

Gyula-
Fehervars

CROATIA

SLAVONIA

Banat of
Bosnia

BOSNIA

Banat of
Macva

B.nat
of
Szereny

C U M A N S

B U L G A R I

Zador

Bielgrad

Split

SERBIA

SAMOGITIA
(ZHMUD)

Memel

COURLAND

SEMIGALLIA

KNIGHTS OF THE SWORD

Mittau

LIV

Vendon

Kokenhau

L I T H U A N I A

Tilsit

Kovno

Troki

B L A C K

Russian
refugees

Novgrodok

NADROVIA

SAMBIA

Königsberg

NATANGIA

BARONIA

GALINDIA

P R U S S I A

SUDAVIA

Plock

VII.

CONTINUOUS INFILTRATION AND MULTIPLICATION IN THE LATE MEDIEVAL AGES.

After the extinction of the Árpád Dynasty Czech, German and Italian parties attempted to put their own candidates on the Hungarian throne. Finally, the Italian-French Anjou family was elected, and for about eight decades, the Anjous (*104) continued the traditions of the Árpáds to establish Hungary as one of the most powerful states in Europe.

Under Charles Robert of Anjou the "Latinization" (which was typical in official, ecclesiastical, literary, etc. affairs in Christian Hungary for three hundred years anyway) continued and strengthened. Charles introduced Italian chivalry in his capital (Visegrad), and Latin, Italian, French became the languages of the law, church and learning. One would think that the Transylvanian Vlachs would welcome these changes; after all, people who were "Roman by origin" should be happy when their new, adopted country became more and more "Roman" in its culture. The new king realized the multinational character of Hungary, especially Transylvania, and he attempted to please the minorities including the Wallachians.

"Magyar, Saxon, Slovak, Roumanian, Serb, all met in friendliest terms and learned to respect, and understand one another." (*105).

Charles Robert encouraged settlements on the North-East Carpathians too, and he guaranteed their freedom. He subdued László (Ladislas), the powerful lord of Transylvania, not only to preserve royal overlordship, but protecting those nationalities, whose relative freedom was endangered by the "little king". (*106).

In spite of all efforts of Charles Robert (and of his successors) the Wallachians still did not show any willingness to become an integral part of the kingdom. They considered "Latinization" as a cultural invasion against their (basically Slav) primitive culture, and as undermining tendencies by Roman Christianity against their Greek-Slavonic religion. They remained isolated and hostile. Since the king needed a large army to secure Hungary's international position and to protect royal power from the "little kings", he introduced the first "direct tax", and encouraged trade. These activities were quite welcome in Transylvania to the Magyars and Saxons, but the Wallachians (whose life in the Balkans was associated with endless flight from military service, from urbanization and from taxation) did not sympathize with the new order at all. Isolating themselves on the mountains more sternly than ever before,

---

104. Charles Robert I (1308-42), Louis ("the Great") (1342-82), and Mary of Anjou (1382-85).
105. A.B. Yolland: *A History of Hungary*. p. 50.
106. Mathios of Csák, and Ladislas of Transylvania were the most powerful of these "little kings"

the Vlachs became an even more mobile and more separated sub-society.

The years between 1324 and 1330 marked the real beginning of Wallachian history, south of Transylvania. Radu Negru's successor

... Ivanko Basaraba, the ally of the Bulgarians in the campaign of 1330, extended his authority over "little Wallachia", completely routed the Hungarians, and strengthened his position by marrying his daughter to the new Tsar of Bulgaria. (*107).

When Stephen Dechanski (who became king of Serbia as Stephen Urosh III in 1321) attacked the weak Bulgarians, a considerable number of Bulgarian Vlachs left their former patrons by joining Wallachia, which made Wallachia somewhat more populous and slightly stronger. Basarab I attempted to side with the Bulgars against Serbia, but Urosh defeated the Bulgarians near Kustendil, occupying the Vardár Valley, and practically putting an end to the Bulgarian power. Since his Balkan policy did not work out, Basarab turned his attention to Transylvania. In 1324, he surprisingly invaded the Bánság of Szörény (S. of the Transylvanian Alps) and attached it to Wallachia. This "Bánság" was partially inhabited by Hungarians since Béla IV (1247).

A number of Hungarian settlements, like Hosszúmezö, now Campulung, were signs of Hungary's ethnic expansion. Contemporaries called this territory Ungro-Wallachia, the westward portion of which was directly under the jurisdiction of Hungary. (*108).

Charles Robert reconquered this "Bansag" again, but this Wallachian-Hungarian confrontation became another stimulus in the Vlach-Magyar hostility, which gradually became traditional both on the Wallachian-Szörény frontierline and in Transylvania itself.

Nevertheless, Basarab had to recognize Hungary's sovereignty over Wallachia. In exchange, however, Hungary agreed to an enlargement of his domain. The Wallachians then secured authorization for the establishment of an Orthodox metropolitan in Wallachia. Such recognition by the Greek Patriarch affirmed the creation of the Principality of Wallachia to which it granted an ecclesiastical seat. (*109).

In 1330, Charles Robert was forced to realize that he could not compete with Vlachs who knew the hidden routes of Wallachia so well. Visiting the "Bánság of Szörény", he fell into a trap prepared by Basarab and the only way of escape was by changing armour with his man, Dezsö Hedervári. The self-sacrificing hero was murdered by bloodthirsty Wallachians, but the king, dressed as Hedervári, returned to Hungary safely. From now on, the Anjous abandoned the "Bánság of Szörény", and recognized the independence of Wallachia, which was called by Basarab as "Tara Romanesca". (This denomination was probably connected with

107. W. Miller: The Balkan States. (The Cambridge Medieval History. Vol. III. p. 540)
108. D.G. Kosary: History of the Hungarian Nation. p.40.
109. R. Ristelhueber: A History of the Balkan Peoples. p.50.

the fact that a few decades earlier, Pope Clement V (1305-14) recognized the Latin elements in the Wallachian language and called Vlachs "Olahi Romani"). (*110).

Charles Robert's son and successor, Louis (called by Hungarians as "Louis the Great"; 1342-82) concentrated his attention on Transylvania even more than his father did. The first interesting act of the new king, who ascended the throne at the age of seventeen, was a visit to the tomb of Ladislas (László) I (canonized by the Church in 1192) at Nagyvárad which was regarded traditionally as the city of this important king of the Árpád house. (Nagyvárad is called "Oradea" today. The Rumanians did not have their own name for this city, thus they deformed the Hungarian expression.) By this ceremonial visit, the young king wished to symbolize his intention of imitating his great predecessor, by devoting his life for Hungary, and especially for Transylvania.

In the age of the Anjou kings not only Wallachia, but also Serbia received a growing number of Vlach population. This Balkan country of Greek-Orthodox Southern Slavs attracted Vlachs from two directions. All those Vlachs who were still on the Dalmatian coast, or in Epirus, or in Thessalonica, rapidly migrated to Serbia, when this Slav country gradually extended its possessions, taking full advantage of the growing weakness of the Byzantine Empire. The other wave of Vlachs came from Bulgaria, when Kaliman II, the last of the Asen Dynasty was deposed and expelled. In Serbia

> ... the Vlachs constituted an important element and a rich source of income for the sovereign and the other landlords. By then the larger mountain pastures were made the most of and indeed devastated and disforested by the reckless grazing-off of the new growth, by the searing of the grass to freshen pasturage, and by the peeling of young beech-trees as a substitute for honey to sweeten milk foods. (*111).

Stephen Dechanski (Urosh III; 1321-31), and Stephen Dushan (Urosh IV; 1331-1355) were the kings of Serbia, when the Vlachs provided their state with excellent horses of small stature but hardy, and good cavalry for the army. The Vlachs also managed the commerce with these pack-horses, and traded in wool, skins, and famous Vlach cheese, which even served as a substitute for money.

> By trading the Vlachs acquired knowledge of the world, and became far superior in experience and shrewdness to the boorish Slav peasant. They grazed the mountain pastures (planina) to the height of 5000 ft., from the end of April to the middle of September, and then slowly made their way, often taking two months, to winter on the

110. Inf. from M. Ghyka: A Documented Chronology of Roumanian History. p. 60.
111. T. Peisker: Expansion of the Slavs. (The Cambridge Medieval History. Vol. II. p. 440).

coasts on account of the mild snowless climate and the salt which splendidly nourishes the sheep. They lived chiefly on milk and cheese. (*112).

The problem of Serbia with the Vlachs came when they became a heavy burden for the peasantry, especially through their destruction of the cornfields. The Serbian peasants and the Vlach herdsmen were in a growing opposition, there was no more intermarriage between them, and the Serbian State had to regulate the wandering shepherds and to protect its own Slav peasants with draconic laws. King Stephen Dushan's lawbook (1349) states that

"Where a Vlach or an Albanian camps in a village district, there another who comes after him shall not camp; if he camps there by force, he shall pay the fight-fine (100 hyperpyres, that is fifty gold ducats) besides the value of what he has grazed off." (*113).

This situation embittered the Vlachs and many of them migrated to Wallachia (where the Basarab Dynasty welcomed them), or to Transylvania (where King Louis tolerated them and where their life standard was still higher than in any Vlach-populated area of the Balkans.)

The northward migration of the Vlachs reached (the previously Cuman) Moldavia too, and

... about the same time as the foundation of the Wallachian principality, a second principality, dependent however on the Hungarian crown, was created in Moldavia by another colony of Roumanians from the north of Transylvania under a chief named Dragoche. This vassal state threw off its allegiance to Hungary about 1349, and became independent. (*114).

This independence was declared by Bogdan, a Vlach, who succeeded Dragoche (Dragosh). Transylvania, from now on, had to exist as a Hungarian province with growing Vlach population, and as an area partially encircled by Vlach principalities. Additionally, the Patriarch of Constantinople delegated a large number of Orthodox priests to the Transylvanian Vlachs, appointing Hiakinthos to be Archbishop of "Ungro-Vlachia". Beginning with this period, most of these priests became not only the religious but the "national" leaders of the Transylvanian Vlachs. When the king, who realized that these priests were acting as national agents of Wallachia and Moldavia, trying to undermine Hungarian authority, expelled Hiakinthos, Vlach hostility grew considerably in Transylvania again.

Differences between national (linguistic, cultural) traditions could, of course, become reasons for national hostilities, and we could see several examples of these problems in European history. This factor was very

---

112. T. Peisker: *Expansion of the Slavs.* (The Cambridge Medieval History, Vol. II. p. 441).
113. Ibid.
114. W. Miller: *The Balkan States* (The Cambridge Medieval History, Vol. III, p. 540).

noticeable in the Magyar-Vlach case by two significant elements. One of them was the difference between the Roman and Byzantine Christianity, which was intrigued simultaneously by Catholic (later also by Protestant), and by Greek-Orthodox priests, respectively. In this controversy, not simply of opposing religions, but of the West (Catholic, later Renaissance, later Protestant) and the East (Byzantine, semi-Oriental) as sharply opposing socio-political views faced each other with hostility. The other additional element was the anger of the poor and illiterate observing the rich and educated, and occasionally, the irritation of the serf living under the feudal lord. Feudalism as a new social order included many good elements, but obviously created many new problems. These problems were especially complicated in multi-cultural areas. Transylvania was a province with a relatively high life-standard, where feudal lords (mostly Hungarians and Saxons) were usually wealthy and educated, and the Saxon burgers and Magyar and Székely peasants were hard-working. On the other hand, the Transylvanian Vlachs were still illiterate, they still continued ther semi-nomadic life, they still attempted to escape from citizenship duties, like military service and tax-paying. Most of them remained very poor, because a nomad life on unproductive mountains really did not offer too much opportunity. Since trade was occupied mostly by Saxons and Jews, they could not create a privileged position for themselves as they did (temporarily for a few decades) in Serbia, but hostility between the Hungarian peasants and Vlach shepherds was very similar to the Serbian situation, and for the same reasons. The society of farmers and artisans was irritated by the appearance, disappearance and reappearance of these semi-nomads, who did not consider any part of Transylvania as their permanent home. The Vlachs hated those who admitted them, with the hatred of the nomad against the settled, with the hatred of the illiterate against the educated, with the hatred of the poor against the well-to-do, and (in the case of feudal relationship) with the hatred of the serf against the lord.

Economic situations in Wallachia and Moldavia were no better for the Vlachs. In these principalities the Vlachs were suffering under the domination of their own (Vlach) landlords, and they were even poorer than their relatives in Transylvania.

> Conditions in both Wallachia and Moldavia remained extremely primitive for a long period after their foundation. There were no real towns. Both countries were completely isolated. Education was almost unknown. Even the Church was backward and unorganized, served mainly by Slav priests. (*115).
>
> ... With us, said Bratianu, one of the prime ministers of Rumania, in the course of a lecture, the Middle Ages began when they ended in

115. R. W. Seton-Watson: *History of the Roumanians.* (p. 29)

other countries ... We were outside the civilization of Europe.(*116).

As a historical paradox, when the Ottoman power advanced on the Balkans, swallowing the small, powerless countries one-by-one, the Vlachs depended on the protection of the hated Hungarian State in Wallachia, Moldavia, and, of course, in Transylvania.

Osman I (1290-1326), the traditional founder of the Ottoman dynasty, already extended his territory at the expense of the Byzantine Empire. Under Orkhan I (1326-59), the Muslems conquered Nicaea (1331), and Nicomedia (1338). In 1345, the Ottomans crossed into Europe and settled in Gallipoli in 1354. Murad I (1359-89) took Adrianople and made the city his capital (1366). In the same year the Turks were confronted by the Hungarians of Louis the Great, and the king defeated them near Vidin (at the Lower Danube, on the Wallachian-Bulgarian frontier). Thus, in the time when the Bulgarians were already paying tribute to the Sultan, Wallachia was being defended by the Hungarian Kingdom. Lajk, the local voevod, showed some gratitude to the Hungarian king, but members of the Basarab family were already speculating about the possible opportunity against Hungary in the situation of possible further Ottoman advance. Moldavia was still far enough from the advancing Turks, it became stronger by the annexation of Bessarabia (1367), and the neighbourhood of the strong Hungarian army gave them more feeling of security.

In the years of 1367-72, Murad conquered Bulgaria, and up to the Balkan mountains the Balkans became part of the growing Ottoman Empire. At this time, those Vlachs who still hid themselves in these mountains, joined their relatives in Wallachia, Moldavia and also in Transylvania.

In 1370, Louis, the king of Hungary, became king of Poland too. He paid little attention to his Polish obligation, but used his extended military power as the protector of Christian civilization against the approaching Muslems. In 1371, the Turks defeated a combination of Serbian lords in the battle of the Maritza river, and this victory secured their domination in Thrace, Macedonia and Bulgaria. In 1380, the year when the great shadow of the Ottoman Empire actually reached Wallachia, Mircea (the Great), one of the Basarabs was expected to join Hungary in the Christian defence-line against the Muslems, but in these critical times, he began a policy to act as the balance of power between Hungary and the Turks. His Wallachian army, seemingly, stood beside the Hungarian forces, but when the Turks captured Sofia (1385) and Nish (1386), the Wallachian leader considered the opportunity to become king of an extending Wallachia, under Ottoman suzerainty. After some hesitation, Mircea participated in the collective defence of Greek-Orthodox states, but with definitely less effort than the Serbians. (Already in 1371, Lazar I of the

116. inf. from Szombor Szász: *Rumanian history.* (p. 205). (Note: J. Bratianu (1864-1927) was prime minister of Rumania three times (1909-11, 1914-18, and 1922-27).

Hrebelyanovich family became the Prince of Serbia, who in association with Tvartko I, Lord of Bosnia, became a very able defender of his Slav state.) On June 15, 1389, however, Murad defeated a coalition of Serbs, Bulgars, Bosnians and Wallachians in the battle of Kossovo (Hung: Rigómező). The Serbians fought with great heroism, but they were not suppourted well enough by their allies.(*117).

After this decisive battle, the Turks arrived at the Hungarian border, pursuing thousands of Vlach and Serbian refugees, who found asylum in Transylvania again. Sigismund of Luxembourg (husband of Mary of Anjou), was king of Hungary at this time (1387-1437). (*118). Following the unfortunate battle of Kossovo, he began to organize a crusade against the Muslems, who conquered Bosnia (after Tvartko's death in 1391), and Bulgaria (after the fall of its capital, Trnovo in 1393), and blockaded Constantinople (since 1391).

On Sept. 25, 1396, the Christian forces, led by Sigismund of Hungary, and supported by Balkan rulers and by French, German and English knights, were disastrously defeated at Nicopolis (Nikopol; it is a town of N. Bulgaria today, on the Lower Danube, opposite Rumania). When the Hungarians were forced to withdraw, Mircea realized that perhaps the time arrived for a better Turkish-Wallachian co-operation. (He probably suspected that if his people survived as "Roman-Vlachs", "Byzantine-Vlachs", "Bulgaro-Vlachs", "Cuman-Vlachs" and "Serbo-Vlachs", the time was ripe to expect further influence, even power and more territories by becoming "Turko-Vlachs" at this critical time.)

The consequences of Nicopolis obliged him to pay tribute to the Turks who in turn granted him a degree of autonomy. His people were grateful to Mircea for all his exploits and aggrandizement of the country by annexing the Dobrudja (Dobruja, Dobrogea), a region south of the Danube which furnished Wallachia with outlet to the Black Sea. (*119).

While Mircea was negotiating with Sultan Bayazid and his successors, hoping for Dobrudja (area of his previous ally, the Bulgars), and for other territories, some other Wallachians took refuge in Transylvania. The Ottoman leaders must have had good reasons to assume that Wallachians on both sides of the Transylvanian Alps (in Wallachia and Transylvania itself) could represent some sort of bridge into the heart of Europe. Meanwhile, King Sigismund founded a society of knights, the "Order of the Dragon" (1408), to fight Turkish invasion. Several members of this new military order were noblemen of both Hungarian and Vlach origin. One of them was Vlad "the Impaler", who obviously disagreed

117. Sultan Murad was killed by a Serb who posed as a traitor, but Murad's son Bayazid I (1389-1402) won a victory. Lazar was captured and killed. Serbia became a vassal state of the Turks.
118. Beginning with 1410, Sigismund also became German Emperor, and in 1436 the King of Bohemia.
119. R. Ristelhueber: *A History of the Balkan Peoples.* p. 51.

with Mircea at this time. (*120). Mircea agreed with Mohammed I (1413-1421) to become a faithful vassal of the Sultan (1415), but Vlad was still ready to fight on the Christian side.

Vlad the Impaler's military and political appearance on the Wallachian scene was associated with the confusion following Mircea's death (1418). When Moldavian and Wallachian noblemen struggled over the question of succession, in spite of Mircea's previous agreement with the Sultan, many of the candidates sought support from Sigismund. Vlad was one of them, and, of course, he attempted to prove to the king that he (Vlad) was on his side. When Mohammed sent a strong army to pacify the restless population of Wallachia, Vlad disguised himself as a Turk and engaged in such successful espionage that he was able to secure himself from Turkish defeat. Following this, Vlad, called "Dracula" by his superstitious peasants, justified his nicknames (Impaler and Dracula), by impaling the Turkish prisoners with unprecedented cruelty.

> The hostility between the two groups of Rumanians did not prevent some princes from occasionally playing significant roles. Such was the case of a Wallachian prince, Vlad the Impaler, whose nickname sadly indicated his barbarism. He warred in brigandage, intimidated the nobles into obeying his authority, and considered himself sufficiently strong to refuse tribute to the Turkish sultan.(*121).

Vlad the Impaler was the greatest authority on Wallachian areas between 1456 and 1462. But before we describe events in Wallachia after his rule, let us return to Transylvania.

In 1437, a peasant revolt broke out amoung Transylvanian serfs against the nobility. Some Rumanian historians introduced this event as the revolution of the Vlachs against Hungarian domination. Actually it was a revolt of serfs (both Hungarian and Vlach) under the leadership of Antal Budai-Nagy, a Hungarian. It was true, however, that the "border union" (Magyar, Székely and Saxon noblement) did not include serfs. The Union of Kapolna

> was really a sort of defensive alliance against all social, political and foreign enemies: peasants, Turks, and royal encroachments. This "union" developed into a sort of Federal Diet for settling the common affairs of Transylvania (each of the partners continuing to enjoy self-government in its internal affairs.)(*122).

This year of 1437 also marked the first victory of János (John) Hunyadi over the Turks. Also in the very same year Albert of Habsburg, son of Sigismund (1437-39) followed his father on the throne.

According to some sources, Hunyadi was a frontier lord of "uncertain origin". It is very probable that he was actually a common-law son of

120. The name of the Order was "Miles Draconis". Vlad actually joined the Order only 1431. (Inf.S. Csabai: The Real Dracula. (The Hungarian Quarterly, 1941. p. 327-28.)

121. R. Ristelhueber: A History of the Balkan Peoples. p. 52.

122. C.A. Macartney: Hungary and Her Successors. p. 257-58.

Emperor Sigismund himself. (The large royal grants he received at a very young age seem to strengthen this theory.) The most widely spread version is that he was son of a Vlach "Kenez" named Vajk, who had considerable authority in south-eastern Transylvania. Hunyadi became the most outstanding Hungarian hero of his age. He served several kings, but most of these rulers were nothing but shadows behind him. (*123). He became Bán of Szörény in 1439, voevod of Transylvania in 1441, and became chief captain of the southern frontiers at about the same time, thus making him the holder of about four million acres. His main duty was the military protection of Transylvania, later of Hungary and actually he became the protector of the whole of Christian Europe, when his victorious campaigns stopped the Ottoman advance for eight years. Although he was defeated at Varna on the Black Sea on Nov. 10, 1444 (King Ladislas III died in this battle), he became Governor of Hungary and protector of the child king, László (Ladislas.)

His greatest victory against the Turks was in 1456, defending Nándorfehérvár. (It is called Belgrade today, and it is the capital city of Yugoslavia. John Capistrano, Franciscan hero (later canonized by Rome) led one wing of Hunyadi's army. This heroic defense was not only of Hungary, but was the glorious defence of the Christian culture of Europe. (Following the declaration of Pope Calixtus III, church-bells at noon still honour the memory of Hunyadi's heroic victory all over the world.)

As we mentioned, Hunyadi's origin is still very questionable. Rumanian historiography was attempting to introduce him as a "Rumanian". Considering his possible Vlach origin, Hunyadi was a person who assimilated completely to the Hungarian culture, customs and language. He was Catholic, and he lived and died Hungarian. (He died August 11, 1456, of the "black death".) (*124).

Mentioning the assimilation of Hunyadi, it should be pointed out that the Hungarian governments did not force the assimilation of the Vlachs, only expected their peaceful settlement and moderate integration. All those who voluntarily integrated, even those who assimilated, did it as a humanly natural effort for better social, economic, educational opportunities. Obviously, the integrated Vlachs could become one of the respected groups under the Holy Crown of the Hungarians. Integration itself did not mean the abandonment of their native language, their original religions and customs, but the integrated Vlach was expected to be a good neighbour and a faithful citizen. Unfortunately, most of the Vlachs never attempted this sort of social behaviour in Transylvania.

Stealing, creeping across the Carpathians, settling in the high, mostly unpopulated areas, endlessly moving from place to place, most of them did not adopt Transylvania as their land in the late Medieval Ages. They

123. Albert (1437-39), Vladislav I (King of Poland and Hungary; 1439-44), and Ladislas V (1444-57).
124. His younger son, Mathias (Corvinus, "the Just"; 1458-1490) became a great Renaissance king of Hungary.

remained not only isolated, but hostile. They used the better pastoral opportunities of Transylvania in contrast to the dangerous and primitive Balkans, but they remained some sort of "Balkanic" community in the heart of Transylvania too. Their separation was encouraged by their Byzantine-minded priests, who were looking at Western Christianity with jealousy and hostility. These priests gradually became political leaders too, and under this leadership, Transylvanian Vlachs communicated more and more with their relatives in Wallachia and Moldavia. Although modern Rumanian historians discuss John Hunyadi, a Hungarian hero of the Christian world, as "Rumanian", Transylvanian Vlachs of the 15th century were hoping for the support of Vlad the Impaler (who trapped Hunyadi after 1444, perhaps because Vlad attempted to please the Sultan at this time), or for the support of Stephen, Prince of Moldavia (1457-1504), who did his very best to encourage Vlach nationalism in Transylvania. He received the epithet of "the Great" from some Rumanian historians.

Under the shadow (and occasionally under the protection) of the Ottoman Empire, puppet-leaders of Wallachia and Moldavia realized the growing population of Vlachs in Hungarian Transylvania, and probably they already visualized a great dream that was becoming clearer after every passing decade; the dream of a greater Wallachia (Rumania) in the future.

The planned framework of this essay is not intended to describe detailed Wallachian history, or to detail Vlach history in Hungarian Transylvania, but only to discuss the origin, migration and Transylvanian infiltration of the Vlach people, from the disintegration of the Roman Empire to the end of the Medieval Ages. Thus, let us end this outline-chronology with (the mentioned) Stephen of Moldavia, who was fighting against Mathias the Just, the great king of Renaissance Hungary, son of Hunyadi. Mathias was not only a great supporter of renaissance culture, but he was the recognized defender of Christian Europe at this time. Stephen "the Great", the Vlach prince of Moldavia did really his very best to undermine the political activity of Mathias. Although in his younger age he was also trying to defend Moldavia against Ottoman penetration, after the fall of his principality (1456), he became a vassal of Mohammed II (1451-1481) and later of Bayazid II (1481-1512). In his vassal position, he also adopted the great plan of the Wallachian leaders, which was to create a great Wallachia some day, a Wallachia which embraces all Vlach populated countries of Eastern Europe.

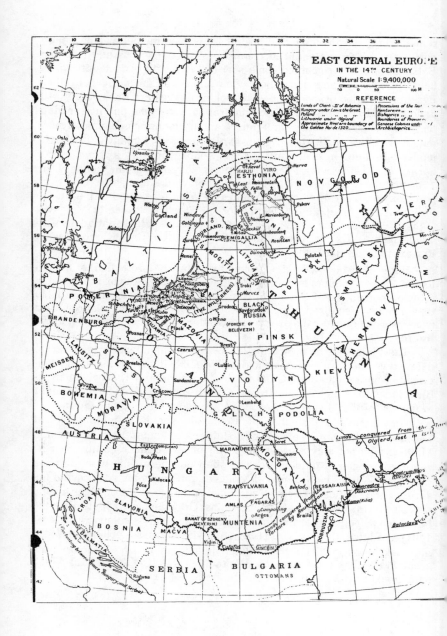

EAST CENTRAL EUROPE
IN THE 14TH CENTURY
Natural Scale 1:9,400,000

REFERENCE
Lands of Charles IV of Bohemia
Hungary under Lewis the Great
Poland
Lithuania under Olgierd
Approximate Western boundary of
the Golden Horde in 1320.........

Possessions of the Teut...
Komtureien...
Bishoprics...
Boundaries of Provinces...
Genoese Colonies under...
Archbishoprics...

VIII.

CONCLUSION

The history of Transylvania (since the end of the Medieval Ages) and the history of the Valch peoples in all Vlach-populated areas (since the same time) was (and will be) discussed in various, detailed approaches. Instead of going into further details, let us conclude this brief study only with a few additional comments.

Wallachia and Moldavia came under Turkish influence and domination in the 15th century, which served as bases of Ottoman military campaigns, Central Europe.

After the downfall of the medieval Hungarian Empire, (*125). these two Rumanian provinces did not see any hope for resistance, and turning their back to the West, they became an active part of the Balkan. (*126).

Before the Turkish Conquest, at the beginning of the 16th century, the population of Hungarian Transylvania consisted of 425,000 people. Of these numbers only 100,000 were Vlachs. (*127). At the end of the same century due to great loss of life in the Turko-Hungarian wars, the Transylvanian population dropped to 400,000 but the number of Vlachs remained at 100,000, (*128), which seems to prove that defence was mainly a Hungarian responsibility and the Vlachs were almost untouched by the war.

... whether by natural increase, by immigration, by the fact that their mountain fastnesses they suffered relatively little from the Turkish and Tatar inroads, or, what is most probable, through a combination of all these causes, they increased very rapidly. (*129).

The increase of the Vlachs was significant in the age of the semi-independent Transylvanian Principality (16-17th centuries). The princes of Transylvania secured a relatively comfortable and prosperous life for the Vlachs. Obiously in this period thousands of them poured into Transylvania from Moldavia and from Wallachia again, crossing the Eastern and Southern Carpathians. In Transylvania they found protection from their Turkish overlords, better pasturages, and much more freedom to live their traditional way of life.(*130). In the middle of the 17th century, the Vlachs represented one-third of the Transylvanian people (*131). Fifty years later, when the population of Transylvania reached a half

125. On August 29-30, 1526, the Turks defeated the Hungarian forces at Mohács. In 1540 Hungary disintegrated to three parts: Royal (Habsburg) territory, Turkish-occupied Hungary, and the semi-independent Transylvania. Hungary was liberated and unified only after 1686.

126. Gy. Zathureczky: *Transylvania, Citadel of the West.* p. 40.

127. Zs. Szasz: *Hungarians - Rumanians (Hungarian Quarterly,* 1941, p. 590).

128. P. Teleki: *Evolution of Hungary, and its Place in European History.* p. 83.

129. Macartney: *Hungary and her Successors.* p. 259.

130. The first (non-Slavic) Vlach document was the Bible, which was translated from the Hungarian version to the Vlach language by Michael Tordasi, a Hungarian Calvinist bishop (1581-82), following the order of the Hungarian Prince of Transylvania.

131. Gy. Zathureczky: *Transylvania, Citadel of the West.* p. 401.

million, the Vlachs comprised about half of this number. (*132).

Finally the Vlach population increased so much
*that the Saxon and Székely settlements, and even some of the Magyar
groups in the west (of Transylvania), had become islands in the
Roumanian sea - a singularly unfortunate matter for ths Székelys in
particular, who, being by now at least true Magyars, found themselves isolated from their kinfolk.*(*133)

The rest of the Vlach story is well known in the history of Modern
Europe. The Congress of Paris (1856) gave to Wallachia and Moldavia vir-
tual independence under nominal Turkish overlordship, and in 1861,
these principalities were united as "Rumania". At the Congress of Berlin
(1878), this new country obtained full independence, and in 1881, it was
obtained as a kingdom. As a consequence of the Second Balkan War
Rumania occupied South-Dobrudja from Bulgaria (1913). In 1914,
Rumania proclaimed neutrality, but in 1916, she surprisingly joined the
Entente in World War I. The Treaties of St. Germain (1919) and of Trianon
(1920) awarded Transylvania, Eastern Bánát, Crisana-Maramures, and
Bukovina to Rumania. Thus, the imperialistic dream of "Greater
Rumania" became a reality.

In 1940, Rumania joined Hitler's Germany, hoping for the defence of
Transylvania from Hungarian revisionism, and for the possible further
conquest (from the Ukraine). In the same year, however, when Nazi-
Rumania already withdrew from the League of Nations (July 11, 1940),
Premiers Teleki of Hungary and Giurtu of Rumania were called to Vienna
to acknowledge the decision which returned the northern part of Transylvania to Hungary. By this decision the Axis Powers wished to satisfy
Hungary (which was already an unwilling satellite of the Axis), and still
keep the support of the Rumanian fascists. Under German influence, on
June 22, 1941, Rumania attacked the Soviet Union, hoping again that
perhaps the Germans would let them bite a piece off the Ukraine, and also
hoping that Hitler would return North Transylvania to them as a reward
for their loyalty. Five days later, the Hungarian Government also declared
war against the Soviet Union, partly under pressure from Germany, partly
because any resistance at this point would have surely resulted in the immediate return of N. Transylvania to the "more loyal" Rumanians. In
August, 1944, however, when the Russian forces attacked Rumania from
the north, King Michael quickly dismissed the pro-German Antonescu
government and ordered his troops to align to themselves with the United
Nations against the Nazis. Hungary could not follow this example at the
same time, since Hitler's troops occupied the country on March 19, 1944,
degrading this unwilling satellite into a helpless colony.

The quick transformation of Fascist Rumania into Pro-Soviet-
Rumania was rewarded by Moscow. By the Peace Treaty which was

132. Zs. Szász: *Hungarians-Rumanians.* (The Hungarian Quarterly, 1941, p. 590).
133. C.A. Macartney: *Hungary and Her Successors.* p. 259-60.

signed at Paris in February, 1947, Northern Transylvania (where the Hungarian population represented 52.3% of the whole population) was restored to Rumania. (*134).

How many Hungarians are still living in Transylvania? There are certain reasons which make it very difficult to estimate their numbers. The Rumanian governments transferred thousands of them to Wallachia and to Moldavia. Hungarian families were forced to "Rumanize" their family names by intimidation in jobs and in schools. These factors and the "official" but unreliable census could prevent any objective investigation by individual historians. Only a well prepared group of professionals, authorized and protected by the United Nations Organization, or by another international body, could measure the true situation in this humiliated and tortured country.

The future of discriminated minorities in Transylvania is hopefully not only in the hand of the Rumanian Government, but also in the hand of the United Nations and of the leaders of the World. In the days, when this study was written, Hungarians of Transylvania are exposed to terror and genocide in their own land, which was the land of their forefathers for much more than a thousand years. They are exposed to a people which was originated in the Balkans, which migrated and infiltrated to Transylvania, and which was permitted to settle down by generous Hungarian rulers. Hungarians of Transylvania are exposed to an alien and rancorous administration, which was clever enough to cover and justify Wallachian imperialism introducing the "theory" of Dako-Roman continuity. In light of this theory the Wallachian conquest of Transylvania became actually a "re-conquest" of the "descendants" of those Daks, who were almost completely exterminated by the Romans in 117 A.D., and of those Romans, who evacuated Transylvania in 271 A.D.

To study, to understand the true history of the Wallachians is very important, because in our complex world objective historiography and education should be the only basis of international justice. Objective historical writing must replace political propaganda in connection with Transylvania and in association with true Vlach history. Only purified historical writing could restore the reputation of professional historians all over the world, and only an objective historical approach could become a base for a restoration which will grant justice for Transylvania.

134. The Census of Transylvania found 2,678 people in this province, in 1910, of which 1,472,021 were Vlachs (51%) (C.A. Macartney: *Hungary and Her Successors.*p. 246-65) According to the Census of 1941, of the 2,577,291 population of North Transylvania 1,347,012 were Hungarians (52.3%), 1,066,330 were Rumanians (41.3%), and 6.4% were other Nationalities. (C.A. Macartney: *October Fifteenth* p. 423.)

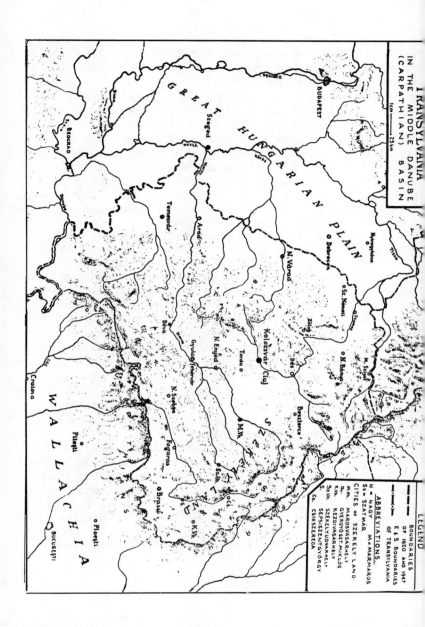

TRANSYLVANIA
IN THE MIDDLE DANUBE
(CARPATHIAN) BASIN

1cm ——— 25 km

BUDAPEST
BEOGRAD
GREAT HUNGARIAN PLAIN
Szeged
Temesvár
Arad
Debrecen
Nagybánya
N.Várad
Sz.Németi
M.Sziget
N.Bánya
Déva
Gyulafehérvár
N.Enyed
Torda
Kolozsvár Cluj
Dés
Beszterce
N.Szeben
M.V.
Fogaras
Sz.Ih.
Brassó
o K.Vh.
Ploești
BUCUREȘTI
Craiova
WALLACHIA
TRANSYLVANIA

LEGEND

– – – BOUNDARIES
OF 1920 AND 1947

···│··· E & S BOUNDARIES
OF TRANSYLVANIA

ABBREVIATIONS

N = NAGY   M= MARMAROS
Sz = SZATMÁR, M= MARMAROS

CITIES OF SZEKELY LAND:
M.V. MAROSVÁSÁRHELY
Gy. GYERGYÓSZT.MIKLÓS
K.Vh. KÉZDIVÁSÁRHELY
Sz.Ih. SZÉKELYUDVARHELY
S. SEPSISZENTGYÖRGY
Cs. CSIKSZEREDA

130

BIBLIOGRAPHY

Alfoldi, A.: The Invasions of Peoples from the Rhine to the Black Sea. (From The Cambridge Ancient History, The University Press, 1936, Volume XII, Chapter V.)

Alfoldi, A., and Ekholm, G.: The Peoples of Northern Europe. The Getae and Dacians. (The Cambridge Ancient History. Vol. XI. Ch. II)

Bang, Martin: Expansion of the Teutons. (To A.D. 378.) (From The Cambridge Medieval History. The University Press, 1936., Vol. I.)

Bang, Martin: A History of the Late Roman Empire form Arcadius to Irene. (395-800) London. 1889.

Brooks, E.W.: The Eastern Provinces from Arcadius to Anastasius. (The Cambridge Medieval History, Vol. I. Chapter XVI.)

Bury, J.B.: History of the Later Roman Empire, London, 1923.

Cholnoky, Eugene: The Geographical Unity of Transylvania (In The Hungarian Quarterly, 1940-41.).

Collingwood, A.: The Central Danubian Provinces. (The Cambridge Ancient History. 1939, Vol. XIII. Ch. III.)

Csabai, Stephen: The Real Dracula. (The Hungarian Quarterly, Autumn, 1941. Vol. VII. No. 2.)

Diehl, Charles: Byzantium; Greatness and Decline. Ruthgers, New Brunswick, 1957.

Dinic, M.: The Balkans. 1018-1499. (From The Cambridge Medieval History. Vol. IV. Ch. XII.)

Dominian, Leon: The Frontiers of Language and Nationality of Europe. American Geographical Society of New York, Henry Holt & Co., 1917.

Durant, Will.: The Story of Civilization. Simon and Schuster, New York, 1950, Vol III: Caesar and Christ, Vol. IV: The Age of Faith.

Dvornick, F.: The Making of Central and Eastern Europe., London, 1949

Élekes, Louis: A Magyar-Roman Viszony a   Hunyadiak korában. (Eng.: The Hungarian-Rumanian relationship in the ages of the Hunyadis) Mátyás Király Emlékkönyv, Imre Lukinish, Budapest, 1940.

Élekes, Louis: The Development of the Rumanian People. (The Hungarian Quarterly. 1941. Vol. VII.)

Erdei, Ferenc, Ed.: Information Hungary. Pergamon Press, New York, 1968.

Forbes, N.: The Balkans. A History of Bulgaria, Serbia, Greece, Rumania and Turkey. Oxford, 1915.

Franzius, Enno: History of the Byzantine Empire. Funk & Wagnalls, New York, 1967.

Ghyka, Matila: A Documented Chronlogy of Roumanian History, B.H. Blackwell, Ltd., Oxford 1941. (Translated from the French by Fernand G. Renier, and Anne Cliff)

Gibbon, Edward: The Decline and Fall of the Roman Empire. Bennett A. Cerf & Donald S. Klopfer, New York, 1783.

Gregoire, H.: The Amorians and Macedonians (From The Cambridge Medieval History, Vol. IV. Ch. IV.)

Haleszki, Oscar: Borderlands of Western Civilization. A History of Eastern Central Europe, The Ronald Press Company, New York, 1952.

Haraszti, Endre: The Ethnic History of Transylvania, Danubian Press, Inc., Astor Park, Florida, 1971.

Homan, Bálint: Hungary. 1301-1490. —From The Cambridge Medieval History. Vol. VIII. Ch. XIX.)

Hussey, J.M.: The Later Macedonians, the Comneni and the Angeli. (From The Cambridge Medieval History, Vol. IV., Ch. V.)

Iorga, Nicholas: A History of Rumania, Land, People, Civilization. Dodd, Mead, and Co. New York (Translated from Rumanian by Joseph McCabe.)

Karsa, Tamás: Hozzászólás a Dako-Roman elmélet jogosultságához. (Comment on the justification of the Dako-Roman theory) Article from the Magyar Szabadság (Hungarian Liberty) USA. 1964, June.

Katz, S.: The Decline of Rome and the Rise of Medieval Europe. Cornell University Press, 1955.

Kosáry, Dominic, G.: History of the Hungarian Nation. (Part I: 830-1919 A.D.) Danubian Press, Inc. Astor Park, Florida, 1969.

Lengyel, Emil: 1,000 Years of Hungary, The John Day Company, New York, 1958.

Lessner, Erwin: The Danube. Doubleday & Co. New York, 1961.

Longden. R.P.: Wars of Trajan. (From The Cambridge Ancient History. Vol XI, Ch. VI.)

Macartney, C.A.: Hungary, Edinburgh University Press, 1962.

Macartney, C.A.:Hungary and Her Successors. The Treaty of Trianon and Its Consequences. 1919-1937. Oxford University Press, London-New York - Toronto. Royal Institute of International Affairs, 1937. (Ch: Transylvania).

Macartney, C.A.: National States and National Minorities. Oxford University Press, London 1934.

Macartney, C.A.: October Fifteenth. A History of Modern Hungary. 1929-1945. At the University Press , Edinburgh, 1957.

Macartney, C.A.: Study on Early Hungarian Sources. Sarkany Printing Co., Budapest, 1940. (Vol. III. Chs. IV & V.)

Macartney, C.A.: The Danubian Basin. Oxford Pamphlets of World Affairs, No. 10 Clarendon Press, 1939.

Macartney, C.A.: The Magyars in the Ninth Century. Cambridge University Press, 1930.

Manitius, C.: The Teutonic Migrations (378-412)(From The Cambridge Medieval History. Vol. I. Ch. IX).

Maskin, N.A.: Az Ókori Róma Története. (The History of Ancient Rome). Translated from the original Russian by I. Borzsak & J. Harmatta. Tankönyvkiado. Budapest, 1951.

Miller, W.: The Balkan States (The Cambridge Medieval History. Vol. IV., Chs. XVII & XVIII.)

Miller, W.: The Rise and Fall of the First Bulgarian Empire. (The Cambridge Medieval History, Vol. III. Ch. III.)

Moravcsik, Gyula: Hungary & Byzantium in the Middle Ages. (The Cambridge Medieval History. Vol. IV., Ch. XIII.)

Osterhaven, M. Eugene: Transylvania. The Pathos of a Reformation Tradition. The Reformed Review, Holland, Michigan, 1968.

Peisker, T.: Expansion of the Slavs. (The Cambridge Medieval History. Vol. II. Ch. XIV.)

131

Peisker, T.: *The Origin of the Roumanians.* (*The Cambridge Medieval History,* Vol. I. Ch. XII.)

Ristelhueber, Rene: *A History of the Balkan Peoples,* Twayne Publ. Inc., New York, 1950.

Runciman, Steven: *A History of the First Bulgarian Empire.* G. Bell & Sons, New York, 1930.

Schewill, F. & Gewehr, W.M.: *A History of the Balkan Peninsula.* New York, 1933.

Seton-Watson, R.W.: *A History of the Roumanians. From Roman times to the Completion of Unity.* Archon Books, Camden and Connecticut., 1963.

Sinor, Denis: *History of Hungary.* Allen and Unwin, London, 1959.

Simogyi, Ferenc: *Küldetes. A Magyarság Története.* (Mission, History of the Hungarians). Karpat Publ., Cleveland, 1973.

Syme, Ronald: *Flavian Wars and Frontiers.* (*The Cambridge Ancient History.* 1936., Vo. XI., Ch. IV.)

Szakonyi, István: *As oláhokról szóló elsó történelmi feljegyzések es a Dako-Roman elmélet történelmi alapjai.* (The first historical notes about the Vlachs and the historical bases of the Daco-Roman theory) (Article from the Kanadai Magyarság (Canadian Hungarians), Toronto, Sept. 10 to Nov. 12, 1966).

Szász, Zsombor: *Hungarians-Rumanians.* (*The Hungarian Quarterly,* 1941, Winter.)

Szász, Zsombor: *Rumanian History.* (*The Hungarian Quarterly,* 1941.)

Taeschner, F.: *The Ottoman Turks to 1453.* (*The Cambridge Medieval History.,* Vol. IV., Ch. XIX.)

Teleki, Paul: *The Evolution of Hungary and Its Place in European History,* The Macmillan Co. New York, 1923.

Wanklyn, H.G.: *The Eastern Marshlands of Europe.* George Philip and Sons, Ltd., Liverpool, 1941, (Part III: The Danube Lands.)

Weber, Williams: *Hadrian.* (*The Cambridge Ancient History.* Vol. XI., Ch. VIII.)

Wolff, Robert Lee: *The Balkans in our Time.* Harvard University Press, Cambridge, Mass. 1956.

Zathureczky, Gyula: *Transylvania: Citadel of the West.* (From: Problems behind the Iron Curtain Series No. 1.) Transl. and ed. by A. Wass, Univ. of Florida, Publ. by the A.H.L.G. Research Center, Florida.

GEOGRAPHICAL NAMES IN TRANSYLVANIA, AND THEIR ORIGIN.
Based on the reserch material collected by

Dr. Sandor Torok
and published under the title
"Településtörténeti Tanulmányok"

a Literary Guild publication, 1973.

Starting out from the principle that the names of mountains, rivers, towns, villages, hills, slopes, forests, glades, swamps and other geographical locations carry the "fingerprints" of those who first settled the land, Dr. Torok set out many years ago to scientifically analyze the origin of all the geographical names found in the Carpathian Basin, including Transylvania. It was a long and labourious enterprise, blending geography with history, but the result of this research was more than rewarding. It shed astonishing light on a heretofore obscure corner of our scientific field of vision, namely, on the "modus operandi" of the actual settling of a newly found land by a tribal society.

When the Magyars (Hungarians) entered the Carpathian Basin, referred to in ancient legends as "Attila's legacy", their nation was made up of seven tribes under one national leader elected by and from the seven tribal chiefs. The tribes were again composed of clans, a tight group of blood-related families.

According to contemporary historians, the Magyars entered the Carpathian Basin in the 9th century A.D. with large herds of cattle, horses, and sheep. Since these herds needed right from the beginning a large amount of food supply, pasture lands for the summer and hay fields for the winter had to be divided without delay.

Beforehand, historians assumed that the land was simply divided up in compact units among tribes, and respectively among the clans within the tribal administration. However, the Torok research discovered an entirely different pattern which, if one analyzes it, makes good sense.

Glancing over the Torok map one cannot fail to notice that the names of the same tribal chiefs can be found in the East as well as in the center and the West of the Basin. If we connect these locations with a line it will result in long, parallel lines stretching from east to west, from one end to the other, each belt marked with the geographical names related to only one and the same tribe. Within these belts one also finds names pertaining to clans, but only these clans which were part of that certain tribe whose chief's name marked the territory in question.

The reason for this seems clear. Since the only occupation of the settlers, besides hunting and fishing, was maintaining their herds, it was the need of those herds that prevailed in dividing the land.

Herds needed winter quarters, where hay could be gathered during the summer months. These winter quarters had to be centrally located near woods and water, preferably on low hills, safe from floods and easily defendable. From these locations, as spring arrived, the herds had to be driven eastward and westward across the flatlands where the grass became green first; then up the river valleys to the lower mountain slopes and back again, following the same route as Fall arrived, when the upper pastures ceased yielding, and the grass on the lower locations was again ready for grazing. The families stayed behind in the permanent winter quarters, gathering hay and other necessary supplies, while the young men, led by the older herdsmen who were designated by the heads of the clans, took care of the herds within the boundaries established for the tribe.

The map thus set up by Dr. Torok shows clearly that right from the beginning the occupying Magyar tribes went as far east into Transylvania as the Szatmár, Szilágv, Bihar. Kolozs, Szolnok-Doboka, Maros-Torda and Arad regions, where we can find the names of the original tribal chiefs of the 9th century.

It seems that during the 10th century these "belts" not only became wider, but longer also, penetrating farther into the eastern part of Transylvania. Since it is impossible to drive grazing herds that far from a central location, it must be assumed that some of the clans, moving out of the centralized tribal winter quarters, established separate locations for themselves within the more distant parts of the tribal belts. This assumption is sustained by groups of geographical names relating to these clans.

In Transylvania, names given to locations in the 10th century include Szabolcs, Ond, Kende, Gyula, Csanád, Tetény, Kolozs, Torda, Velek, Elek, Körögy, Telegd, etc., as well as names composed of these elements, like Kolozs-vár (fort of Kolozs); Tetény-árka (ditch of Tetény); Körögy-pataka (Körögy's creek) and so on.

During the 11th century the Magyar settlers reached the very eastern tip of Transylvania, the so-called "Székely land", establishing there 138 names of settlements; 67 names of mountains and hills; 34 names of rivers and creeks and a couple hundred designating fords, crossings, slopes, meadows, etc. These names are still in use today, together with all the other old Magyar names throughout Transylvania. Most of these names were simply taken in later centuries by the newly arrived Vlach (Rumanian) settlers who altered them to their way, such as Torda-Turda; Maros-Mujres; Szamos- Somes, or by their translations causing Maros - Vasarhely to become Targu Mures; Nagy-Banya, Maia Mare, etc.

Original Vlach (Rumanian) geographical names can be found only in certain border regions like Fogaras, Máramoros and the southern and southeastern mountain peaks, proving without doubt that Vlach (Rumanian) presence within the Carpathian Basin before the end of the 12th century was extremely limited.

Moreover, analyzing from a linguistic viewpoint those geographical names which can be regarded as early Rumanian, we find that the words used in giving those names do not derive straight from the Latin, but suggest close contacts with the Albanian, Greek and Slavic languages, which could have happened only during the known Vlach migration northward across the Balkan, between the seventh and twelfth centuries A.D.

SUMMARY

The bibliographies attached to the previous research material, as well as the references which follow here, furnish ample proof that from the 19th century on intensive research work was carried on by Rumanian and non-Rumanian scientists alike with the purpose of establishing the true origin and identity of the Rumanian people. This research was conducted on two main levels, history and linguistics.

A special team of the Danubian Research Center compared and evaluated all the available material, and after checking and double-checking the accuracy of the documentations, came to the following conclusions:

1. The Vlach (Rumanian) people belong to those nations which have developed as conglomerates of several small splinter nations within the Byzantine Empire. The original birth place of the Vlach nation was somewhere in Dardania, near the Albanian border.

SEE: Sudost Forschungen, Band XXI, pages 19, 370-393, 484 and 485. München 1962, Silviu Vladomir: Vlahi din nordul peninsulei Balcanice in evul mediul. Bucharest, 1959, page 139.

J. and W. Grimm: Deutsches Worterbuch, Vol. XIII, pages 545-547, Leipzig, 1922.

M. Eugene Osterhaven: Transylvania, the Pathos of Reformation Tradition, Reformed Review 1968, Western Theological Seminary, Holland, Michigan.

Herbert Van Leisen: Terres Hongroises de Transylvania, Kunding, Geneve, 1941.

J. Peisker: Die Abkunft der Rumanen Wissenschaftlich Untersucht, Graz. 1917.

R. Roessler: Rumanische Studien. Untersuchung zur alteren Geschichte Rumaniens, Leipzig, 1871.

C. Goos: Studien zur Geographie un Geschichte des trajanischen Daciens. Hermanstadt, 1874.

Eudoxius Hurmuzaki: Fragmente zur Geschiechte dur Rumanen, Bucharest, 1878.

Jon Nadejde: Xenopol "Istoria Romanilor den Dacia Trajan", a review, published in the Revista Contemporanul, Jassy, 1888.

Hunfalvy: Le Peuple Roumain Valaque, Tours, 1880.

Hunfalvy: Der Ursprung de Rumanen. Wien, 1888.

2. All research material agrees that: Emperor Aurelianus evacuated the entire population of Dacia between 257 and 271 A.D. From this time, on until the 13th century, there is no trace of any Latin population in that area. However, between 579 and the 14th century Byzantine chronicles and other contemporary sources refer to the presence of a Latin people on

the Balkan peninsula, called Blach, Vlach, or Wallach.

Two documents dated 579 A.D. (Theophilactos Simokkata, II. 15 Ed. Bonn. and Theophanes: Choreographia, 394, Ed. Bonn) mention Vlachs at the "Kalvo Munti" - meaning Bald Mountain in the neo-Latin language - situated in Thracia. Between 976 and 1164 A.D. several documents refer to the presence of the Vlachs in the Pindos mountains (Thessalia), between Kastoria and Prespa as well as Grammos, Nerecka and Sar-dragon in Bulgaria. (SEE: Kendrenos II. 435. Ed. Bonn., Scriptores historiae Byzantineae. Ed. Veneta IX. 7,74,533. XII. 110 and 217. Hunfalvy: Quelques réflexions. Paris, 1892).

The first appearance of the Vlachs in today's Rumania is proven by a document dated 1164, when the fugitive Greek Prince Androkinos was pursued by Vlach border guards stationed at the Nis-region (today's Bulgaria) and captured near today's Suceava, Rumania. Two years later, Leo Vatatzes crossed the Danube River with Vlach troops ("Valachorum ingens multitudo") and broke into the Hungarian Kingdom near the fort of Brasso (Transylvania), on the orders of Emperor Manuel Comnenus. (SEE: Kinnamos, Historiae Byzantine Scriptores XII.68,69,118.)

This is the first historically proven presence of Vlachs in Transylvania.

According to the annals of the Greek Orthodox Church, the Vlachs moved into the "Transdanubian territory" in the year 1234, and renamed it Vlach or Wallachia (in Hungarian "Havasalföld"). Today it is known as the province of Muntenia. From there, migrating Vlach groups reached the Fogaras mountains in the southern Carpathians during the same century.

(SEE: Otto Mittelstrass "Beitrage zur Siedlungsgeschichte Siebenburgens im Mittelalter" München, Oldenbourg Verlag, 1961. and Sudost Forschungen, Band XXI. page 485, 1962)

3. Research carried out in the field of linguistics came to the conclusion that the Rumanian language, regarding its elements, is a "neo-Latin" language, which went through the primary stages together with the Italian. The basic words are formed from the accusative (objective case) of the Latin, similar to the Italian. Contrary to the ancient Latin, however, it uses articles formed from the Latin demonstrative pronoun "ille", "illa", like all the other neo-Latin languages (Italian "il", "la", French "le", "la") **with the significant difference that the Rumanian uses these articles at the end of the nouns and not in front of them, like the other neo-Latin languages.**

Only the Albanian and Bulgarian languages do it the same way as the Rumanian. The Bulgarian language resembles the Rumanian only in principle, while the Albanian both in principle and in form.
Examples:

137

MAN. In Latin: homo; in Italian: il uomo; In Rumanian: om-ul; Albanian: njeri-u

CONVENT. In Latin: conventus (gathering); In Rumanian: cuvent-ul (word); In Albanian: kuvend-u (talk)

NUMBERS. Latin: unus, una, unum -du, duae, dua - decem.

Italian: uno, una - due - dieci
Rumanian: unu, una - doi, doua - zece
Albanian: nje - dju - djete

But from **eleven** on:

Latin: undecim - duodecim
Italian: undici - duedici
Rumanian: un-spre-zece - doi-spre-zece
Albanian: nje-mbe-djete - dju-mbe-djete

From the number ten on the Rumanian follows the Albanian pattern of one-above-ten, two-above-ten and not the compounded Latin system.

It must be assumed, therefore, that the forefathers of the Rumanians, the Vlachs, lived side by side with the Italians during their primitive stage of cultural development. When they reached the stage in which they were able to count further than ten, they learned the method forming the new words from the Albanians.

It is indeed hard to imagine that the descendants of the Roman conquerors of Dacia were unable to count further than ten, just to point out one of the obvious fallacies of the Daco-Roman theory.

(SEE: Andre Du Nay "The Early History of the Rumanian Language: Edward Sapir Monograph Series in Language, Culture and Cognition, No. 3. American edition: Jupiter Press, Lake Bluff, Ill. 60044, 1977.)

Further linguistic proof includes:

The basic Christian expressions in the Rumanian language originate from the Italian - therefore they could not have been picked up in any way in the former province of Dacia.

New words, referring to religion (from the 8th century on) came from the Greek into the Rumanian language, like the words for church, teacher, picture, punishment, etc.

The great quantity of Slavic words entered the Rumanian language only after the basic neo-Latin (Italian) element was established, followed first by the Albanian and then the Greek "borrowed words".

After the Slavic element became part of the Rumanian language a great number of borrowed words and expressions from the Hungarian were added to it, defining objects and acts introduced through contact with the Western culture within the Hungarian Kingdom, such as the expression for, GUN: In Hungarian "puska", Rumanian "pusca", etc.

4. Examining the history of southern Italy and the history of the

Balkan seashore only 55 miles across the Adriatic, we find the following:

Southern Italy, called Apulia, was part of the Byzantine Empire from 553 A.D. to 1040 A.D.

Those parts of the Balkan shoreline which were opposite Apulia were ravaged and left desolate by the Western Goths between 396 and 402 A.D., and again by the Slavs between 572 and 591 A.D.

After the first desolation, Byzantine landowners resettled their lands on the Balkan shore with Albanians. After the Slavic onslaught they introduced new labourers from their own estates in Apulia, settling them next to the Albanians. (SEE: G. Stattmuller "Forschungen zur Albanischen Frungeschichte" 1941, and "Geschichte Sudosteuropas", 1950) Also: (S. Dragomir "La Transylvania", 1946)

Furthermore, keeping in mind that no new language can arise by "Romanizing", only the basic elements of an existing language (in this case the ancient Dak language in Dacia) while leaving untouched the stratum of the vocabulary which related to a higher culture-stage, we must definitely reject the Daco-Roman theory as unfounded and purely politically motivated.

THE RUMANIAN LANGUAGE IS NOT A ROMANIZED LANGUAGE, BUT ON THE CONTRARY — AN ALBANIZED AND SLAVICIZED NEO-LATIN, ORIGINATING FROM APULIA.

5. Since history as well as geography corroborates the linguistic findings, we must declare that **the Rumanians, descendants of the Vlachs, cannot be regarded as the original settlers, and therefore native population of Transylvania.**

The Vlachs (Rumanians) entered the Hungarian Kingdom as migrating herdsmen three centuries after the Hungarians settled the land and established statehood.

(These findings were approved and released by the Danubian Research Center in June 1979).

III. THE PROBLEM

ZATHURECZKY

TRANSYLVANIA

CITADEL OF THE WEST

Translated and Edited by
A. WASS de CZEGE
University of Florida

Documentation checked and approved by the
DANUBIAN RESEARCH CENTER

(Mr. Gyula Zathureczky is a well known Transylvanian journalist, former editor of the largest Transylvanian daily newspaper. the "Ellenzék" (Oppostition), published in Kolozsvár. Today Mr. Zathureczky is working for Radio Free Europe as an expert on East-Central European affairs.)

INTRODUCTION

If you had been born in Transylvania, you would not yet have to be fifty years of age and your citizenship status would have already been changed three times, without your ever leaving the town or village of your birth. You have been "liberated" under different flags, or different party slogans, five times and each time under the pressure of an outside power which knew nothing about your problems and couldn't care less.

If in addition to all this you happen to belong by birth to the almost 3-million Hungarian minority group of that land you have had it even worse. You were forbidden to use your own language in public places. You were discriminated against in every phase of your life. You were treated by government agencies as some sort of inferior type of human being, with no rights, only duties. In time of elections, you were intimidated by gendarme brutality and kept away from the polls with bayonets.

Today, according to the reports reaching us from behind the Iron Curtain, if you were an Hungarian, you would be carrying a double load of suffering compared to those of other nationalities. For in addition to the over-all communist terror and domination, you would have against you the organized efforts of the Rumanian government to eliminate the so-called "Transylvanian Problem", through the total extermination of the Hungarian ethnic group, which according to Rumanian doctrine, is the cause of this problem.

Mr. Zathureczky, the author of "The Transylvanian Dispute", tries to point out in his book that the extermination of large masses of people, whether Jews, Hungarians or any other, is not the way problems should be solved on this earth. Other ways can and must be found through the use of vision and good will. For these problems are not isolated cases, involving only a few millions of people here and a few millions there. We are all involved in them, for every injustice that creates bitterness and hate, and every hate that creates new injustices, must be regarded as an universal problem of the entire human society. These situations create danger spots on the face of this globe from where the sparks of new World conflicts can originate and blow up our entire civilization. Therefore, it is not only our ethical and moral obligation to search for just solutions of these problems, but wisdom also dictates the necessity, if we are to try to make the world a better place in which to live, not only for ourselves, but for all mankind.

In this condensed edition of Mr. Zathureczky's book, we are trying to present a clear and unbiased picture of the facts concerning the Transylvanian problem and the reasons and causes for these conflicts. Carefully examining these reasons and causes, we shall attempt to point out the only workable solution which can bring peace and justice, not only to this particular geographical location, but which can be used as a guideline in solving similar problems in many different parts of the world. However, in order to be able to reach such solutions, we must first accept as individuals and as nations, the collective responsibility for the life, liberty and the pursuit of happiness of every group of human beings within our organized human society. This must be done even if it means changing our concepts of certain established systems which may be useful to us, but harmful to others.

June, 1964
Prof. Albert Wass de Czege
University of Florida

I

THE FACTS OF THE PROBLEM

After World War I, the three great powers, the United States of America, Great Britain and France, reshaped the face of South-Eastern Europe. The Austro-Hungarian Monarchy, and with it, the unity of the Danubian Basin, was dismantled and broken into small national states. This re-organization took place through the application of the two main ideas of our age: the democratic principle of majority rule and the people's right to self-determination. In practice, however, only the first was put into effect. The question of self-determination has never been probed.

Transylvania, an integral part of Hungary for almost one thousand years, was given to Roumania, in accordance with the principle of majority (53.8%). A territory as large as Portugal, and two and a half times as large as Switzerland, with a population of 5,257,467, of which 2,838,454 were Roumanians (53.8%), 1,661,805 were Hungarians (31.6%), 564,789 were Germans (10.7%), and the remaining 3.9% were Jews, Gypsies, Bulgarians and other nationalities.

Due to the ever increasing pressure and discrimination imposed by the Kingdom of Great-Roumania against the Hungarian minority, the situation between Hungary and Roumania became more and more dangerous. In 1940, after the deliberations between the two countries failed to bring any results, the Royal Roumanian Government asked the two ruling powers of Central Europe, Germany and Italy, for an arbitration. These two powers decided on August 31, 1940 to divide Transylvania between the two litigants. The Axis-powers, already being at war, could not tolerate the development of a serious crisis in South-Eastern Europe. In their decision, they were led by the same view-points of power-policy as had been the Entente Powers twenty years before.

Finally, the last dictatorial changes in the status of Transyhlvania were accomplished by Stalin, who declared the Vienna arbitration void and gave the entire territory back to Roumania. With this decision he was trying on the one hand to compensate Roumania for the Eastern territories annexed by the Soviet Union, while on the other hand, the cause of Bolshevism in South-Eastern Europe seemed to be served more effectively by this decision.

Since the first ruling of the Western Powers which gave the Roumanian Kingdom jurisdiction over Transylvania after World War I, the population of the country increased by approximately 1 million, and the distribution of the nationality figures shifted somewhat in favour of the Roumanians.

It seems strange that while this population increase between the years 1910 and 1941 totalled only 665,717 (increasing the ratio of the Roumanians from 53.8% to 55.8% (464,529 souls), and decreasing the ratio of Hungarians to 29.5%), the new statistics of the Roumanian People's Republic in 1956 show only 1,618,246 Hungarians, compared to 4,192,506 Roumanians.

These few figures clearly prove the justification for a deeper look into the Transylvanian problem. Disregarding completely those two-hundred thousand Hungarians (mostly from the middle class), who were forced by the Roumanian Government to leave their country right after World War I, no other mass exodus has ever taken place. Therefore, it is very unlikely that during the last 46 years the Hungarian population of Transylvania has only increased by 57,441 souls, while the Roumanian population has increased by 1,353,052.

Even with reservation and doubts of the reliability of the statistical data produced by the Roumanian People's Republic, it is unquestionable that there appears a very considerable shift today in the ratio of the Transylvanian nationality groups for the benefits of the Roumanians. Such a shift cannot be explained by natural reproduction. It can occur in countries where the ethnic minorities are exposed to the most cruel discrimination and brutality, while on the other hand, the increase of the majority group is being aided by government-organized colonization.

The discrimination against the Hungarian minority in Transylvania during the last decade reached the level of intellectual and economic genocide. Not only have Western newspapermen travelling through Transylvania rendered documeted accounts of this, but even the letter of the American Legation in Bucharest, addressed to the American Transylvanian Federation, verifies it.

It is positively documented that since 1945, the Roumanian government has killed and deported under different pretexts, approximately 278,000 Hungarians. Some of those who were deported died under the most inhumane conditions in labour camps, wether within the borders of Roumania or in the Soviet Union. The others are maintaining an incredibly primitive existence in the swamps of Dobrudja and other places, restricted in their desire to return to their native land. The terror and brutality exhibited by the Roumanian government in its effort to reduce the Hungarian population of Transylvania is increasing day by day. The extermination of the urban middle class is almost completely accomplished. The liquidation of the large masses of Hungarian peasantry is being carefully planned.

As long as the Iron Curtain prevents the West from exercising its influence in the Danubian Basin, there is not much we can do to bring peace and justice into this part of the world. But sooner or later, the time will come when the equalizing effect of a fast shrinking world will overcome the barbed-wire fences and artificial barriers and bring the different fractions of human society closer to each other. When this time arrives, Western Democracy must be ready to solve this problem, with many other problems waiting for wise and fair solutions.

II

THE ESSENCE OF THE PROBLEM

Until now, the big powers ruling our world have always been inclined to regard the problems of smaller nations as unimportant, best solved by dictatorial measures. However history has proved again and again, that such dictatorial solutions are only of a temporary nature and create political danger-spots for new world conflagrations.

For almost a half-century the Western World regarded the Transylvanian problem as a mere border dispute between Hungary and Roumania. From this view-point, it was settled and re-settled three times, without success. It is obvious that behind each settlement there were foreign power-interests in the background. However, the main reason for the apparent insolvability of this acute problem lies much deeper. It can be found in part in the political system of our age and its practices, and in part in the complete disregard of the natural, historical and spiritual laws which co-ordinate the evolution of human society.

After World War I, in the place of the Austro-Hungarian Monarchy which had kept order in the Danubian Basin, small nationalistic countries were left facing each other, with large groups of ethnic minorities in every one of them. The place of a liberal, international and constitutional State-system, which had stood above narrow national horizons, was taken over by small nationalistic democracies.

Since the Monarchy did not exercise its balancing role in the Danubian Basin any longer, neither was there a protecting wall toward the East, nor any serious power standing in the way of German expansion. First Hitler took over, then Stalin. Both needed these territories for a base of operations. One against the East, the other against the West. The universal European importance of South-Eastern Europe, and within its range, the importance of the Transylvanian problem, was clearly documented again.

Transylvania has been in all times, the fortress of Western Europe and the Western Christian culture-circle. Its frontiers, the two-thousand meter high ridges of the Eastern and Southern Carpathians have always been the Eastern frontiers of Western Europe. Beyond them lay the East: an entirely different culture, different in its way of thinking, different in its way of life. The re-organization which followed World War I abolished this frontier and terminated thereby the West-European role of Transylvania.

The resolutions passed by the Roumanian National Council in Gyulafehérvár (Alba Julia), were accepted as the voice of the people, in spite of the fact that neither one of the two other Transylvanian national groups were represented at that convention. The first point of that resolution declared, "unification of all Roumanians and the territories inhabited by them with the Kingdom of Roumania."

From this situation arose the Transylvanian problem. Since the reasons for the controversy are not solely political, but are deeply rooted in principles and ideas of the all-European background, the cause of Transylvania must be regarded, par excellence, as a European problem.

From the point of view of fair play, principles of democracy based on the majority rule can only be successfully applied in the governments of homogeneous societies, where the chance to become a majority is always open to the minority groups. Ethnic minorities, however, do not have this opportunity. Let us not forget that "because the majority rule is the strict consequence of democracy, democracy is always inclined to become an oppressive domination toward those elements of society which, due to some conditions originating in their very nature, are of a permanent minority status." (L. Ottlik: "The Minority Problem Yesterday and Today", Szemle, page 106.)

Exactly this happened in Roumania and the ever-increasing discrimination against the almost two-million Hungarian minority in Transylvania became the source of conflicts between Hungary and Roumania. The anti-minority attitude of the Roumanians "finds its explanation in the modern doctrine of nationalism, the essence of which can be expressed by saying that it upsets the former relations between the two definitions 'country' and 'people'. Originally, the word 'people' meant the inhabitants of the 'country' as a historic-geographical unit. Today, the word 'country' means the space in which one 'people', meaning ethnic unit, lives." (L. Ottlik: "Pax Hungarica", Szemle 1934, page 87).

This doctrine of nationalism prevails today in all the national states of Europe, in opposition to the former imperial State-Concept, based on the co-existence of several nationalities. The goal today is to create a homogeneous society, an indivisible nation state, and for this reason, the ethnic groups caught inside of the borders are being treated as foreign elements which must be eliminated.

It is also a weakness of democracy in relation to ethnic problems, that its practice of government is highly centralistic. Therefore, it would come in direct conflict with its own self in case it should try to apply the only solution concerning the problem of ethnic groups, namely, the introduction of self-government for the minorities. Which, of course, is still not a final solution, but at least a modus vivendi between the majority and the minority groups. Since "government on the local level is not only the best protection against the transgressions of national egotism, but also the best medicine for local differences." (Lyon Blease: "Short History of English Liberalism", page 17.)

It is obvious that the main reason for the apparent insolvability of the

Transylvanian problem can be found in the political system of our age and its practices. The rejecting attitude of the big powers, which they evidence in connection with this problem, exhibits a great measure of hypocrisy and is in complete opposition to the substantial interests of Europe. Nevertheless, by pointing out that the questions involved here are not a mere border dispute between two nations, we have exposed only one side of the problem. The roots of the controversy go much deeper. Its bearings are potentially more of a continental nature, and are closely interwoven into the life of entire Europe. In order to understand and solve this problem, we must closely examine the relations, causes and effects of these factors, to which our world, of late seeming to turn more and more materialistic in its view-points, has paid little attention.

Salvador de Madariaga, the famous Spanish writer and philosopher, described Europe as the "unity of diversities". (S. de Madariaga: "Portrait of Europe", 1952). By "Diversity", he means the multitude of the colourful living units, which all together form the continent of Europe. Under "unity", he means harmony, the most important law of nature, to which the entire Universe is subordinated.

The living units of our human world are the regions and the people inhabiting these regions. The more marked such a unit is and the more crystallized its individuality appears to be, the more able it becomes in creating harmony by its functions. Because "there is no harmony without diversity ... and without the concept of delimitation, harmony cannot be achieved". (Raul H. France: "Lebenslehre fur Jedermann", Berlin, 1952).

When any such unit is prevented by outside force in exercising its natural functions, which give reason for and meaning to its existence, the harmony becomes disrupted and catastrophe sets in. This cannot be avoided by any means of power and brutality.

The essence of the Transylvanian problem can be formulated therefore, in the following two questions:

I. How can the problem of government be solved in such a way that every enterested group would be satisfied?
II. How can the undisturbed and productive co-existence of the three Transylvanian nations best be achieved?

It must be clearly understood that neither of these problems is of a local nature, and cannot be solved by border discussion. The problem of government and statehood can find its solution only in the spirit and within the framework of a new European unity, through the evolution of Europe as a whole. On the other hand, the symbiosis of the three Transylvanian nations can be promoted only through a complete revision of today's prevailing concepts and practices concerning the treatment of ethnic minorities.

In order to reach any workable solution, two main issues must be clarified:

    I.   Just how far can Transylvania be regarded as a "living unit" in its own right, and

    II. What are its functions within the European community?

In order to answer these questions, we must examine the geographical, historical and cultural-spiritual framework in which Transylvania maintains its existence, built into the unity of the past, present and future.

III

TRANSYLVANIA: THE SPECIFIC UNIT WITHIN
THE DANUBIAN BASIN

Geographical units are living units all over the world, having their own individuality in space and time. In space, because they are different from all other regions. In time, because their inhabitants adapt themselves to the land and natural endowments of the geographical location and create thereby the historical individuality of the region. The limitations and possibilities of the location determine the way of life and all its manifestations, and these manifestations build up into tradition under the influence of time. The economy and structural development of human society are determined by the unchangeable laws of nature - climate, flora and fauna. People inhabiting the prairies have an entirely different way of life than those who are settled in mountain regions or on the seashore. Thus, the borderlines of geographical units automatically turn into the borderlines of human society also, dividing races, languages and administrative organizations such as countries and states.

Geographical units coexist in a functional symbiosis within the greater units of the Continents. Wooded mountains regulate the water supply of the plains. Plain and mountain therefore climatically complete one another. Our human world, rooted into geographical regions, adapts itself to this great harmony of nature. As time makes history, the political and cultural manifestations of human societies follow closely the dividing and connecting laws of geography, creating thereby the historical individualities of the different regional units.

One of the most delimited and firmly outlined living units of Europe is the Danubian Basin, with its particular and specific historical individuality. Surrounded on the North, East and South-East by the chain of the Carpathian Mountains, the Danubian Basin stands leaning with its Western elbow on the Alps like a fortress facing the vast plain of Russia, which has been through all history the highway of barbaric invasions. In that Basin, which is open toward the West, though separated from the Balkan Peninsula by the lower course of the Danube River and by the bare, rocky ridges of the Karst, was the meeting place of the different climatic zones of Europe. The deep humus of the Central Hungarian Plain served for centuries as the granary of Europe. The treasures of the mountain regions, which are rich in gold, silver, iron, salt and wood are equally balanced by the oil wells, bauxite and uranium mines of the fertile hill-country West of the Danube. The natural water system of the Basin is centralized: all the rivers, except the Olt, run toward the central plain. The diversity of the Danubian regions makes every production possible. The Basin is a closed, compact living unit, not only geographically, but economically also. Its separate regions cannot survive without one another, but as one living unit, the entire Danubian Basin fits into a perfect economic balance. Consequently all through history, it was a firm cultural, spiritual and political unit also.

Through centuries it was the melting pot of the great opposing spiritual and intellectual currents of the European continent. Roman Catholicism, Northern Protestantism, and Oriental Orthodoxism reached hands here, to build the foothold of religious freedom and tolerance in Europe. Here was where nomadic traditions and the Western way of life first mixed, in order to create a new and specific Danubian culture, spiritually and politically in the same time. It is the Danubian Basin which separates the Slavic bloc from the Germanic, serving as a bridge between the four great cultures: the Latin, the German, the Byzantine and the Slavic.

None of the nationalities living in this geographical unit was ever able to withdraw itself from the influences of this synthesis. The Danubian German is different from the Austrian or the North German. The Serbian, settled on the Southern plain is different from the Serbs in Serbia, and the Transylvanian Roumanian is of an entirely different background and mentality than those from Moldova or Muntenia, across the Carpathians. Even the Transylvanian Hungarian seems different from the other Hungarians who inhabit the Central plain or Transdanubia. For within the Danubian Basin, Transylvania is the region with the most individuality.

A single glance at the map of Transylvania gives the feeling of an advanced fortress nesting in the bend of the Carpathians, guarding the Danubian Basin from the East. In such a frontier position, everything happens under heat and pressure. The crystallization of historical individualities is accelerated. If we accept the concept that the Danubian Basin is the fortress of Western Europe and at the same time the bridge between the East and the West, we can also say that Transylvania has been, and still should be, the transmitting antenna of Western culture toward the East.

Such is the location, the geographical framework which determines the European functions of the Danubian Basin, and also of Transylvania, as an integral part of this unit. History, as the recorded chain of events, actions and re-actions performed by human society, proves the validity of this natural law.

IV

HISTORICAL BACKGROUND OF THE DANUBIAN BASIN

The recorded history of the Danubian Basin begins with the continental conquests of the Roman Empire. In 50 B.C., the borders of the Empire were drawn from the River Rhine down to the Italian Alps. The South-Eastern part of Europe, from the Bohemian Basin down to the Black Sea was in the hands of the Barbarians. Thus, the frontiers of Julius Caesar's Empire were almost identical to the Iron Curtain of today.

Rome recognized the danger which threatened the Empire from this direction, and as a preventive measure, the Emperors Augustus and Trajanus took possession of Bohemia, Moravia, Pannonia (today's Hungary) and Dacia (today's Transylvania). Dacia, however, was used only as an outpost, while the main defense line was established at the banks of the Danube River.

The wars involving the possession of these territories were extremely bloody. The Roman Legions, drafted from all parts of the Empire, destroyed the Markomanns in the Bohemian Basin and almost completely exterminated the Daks of Dacia.

The historical significance of these conquests lies, first of all, in the fact that Rome outlined and determined for all time the boundary between the Greek and Latin culture circles on the Eastern ridges of the Carpathians. Thus, the Danubian Basin became integrated into the Empire as the provinces of Pannonia and Dacia, establishing thereby the Western political status of this territory. During the two thousand years which have passed, the Danube River remained the main defense line of the West throughout a very lively history. Just as Transylvania, intended to become an outpost of the West, kept this role through all the centuries, and developed it into a unique historical individuality within the Danubian Basin.

After the fall of the Roman Empire, the Danubian Basin became the bridgehead of Eastern invaders for several centuries. From the South-East, huge waves of nomadic nations broke into the area, mostly through the Focsani gate. Sweeping across the unprotected basin they invaded the West, in order to melt by and by into the Latin and Germanic culture circles, and, after mixing with the original inhabitants, create the nations of today's Europe.

The first serious danger which threatened the entire West with total destruction was the appearance of the Huns in the Danubian Basin. King Attila, the "Whip of God", as he was called by Rome, established his headquarters on the wide plain between the Danube and the Tisza Rivers. His empire, however, stretched out from the Alps to the Baltic Sea, from the Rhone to the Aral Sea. When Attila died in 453, his empire fell apart. Around 480, the rest of the Huns merged into the Bulgarian-Turk tribal federation, to which the Hungarians also belonged. According to folk legend, one of the Hun tribes under the leadership of Attila's youngest son took refuge in the bend of the Eastern Carpathians. The "Székely" nation, still inhabiting the Eastern part of Transylvania and speaking a dialect of the Hungarian language, are supposed to be the descendants of these Huns.

In the middle of the sixth century, the Avars, a nation closely related to the Huns, moved into the Danubian Basin and organized a new empire which reached from the Black Sea to the Baltic Sea, from the Enns to the Don. After two and a half centuries their empire fell under the pressures of Charles the Great from the West and the Bulgarians from the East. For more than a century, no one was able to occupy the Danubian Basin and organize it into a stable unit. Until at the end of the ninth century, the Hungarians appeared.

When they crossed the Carpathians in 896, they had behind them as a rear-guard, a closely related nomadic nation, the Kazars, whose huge empire included today's Russia and Poland. The invasion of the equistic and bellicose Hungarians into the Danubian Basin caused panic in the West. The Christian World declared their lightning-fast attacks the "end of the world", and the Pope himself saw in them the executors of the "last judgement".

The Hungarians undertook several ravaging incursions into the West, crossing the Alps seven times on horseback, and twice reaching clear to the shores of the Atlantic. These incursions served three purposes, looting, reconnoitering, and preventing the formation of a united Western front. Nevertheless, it was due to these attacks that the German unity became consolidated and the West Roman Empire of German Nations rose to the peak of its power.

German historians like to claim the credit for the Christianization of the Hungarians as a result of the defeat they suffered in 955 near Augsburg from the united German armies. The truth is that of the eight Hungarian tribes, only two were involved in that battle, and therefore the loss they suffered was not serious enough to justify the abandonment of their former political concept. This came as a result of other causes. One was the inner dissention between the Hungarian tribes. The other, and even more important, the fall of the Kazar Empire in the East, who were beaten and destroyed by Szjatoslav, Norman-Russian Archduke, in 969. He became the ruler of today's European Russia. With this, the nomadic culture disappeared from Eastern Europe, and the Hungarians became isolated in the Danubian Basin. They had no other choice but to compensate for the lost connections with new connections in the West. Thus, the

Christian Hungarian Kingdom, joining the Western culture-circle, came into existence as a political necessity for survival.

We shall not enter here into the detailed history of the medieval Hungarian Kingdom. Nevertheless, we must point out the factors which made it possible for the Hungarian nation to survive until now in the Danubian Basin, in spite of the complete isolation through language, habits, mental attitude and spiritual values, while all the other nations which had entered the same territory before disappeared in a very short time.

The conversion to the Christion faith, and through it, the acceptance of Western civilization, does not furnish sufficient answer for that. It would also be a mistake to claim that the Hungarian nation possessed such extraordinary qualities which enabled them to organize and maintain statehood and national life against the will of the entire Europe and in opposition to the interests of bigger powers. But if we look at the European role of the Danubian Basin, which we have discussed before, it follows automatically, that the functions of the geographical location could be fulfilled only by certain qualities. In other words, in that certain time when Europe took its permanent shape and form, only such nation was able to meet the need of the geographical location, which had its own particular individuality delimiting it from any other nation, thus making its absorption impossible into any other European culture-circle or any other nation, yet still enabling it to become exclusively and universally European.

The medieval Hungarian statehood and social system resulted from the mixture of Eastern nomadic traditions and Western influences.

The Hungarian kings did not inherit the throne as the right of the first-born as was the practice in the West. They were elected. This unwritten law of early nomadic tradition became a written law in 1222, when the Hungarian Constitution was formulated. The legitimacy of the royal power was invested into the Hungarian Royal Crown (Stephen's Crown), and during the entire existence of the Hungarian Kingdom, up to 1918, only those kings were regarded as legal rulers who were crowned according to the regulations prescribed in the Constitution.

The country belonged to the Crown, and constitutional dialectic called the annexed territories at all times, "countries of the Holy Crown". In case the king disregarded or violated the Constitution, the people had the right to resist with the use of weapons (Jus armis resistendi). This clause of the 1222 Constitution, together with the free election of the king, was repealed arbitrarily by the Habsburgs at the end of the 17th century.

The Hungarian king did not have the power to send troops onto foreign soil or to start war without the consent of the nation. The medieval term "nation", included the entire political nation, in other words, all the voters. Just as before in the nomadic society, the power of the elected chief was based upon the whole society of free warriors, so the power of the Hungarian kings was established on a wide base of free men and small nobility, and did not wobble at the top of a pyramid-like social structure like the power of the Western kings.

While the tribal structure of the early Hungarian society was demolished by the formation of a Christian Kingdom, the clan-system survived with its patriarchal order of succession, based on bloodline. This ancestral system proved to be stronger than the Western "jus regium", and for centuries prevented the development of the feudalistic system and the formation of a privileged aristocracy, separate from the nation. These Western ways were introduced into Hungary only under the foreign rulers of later centuries.

The administrative and political organizations of the Hungarian statehood, based on autonomy and self-government, was also the inherited legal system of the nomadic tribal life. While the nomadic tribes included all the free warriors of the clans, so were the nomadic nations formed by the federation of free tribes. The association of free nations, created through the federation of free tribes, built the huge nomadic empires like those of the Huns or the Mongols. This association was usually forced upon the smaller nations by a stronger one. However, the submission of the weak did not touch its social system, religion, legal customs or administrative procedures, and in most cases, the weaker nation forced into a nomadic empire did not even have to change its leaders. Thus, the nomadic empires were built on autonomy and self-government, and the concept of discrimination against different racial or language groups was unknown.

This principle of self-government and tolerance toward foreign groups, together with the respect for the liberty of others, prevailed in the same way within the Christian Hungarian Kingdom. It became expressed in the autonomous district system, in the self-government of the "free royal cities", and later in the territorial, political and cultural autonomy given to those ethnic groups which came to find refuge under the Holy Crown. The constitutional relationship between the "countries of the Holy Crown" were similar to the structure of the British Commonwealth.

These were the reasons which made the Hungarian State-concept suited to fulfill the role of a bridge between the East and the West in the Danubian Basin. Other nomadic nations, pushing from the East, clear up to the 13th century, were just as able to fit into this State-concept as the German and Vallon settlers, or members of certain royal escorts entering the country with royal brides from Western and Northern Dynasties and deciding to stay in the country. With them the different national cultures of Europe entered Hungary. From London to Moscow, from Lithuania to Byzantium, from Rome to Paris, this lively cultural exchange between the Danubian Basin and the rest of Europe went on for centuries. Hungarian students could be found in great numbers at every European University (The first officially registered student in Oxford was a Hungarian.) The first Hungarian University opened its doors in the 14th century to accommodate thousands of foreign students.

During the two and a half centuries following the millennium, a unity of diversities came into existence in Europe, from the Atlantic to the Urals, from Scandinavia to the Mediterranean. Races, nations, languages, countries and empires divided this Europe into living units, but they all met in the synthesis of Christianity. They were all built on the spiritual heritages of Rome and Byzantium.

In South-Central Europe, two great powers were facing each other as the representatives of racial and religious differences: the orthodox Byzantine Empire, representing the Eastern Slavs on one side and on the other the German Holy Empire. Between these two powers arose in the Danubian Basin the Hungarian Kingdom as a dividing and, in the same time, a balancing power between the Latin-German and the Greek-Slavic worlds. In order to fully understand the importance of this role, one must keep in mind that medieval Hungary belonged among the great powers of Europe. The wealth and prestige of the Hungarian Royal House were equal to those of France and England. There were only 2/3 more Germans than Hungarians and up to the 16th century there were just as many Hungarians as there were English on this earth. It is understandable therefore, that the Hungarian Kingdom was able to block German and Byzantine expansion, either by diplomacy or by the use of arms.

The natural evolution of Europe was interrupted by Genghis Khan's invasion in the middle of the 13th century. In 1240-41, he occupied the Danubian Basin, causing terrible destruction, but in the same year he left again. There are several theories for his fast withdrawal. The most plausible seems to be that in Hungary the nomadic Mongolians met with Western-type fortifications for the first time which they were unable to surmount. Upon learning the fact that the West was fortified, Batu Khan gave up his plan for conquering the rest of Europe. Therefore, the occupation of Hungary, as a march route toward the West lost its purpose. They did not give up Russia, which remainded for centuries under Mongolian rule.

Thus the nomadic social system, statehood, world concept and morality forced upon the nations East and North-East of the Carpathians left unalterable changes in this part of the continent, destroyed the unity of Continental Europe and pushed the frontiers of the Eastern World to the Carpathian Mountain ranges, as part of the dividing line running bet ween the Baltic Sea and the Black Sea. Hungary, a corresponding partner to Eastern Europe before, now became a solid part of the West, making the Carpathians one of the most significant cultural dividing lines of the European Continent. This situation became solidified for seven hundred years.

Following the Mongolian invasion, the formation of the medieval Hungarian Empire came as a natural reaction to the ever-present danger in the East. With the appearance of the Turks in 1358, this danger increased on the South-East corner of the continent. A chain of wars began against the Turkish invaders for the possession of the Danubian Basin, and lasted to the 18th century.

After the Hungarian Royal House of the Árpáds died out in 1305, on the constitutional right of free election, the nation chose kings from the female lines. Thus came the Anjous to the Hungarian throne. Their empire reached from the Baltic Sea to the Black Sea and to the Adriatic, forming a bulwark against the East. Following the Anjou line, Sigismund Luxembourg joined the Holy Crown of Hungary with the Crown of the Holy German Empire. As ruler of this enormous power, Sigismund was able to bring Western troops into constant battle against the Turkish aggression. Nevertheless, the weight of protecting Europe from the invaders fell mostly on the Hungarian nation. In 1456, János Hunyadi won a world-renowned battle over the Turks at Belgrade, remembrance of which is still being expressed in the Christian world by ringing the church bells at noontime.

The Turks were kept away for several decades, while Hunyadi's son, the Transylvanian-born king, Mathias Corvinus, built an empire of strength and culture in the Danubian Basin. After his death, however, the power of the Hungarian Empire began to wane. The political forces within the country turned against each other and the Jagello House, which inherited the Hungarian throne, was not able to unite the nation.

In 1526, the Turkish army, a hundred-thousand strong, broke into Hungary and defeated King Lajos II in the famous battle of Mohács, in which the young King himself fell on the battlefield. The Western part of the country elected his brother-in-law, Ferdinand von Habsburg, to fill the throne, while the Central portion, under Turkish occupation, elected János Zápolya. In the East, the autonomous Transylvanian Principality was formed, as the custodian and further developer of free Hungarian statehood.

The Turkish wars went on for one century and half within the borders of Hungary. From the approximately five million Hungarians who made up more than 80% of the country's population in the 15th century, at the end of the century were only one and a half million. Fugitives from the East and new settlers from the West moved in, and the Hungarian National State turned into a State of nationalities.

161

After the end of the Turkish wars, the Habsburgs regarded Hungary as "conquered territory". They did not re-instate the unified Hungarian Kingdom but ruled over it from Vienna, as part of the Habsburg Empire. From that time on, to speak about Hungarian Statehood and sovereign Hungarian policy is nothing but fiction. (Andrássy: "Ungarns Ausgleich Mit Osterreich von Jahr 1867", Leipzig, 1897, page 215.)

A long series of Hungarian liberty wars tried in vain to re-establish the unity of the country and the continuity of its independent statehood. Just as one and a half thousand years before, in the days of the Roman Empire, the Danubian Basin sank to the level of a province and its functional capacities became paralyzed for centuries. It yielded completely to the policies of the German Empire, which no longer regarded it as a fortress toward the East, but only as a "no man's land", for impending operations.

Only in 1867, after the Holy Roman Empire of German Nations disintegrated and the Habsburgs had lost their German and Italian possessions, did there come a conciliation between Crown and Nation, as the late result of the 1848-49 Kossuth uprising, in the form of the Austro-Hungarian Monarchy.

V

TRANSYLVANIA, IN LIGHT OF HISTORY

In order to understand the regional role of Transylvania within the Danubian Basin, we must know the conditions which created that role. As was mentioned before, the Roman Empire drew a strategic line of defense on the banks of the Danube River, using Transylvania as an outpost. After the Hungarians settled the country, Transylvania was ruled by the clan of Gyula, which pursued a separatistic policy under the influence of Byzantine Christianity. King Stephen made an end to this tendency and forced Transylvania under the royal authority. Yet its role of being an outpost of the West did not change within the Hungarian Kingdom either. Due to military, administrative and most of all communication reasons, the Hungarian kings ruled Transylvania through their agents, called "vajda" or "princeps". Often the younger brother or the son of the king carried the title and the responsibilities which went with it. This practice was in force from 1074 until 1526, the fall of the medieval Hungarian Kingdom.

This de-centralized almost federative, form of government, lay in the very structure of the Hungarian Empire. Croatia co-existed from 1091 to 1918 in a specific form of union with the Hungarian Kingdom. The Southern belt, called "Bansag", which was originally a defensive organization, was ruled under its own administrative autonomy by a "Bán". The cities of the Dalmatian seashore joined the Kingdom as autonomous cities, while the belt of subjugated principalities, encircling Hungary from the South, East and North, including today's Yugoslavia, part of Poland and Roumania, were ruled either by their own dukes or by centrally nominated royal representatives, and were attached thereby with the central power, seated in the Danubian Basin.

Thus the indirect government of Transylvania did not suggest in any way a separation, because the king could take into his own hand at any time the administration of the land. Transylvania was an integral part of the Kingdom. When, as a result of the Turkish occupation, the Kingdom itself fell apart, and in accordance with the Speyer treaty in August, 1570, the independent Transylvanian Principality was established, even the people of Transylvania regarded the situation as interim and born of necessity. In the said treaty, János Zsigmond, the nationally elected king, abdicated voluntarily from the Hungarian throne for the benefit of the Emperor Maximilian, and, recognizing the sovereignty of the Hungarian Crown over Transylvania, took the title of "Duke of Transylvania" (Serenissimus Princeps Transylvaniae.)

This Transylvanian attitude was classically expressed in the "Last Will and Testament" of the Duke István Bocskay, 1604-1606, who was the

163

creator of the authotelic policy of Transylvania, caught between two competing forces, the German and the Turk.

"As long as the Hungarian Crown shall be in the possession of the Germans, a nation more powerful than we are, the presence of a Duke in Transylvania will always be practical and needed in support of Hungary. But when God shall be willing to return the Hungarian Crown to Hungarian hands and within an Hungarian Kingdom, we urge the people of Transylvania not to secede from or turn against that Kingdom, but to aid it with all their power and in complete agreement, and render themselves under the Crown according to old customs."

The independent Transylvanian Principality came into existence under outside pressure. The regionalism, as such, has evolved out of the specific natural endowments of the region, a particular living unit of its own within the unity of the Danubian Basin. This regionalism became deeply engraved into history during the short era of independence, when Transylvania was forced to become the sole heir of the Hungarian Statehood in the Danubian Basin and to carry alone the burden of torchbearer and developer of this concept.

The basic principle of this statehood was the "una eademque libertas", the same and equal liberty for all. This liberty-ideal was not only expressed by the continuous liberty wars of the Transylvanian Principality against the Habsburgs, but most of all in the very statehood of Transylvania itself, in its political system and mental attitude.

The evolution of this specific Transylvanian State-concept was determined mostly by the fact that it was not a national State, but consisted of three nations living within the land: The Hungarian, the Székely and the Saxon (German settlers).

Of course, contrary to today's ethnic concept of the word, "nation" meant exclusively a political nation. That part of society which possessed the political rights - free men and nobility. The political system of Europe was based on the two polarities of free men and serfs. This was the era when the privileged classes (nobility, patricius) referred to in the legal language as "Status and Ordines" stood in opposition to the masses, rightfully called "misera plebs".

The fall of this social and political system was caused by the very fact that it did not include the people into the nation. However, anyone could become a member of the nation, for every member of the "misera plebs" had the free opportunity to raise himself by virtue of deeds into the privileged classes, completely disregarding his ethnic origin, language or religion. Act VI of the 1540 Law of Transylvania clearly stated that "there shall be no differences between the Hungarian members and the Roumanian members of the nobility". (Valachus ipse nobilis cum Hungaris nobilibus et verificationem et juramenti depositionem in Judiciis facere peregareque tenentur". (Puscariu: "Disertatiune Despre Impartirea Politica Ardealului", Sibiu 1864, page 36.)

The three Transylvanian nations, already united in 1437 at Kapolna, agreed to aid one another and to administer their affairs jointly. This agreement of Kapolna later became the foundation of the Transylvanian Constitution.

The Székelys, who had been detailed there by former Hungarian kings as frontier guards, and the Germans (called Saxons), who had settled later for the same purpose "ad retinendam Coronam", lived in privileged regional, political and cultural autonomies, called "Universitas". The administrative organization of the Hungarians was the district or county-system. The Roumanians, who moved across the Carpathian Mountains in an always increasing number seeking refuge from Turkish oppression, lived under similar administrative and legal circumstances as did the Hungarians, but without the possibility of becoming a fourth nation. For their benefit were created, on the pattern of the Hungarian districts, the "Universitas Nobilorum de Krasso", the "Universitas Nobilorum de Hunyad" and the "Universitas Nobilorum de Fogaras", with Roumanian nobility and serfs. The situation of the Roumanians was best expressed by two leading Roumanian politicians and historians.

"When in 1437, the three Transylvanian nations signed the first Constitutional Agreement of the Union in Kapolna, the Roumanian knesdoms had already crumbled away, and sunk into serfhood after the fall of the patrimonial Kingdom. Thus the Roumanians were not able to develop into an independent national structure and could not be taken into consideration as an equal partner at the signing of the Agreement. Due to this reason, during the era of the Independent Transylvanian Principality, (1542-1690), the Roumanians were not able to become a Transylvanian nation, invested with large scale self-governmental rights and privileges." (Goldis: "About the Nationality Problem", Arad, 1912, page 17.)

Jean Slavici adds to this: "The only notable cultural institution of the Roumanians was the Greek-Orthodox Church, which stood, however, under complete Balkan-Slavic influence. Its official language was not Roumanian, but Slavic. The era of the Roumanian national consciousness began only about 1700, when half of the Transylvanian Roumanians converted into Greek-Catholic religion, and our priests were able to study history in Rome and Vienna." (J. Slavici: "Ardealul, Studiu Istoric", 1893, Bucharest, pages 95-96).

The true state of this nomadic herdsman-people can be best evaluated from the decree of the Duke George Rákóczy I (1631-48), sent to the Roumanian Bishop of Bihar, ordering him "to preach to those poor Wallachians in their own tongue, so they may be edified by it in the knowledge of God, and led out from the shadows of superstitious errings into the clear sunshine." Roumanian culture and civilization had its origins in Transylvania and started with the help of financial aid of Transylvanian Hungarian Dukes and noblemen.

The Constitution of the Transylvanian Principality, based on two separate legal documents, can be summed up as follows:

The country was governed by an elected duke, whose legal authority was determined by the Congress, which Congress also possessed the power to remove him from office. Each nation elected "Counselors" in equal number, to serve beside the Duke. In order to bring a Congressional Resolution, the consent of all three nations was necessary. The nations voted collectively in Congress, as a block. Later, repealing the original vote-right, the constitution ordered that in case of grievances, the nation concerned had to turn to the other two for support, who, in their turn, had to present the case to the Duke through due process of Congress, or in case of lesser grievances, to the Counselors.

The Congress consisted of one house only. Individual representatives had only discussion-rights, while the vote went by nations in block. The majority, therefore, did not necessarily consist of the numerical majority of the members of Congress, but of the votes of the three nations as groups.

The power of the Transylvanian Principality was based on the army, jointly maintained by the three nations. Each nation provided the Duke with 7,000 men. This was the first non-mercenary army in Europe.

At the time of the Transylvanian Principality, Europe was like a boiling pot, torn by ideological wars. The Turkish Empire, commanding the most modern armies of that time, and spurred by the fanaticism of the Islamic religion, made ever newer and newer efforts to run down the rest of Europe. Its base of military operations was the Central Plain of the Danubian Basin.

In the West, new colonial empires arose, aided by the new geographical discoveries, creating great wealth on one side and miserable poverty on the other. Thus the outlines of the later social differences began to take shape. The urge of the human mind for liberty brought forth Protestantism, Pietism, Certezianism and Puritanism. In Italy and Spain the Inquisition raged, along with devastating peasant uprisings. The Thirty-Year War decimated Central Europe.

In these wars, the Transylvanian Principality fought for the freedom of religion as a member of the Federation of Protestant States. First in the world, Transylvania declared religious freedom in 1550, and 1557 added to the Constitution the right of man to change his religion according to his belief. The Transylvanians were fighting the Turks and making pacts with them. They were fighting against the anti-Protestant, Germanizing Habsburgs, who were trying to melt Hungary into the German Empire. But their main purpose still remained - to re-establish the integrity of Hungary, and to secure the recognition of the Hungarian Constitution by the possessors of the Holy Crown.

In the meanwhile, the regional profile of Transylvania became clearly outlined. Its historical individuality developed into a realistic political and mental attitude, which kept its eye only on the final goal, clinging to solid principles. Giving place to the play of opposing forces, this attitude created a specifically collective and particularly regional mentality, known as "Transylvanianism". With the aid of this mental attitude and political flexibility, Transylvania survived as a living unit on the ruins of the Danubian Hungarian Kingdom, ground between the huge millstones of the two opposing empires, the German and the Turk. As the lone fortress of the Western Christian culture-circle, Transylvania, custodian of the Hungarian State-Concept, kept on guarding the frontier of the West toward the East.

As the heir of the humanistic-renaissance kingdom of Mathias Corvinus, the Transylvanian Principality took over the legacy of the Hungarian European culture. The first book printed in Hungarian appeared in Transylvania in 1527. Toward the end of the same century, some 18 printing establishments were at work within the land. Together, they published 380 books, 180 in Latin, 139 in Hungarian, 15 in German, 10 in Roumanian, 9 in old Slavic and 7 in Greek language. In the 17th century, there were already 44 printing establishments at work. Besides the original encyclopedias, guide-books and school-books of Transylvanian authors, they published a large number of translations from French, English, Italian, Dutch and German writers, philosophers and clergymen.

In the same time, the specifically Transylvanian literature appeared for the first time. In 1555, Tinódi Lantos Sebestyén published in Kolozsvár his famous "Verses Kronika" (Chronicles in Verses) and in 1569, appeared the most typical literary work of that era, printed in Abrudbánya, the "Comedy about the Treason of Balassi Menyhért".

The Transylvanian culture, due to its typically Protestant nature, was not the sole property of the higher classes, but it became a popular culture, with a specifically Transylvanian taste and colour, reflecting the reciprocal influences of the three national and racial cultures, tastes and mentalities. The centers of public education were "Collegiums", where side by side with young noblemen, a large number of lower class children became educated. Besides Hungarian professors who received their degrees at foreign universities, many foreign professors of great international prestige taught in these Collegiums, like Martin Opitz, John Alsted, Henry Bisterfeld and Isaac Basire. Young Transylvanians visited foreign universities in increasing numbers, financed by the dukes of Transylvania.

For example, in Wittenberg, between 1586 and 1640, more than 300 Transylvanian students received their diplomas, while in Lynden, between 1620 and 1650, there were 231 Transylvanias enrolled.

While politically, the three official "natio" ruled Transylvania, culturally, the symbiosis of the three peoples prevailed - the Hungarian, German and Roumanian. The mutual influence these three cultures exercised on one another can no longer be separated.

The Transylvanian dukes and noblemen gave powerful aid to the unfolding of Roumanian culture, civilization and education. A hundred years before the first Roumanian book was published in Roumania proper (Moldova), in the year 1564, Benker, German Mayor, and Miklós Forró, an Hungarian nobleman, jointly published the Evangelium in the Roumanian language. Duke Kristóf Báthory established and maintained in Gyulafehérvár, a Roumanian printing shop, where the first Roumanian book appeared printed with Latin letters in 1570. In 1582, as a donation of Ferenc Geszty, the Old Testament was printed in Rumanian, while the New Testament came out from the same printing shop some years later.

This situation did not change, even after the Independent Transylvanian Principality ceased to exist. Among the 587 Roumanian books published in the 19th century, 320 were published in Hungary. The first Roumanian newspaper, the "Gazeta Transylvania" appeared in Brassó in 1839, and Octavian Goga, the great Roumanian poet, who later became the Prime Minister of Greater Roumania, published his literary and political magazine "Luciaferul", in Budapest, 1902.

Professor Torjai-Szabó wrote in his book: "The Hungarian and German Protestantism in Transylvania exercised a decisive influence upon the cultural and political development of the entire Roumanian nation. These cultural influences, coming from the Hungarians, developed in a relatively short time the cultural and political nationalism of the Roumanians."

The Transylvanian Germans, who enjoyed complete territorial, political and cultural autonomy, also produced a long line of scientists, writers and creative artists. In spite of the fact that through all the centuries they stayed loyal to their German origin, creating a very special branch of the universal German culture, they contributed a very particular color to the development of the Transylvanian regionalism and mentality.

Thus, the Principality of Transylvania became the continuity of the Hungarian State-Concept, which was: "to make the Carpathian Basin, as a natural living unit, into a political framework and fill this with the traditional Hungarian Liberty-concept. This is the true Hungarian State-Concept and not the domination of one nation above the others." (Ottlik:

"Pax Hungarica".)

The noted Roumanian historian, Nicolae Balcescu, writes in his "Istoria Romanilor", page 312, "The Problem in Transylvania was not, and is not, how the Roumanians, the Hungarians, the Germans or the Székely must proceed in order that they alone rule this land and eliminate the others. But how to find the ways among themselves to the possibilities of harmony within the framework of a federative state, in which equal rights are enjoyed by all individuals just as by all nations." (Published in 1902, Bucharest.)

When, finally, at the end of the 17th century and the first part of the 18th century, the Danubian Basin was liberated from the Turks by united Western efforts, the Habsburgs regarded the devastated Hungary as a "Crown Dominion". Transylvania started several liberty wars against the Habsburg oppression, but everyone of them failed. In 1691, the Emperor terminated the Transylvanian Principality and incorporated it into the Empire. While he abolished the Transylvanian Constitution, it still retained almost the same principles of "Systema unionis trium nationem".

In a new liberty war, in 1707, the Hungarian Congress of Onod declared officially the dethronement of the House of Habsburg, giving the power of "regent" to the Duke Rákóczy, until free elections could be held. Thus the decree of Ónod restored in principle the National Kingdom and the territorial unity of the country. Due to the fact that the elected Duke of Transylvania and the Regent in whom the Hungarian Congress invested the Royal Powers was the same person, in idea and in practice, the re-unification of Hungary and Transylvania became materialized.

However, with the change in political constellations in Western Europe, the Imperial forces concentrated on Hungary, and the Rákóczy Liberty War ended in defeat. With this, the fate of Hungary was determined for one and a half centuries. During this time, the Hungarian nation, and through it, the seminal forces of the Danubian Basin, were completely paralyzed by Habsburg domination, terror and persecution. Nonetheless, the Danubian Basin itself, framed now into the Great Empire of the Habsburgs, continued its European functions as the fortress of the West toward the East, and as the bridge between the two worlds. Only it had declined to the level of the former Roman provinces.

The Hungarian National State turned slowly into a state of nationalities, and the awakening national consciousness began in the 18th century to create conflicts among the nationalities. The centralized bureaucracy of the Habsburg absolutist system was unable to replace the principles of the Hungarian Constitution which was based on local autonomies and thereby secured the free play of political forces.

All power was in the hands of the ruler, residing in Vienna. He was the instigator and the executor of the reforms. The Emperor Joseph II, who was one of the most modern and most liberal rulers of his age, abolished the Constitution completely, and in an attempt to create a unified Empire, ordered the German language to become the official language of the administration. He tried to organize a unified national state where there was no unified nation.

The French Revolution, the American Declaration of Independence, and finally the plans of Napoleon to unify Europe under French hegemony, brought forth great changes in the life of Europe. The principles of "Égalité, Fraternité, Liberté", the desire of the peoples for a liberal parliamentary form of government and constitutional rule, aided by the increase of national feelings, stirred new unrest.

In many cases, as in Hungary and Transylvania, the nobility itself led in the proclamation of social and political reforms by voluntarily giving up out-dated privileges. A strong mental fermentation began. The initiative was given by writers, and taken over by politicians. In Hungary, this was the era of reform-meetings, which finally ended in the Liberty War of 1848-49, led by Louis Kossuth.

The Revolutionary Congress of 1848 restored the Hungarian Constitution, abolished the privileges of the nobility, created a new, parliamentary government, offically united Transylvania with Hungary and passed liberal laws concerning the nationalities. The new laws included equal taxation, freedom of press and the equality of all religions.

The Emperor Ferdinand V sanctioned these new laws, but the Vienna government feared the reforms for the sake of the Monarchy's unity. They forced the Emperor to abdicate and replaced him with the sixteen year old Franz Joseph, who did not even let himself be crowned with the Stephen Crown, so he would not have to take the oath to uphold the Hungarian constitution. He declared the reforms, already sanctioned by Ferdinand, void, and sent his army into Hungary to remove the freely elected government. The greatest Hungarian Liberty War had seemed for a while to succeed against the Habsburg forces, but Franz Joseph, citing the European Holy Alliance, asked aid from the Czar of Russia. On August 13, 1849, the Hungarians surrendered to the Russian Commander.

After the surrender, the most bloody rule of terror dominated Hungary for two decades. However, in the meantime, the Habsburgs were slowly losing their dominions in Italy and Germany and w ؛re left with the Imperial Crown of Austria and the Royal Crowns of Bohemia and Hungary. In 1860, negotiations began between the Crown and the Nation, which finally led in 1867 to a compromise between the Emperor and Hungary. The Constitution was restored, Hungary and Transylvania officially united again and the Austro-Hungarian Monarchy came into existence.

VI

CHANGE IN CONCEPTS WITHIN THE MONARCHY

The Austro-Hungarian Monarchy, a liberal-constitutional state formation, created in the Danubian Basin a tremendous economic upswing and prosperity. Together with the industrial and commercial urban development, the entire social structure of the country began to change. Sadly enough, the political changes did not keep in step with the social changes.

Every citizen of the Monarchy enjoyed the same rights provided by the law. The change from a feudalistic system to a liberal-constitutional state filled everyone with enthusiasm, and turned the people's attention to legal problems. All the political activities of this era were concentrated on the discussions of constitutional questions.

The booming economy created a prosperous middle class and a tremendously large class of urban bourgeoisie. The large numbers of landholding peasantry also benefited from the wealth of the Monarch, but not the landless farm laborers, who began to emigrate to America to make their fortunes.

Within the Monarchy itself three different state-concepts met in silent struggle: that of the German Holy Empire; that of Stephen's Crown; and the Czech concept of Bohemia.

Hungary, where the regional autonomies had long been repealed by the Habsburgs, yielded to centralistic tendencies of the Monarchy, and so the districts, losing their intended political roles, became solely administrative units. The effect of this change was felt most in Transylvania, where the Constitution had secured for centuries complete self-government to the different nationalities.

Before the establishment of the Monarchy, during the one and a half centuries of unlimited Habsburg domination, the Transylvanian districts were administered by German speaking Austrian officials. After 1868, the administrators were mostly local dignitaries, nominated by the Emperor, who was also the King of Hungary.

The members of the lower house, the representatives in the Parliament, were freely elected by the people. Many Roumanian politicians, who later played great roles in post-World War Roumania, began their political careers as representatives of those districts where the Roumanian population was in the majority. Strangely enough, most of these politicians regarded the Austrian Empire as their homeland, and not the Hungarian Kingdom in which they lived, and of which they had enjoyed the Constitutional rights.

The explanation for this can be found in part in the social changes within the country, and in part, in foreign influences seeping across the borders from the East.

The economic development of the country gave free opportunities to everyone to climb through his own initiative, from the lower classes into the prosperous middle class, and even into the upper class, with absolute disregard of his nationality (János Bud, Anton Mocsonyi de Foen, Dr. Moldovan, Mr. Muntyan, etc.). But because the middle and upper classes in Transylvania were exclusively Hungarian in language, those members of the other nationalities who came up into these classes through their own efforts became rapidly assimilated into these classes, and most of them lost their national identities.

Roumanian politicians called this natural assimilation of the individuals in the group "hungarianization". The fact is that "Hungarization" or "Magyarization", as a planned program, never existed. It would have been against the Hungarian Constitution. Nonetheless, there was a definite assimilative effect at work within the bourgeoisie and the upper class toward the new-comers into these classes. It was simply the law of assimilation exercised by a higher culture on an inferior one.

Public education was centrally organized and financed. Teachers, hired and paid by the Hungarian Government, were ordered to always teach in the native tongues of their pupils. Only high education was exclusively Hungarian, and even that in only the public institutions. Private schools, maintained by the different churches, were free to teach in any language they desired.

All nationality groups were equally entitled to the exercise of free elections, to representation in the Parliament, to their own free press and to any other kind of cultural, economic and religious establishments. Whether this liberal attitude, deeply rooted in the Constitution and in the Freedom-Concept of the Hungarian Nation, was an asset or a liability to Hungary can be argued. The fact is that through these establishments, not only allowed, but generously supported by the Hungarian government, foreign influences moved into the country, undermining its unity and preparing its downfall.

While the Hungarian State-Concept has never changed from its original basic principles, a shifting began to take place in the interpretation of this Concept. It was instigated by Vienna and by the increasing anti-Hungarian attitude of the ethnic minorities.

The law (Sect. 44-1868) clearly stated that "all the citizens of Hungary form one political nation, therefore every citizen of the country no matter to which ethnic group he belongs, is an equal member of the nation." This law meant that in Hungary, not only the majority group belonged to the ruling nation, but even the smallest ethnic group was a

172

member of it. The political structure of Hungary was not based on the rule of one people over the others, but on an idea of civilization, namely to include the entire Carpathian Basin as a geographical unit on the frontiers of Western culture into the political framework of one Western Christian Kingdom. The style of rule was, beginning to end, not "national" but Western Christian, therefore, international. It was not called "Hungary" because it was ruled by Hungarians, but because within its borders, up to the 18th century, Hungarians were in the majority. Just as within the Roman Empire, where Africans, Hispanians, Illirs and even Germanic Barbarians, stepped into the leading ranks of the Roman patricians as the vanguard of Roman civilization, so can we see Frenchmen, Germans, Italians, Croatians and even Roumanians fighting through the centuries for Hungarian civilization and liberty.

In 1848-49, German, Serbian, Irish and Polish heroes fought for the principles of the Hungarian State-Concept. Men who never spoke the Hungarian language. Spiritual leaders of humanity like the English Matthew Arnold, the French Reclus, and the German Heine, praised with enthusiasm the Hungarian phenomenon of unity. The famous epigram for which Hungarians were so frequently accused of being over-patriotic: "Extra Hungariam non est vita, sic est vita, non est ita" (Outside of Hungary there is no life, and if there is life, it is not the same.) was created, not by a Hungarian, but by the Italian Coelius Rhodinginus in the 15th century.

The "One Hungarian People" mentioned as such in the original Constitution and later again in the 1868 law, stood for all the native inhabitants of the Carpathian Basin, framed into one unity by the Constitution of the Hungarian State-Concept.

This State-Concept, however, in the last centuries had a giant competitor - the conception of the Habsburg Empire. The Habsburg civilization embraced a much larger horizon, for it included the entire valley of the Danubian River. It stood in opposition to the Hungarian Liberty-Concept because it was based on the idea of Dynastical rule. In other words, it carried the concept of an overall servitude of the people. From an historical-philosophical viewpoint, the many centuries-long fight of the Hungarians against the Habsburgs was, in reality, nothing less than the clash of these two opposing concepts of civilization. This fight, expressed in the many wars of liberty, had a dynamic current. The peoples in the Danubian Basin saw in the Hungarians the torch-bearers of liberty against the Turk and against the Habsburg oppression, and they were willing to fight side by side with them on the battlefields.

The Nation-Concept of the 19th century became interwoven with the ethnical and the language concepts. Because during the feudalistic era and even after 1868, the political nation was Hungary, the desire became more prevalent that the member nations should speak the Hungarian language. This brought forth the false notion that those who could not speak the language could not be good Hungarians nor good patriots. "This created a big propaganda movement on behalf of the Hungarian language, called 'Magyarization' , which had more noise than effect and the logic of which was in direct opposition to the facts. The great masses of the nationalities never learned the language, but still retained their traditional loyalty to the Hungarian State, while their political leaders used their knowledge of the Hungarian language as a tool against the Hungarian concept of unity within the Carpathian Basin." (Ottlik: "Pax Hungarica".)

As mentioned before, the assimilation was much more effective on the social level. Except for the Germans, especially the Transylvanian Saxons, the large masses of the ethnic groups in Hungary were peasants and herdsmen. Without a certain degree of assimilation they were unable to rise into the commercial or administrative middle-class, since they had no such classes within their own ethnic groups. This lack of a leading class made it impossible for them to become organized into regional autonomies as the Germans or the Székelys, which otherwise would have been the normal procedure, according to the Hungarian Constitution.

The leaders of the ethnic groups, mainly their priests, protested with every possible means against this assimilation, and regarded it as a manifestation of hostility against their interests. They saw the solution of their problems in the creation of ethnic autonomies and in the federation of these autonomies. In spite of the fact that in the concept of the Habsburg Empire there was no place for such autonomies, while on the contrary, the original idea of the Hungarian State-Concept was based on regional autonomies until the Habsburgs abolished them, the leaders of the ethnic groups showed loyalty only to the Vienna court and not to the Hungarian homeland.

In their turn, the Hungarians, prompted by this hostile attitude, regarded the ethnic problem as part of the oppressive Habsburg policy against the territorial integrity and unity of Hungary. Under these mental and political conditions the Pan-Slavic, the Pan-Germanic and the Daco-Roumanian movements of the 19th century infiltrated the public life of the Monarchy. The mutual misunderstandings, local administrative transgressions, and the increasing anti-Hungarian attitude of the ethnic groups created an atmosphere of tension and mutual distrust. Thus the nationalities of the Carpathian Basin, who not only had co-existed for centuries, but had built a country for themselves in peace and harmony, now, under the influence of the new nationalistic ideas of the 19th century, turned against one another.

The faults and merits of the Austro-Hungarian Monarchy have been for many decades the centers of violent discussions. It is not our aim to engage ourselves in this controversy. It will be the task of future historians to deliver an objective evaluation, for all those who are discussing it today are either witnesses or victims of that political era. This explains the mutual accusations, the extremely biased opinions and the many distortions of the truth.

Nevertheless, certain evident facts must be pinpointed here. One, that the former member nations of the Monarchy mutually accuse each other today of everything that went wrong. Second, that the small national states which took the place of the Monarchy, and which contain just as many ethnic groups as did the Monarchy, have been unable to furnish the same status of power and security, the same status of peace and prosperity to their citizens as they enjoyed before, in spite of the inner struggles. The proof of this statement is clearly documented by the ever increasing search in people's minds for the restoration of the old unit in some other form.

This idea of a Danubian Federation or a Federation of Danubian States has often arisen since the fall of the Monarchy. Its realization between the two World Wars was made impossible by the overheated political atmosphere which excluded even the thought of mutal concessions. Today, under the dictatorial pressure of the Soviet Union such an idea cannot even be mentioned. The creation of a Danubian Federation in any form would mean nothing less than the return of the Danubian Basin to its original historic functions as the organizing power of South-Eastern Europe, and the fortress of the Western World toward the East. But as long as the Soviet Union does not give up her plans of World-conquest, her position in the Danubian Basin will serve as her most important bridgehead against the West.

Among the historical heritages of the Monarchy two main problem complexes remain to be solved. One is the question of statehood in the Danubian Basin, and the other is the problem of the ethnic minorities. Both problems are far from being simply regional problems, and belong to the overall synthesis of Europe. In order to deal with these problems, we have to clarify a few concepts.

Under Danubian Basin, we understand those territories around the central course of the Danube River, which formerly belonged to the medieval Hungarian Kingdom, the "Archiregnum". The center of the Danubian Basin, however, is that certain region we call the Carpathian Basin, and the borders of which coincide exactly with the borders of the Hungarian Kingdom itself. For the sake of illustrating these problems, we have discussed on previous pages the past history of the entire Danubian Basin, and the principles of a concept which was able to organize this territory into a strong and propserous unit and to maintain it for many centuries. The objective evaluation of this past proves that the fate of the entire Danubian Basin and all its peoples depends of the functions performed by its natural center, namely the Carpathian Basin. Independent from all the other factors, the charismatic consciousness of this key position explains the stubborn devotion of the Hungarians to their Statehood and the integrity of this Statehood even in times when both were nothing more than fiction.

After the fall of the organizing power of this region, the Hungarian Kingdom, the Danubian Basin became first the Central European basis of the Turkish aggression against the West, and then was turned into a province of the German Empire. Only after the Habsburgs lost most of their powers, was the Danubian Basin re-established again, still under the Habsburg rule, as the living unit of historical individuality.

Unluckily enough, in this revived unity, the original idea which enabled the peoples of the Danubian Basin in the previous centuries to unfold to the full their individualities harmoniously was no longer present Instead, three completely opposing State-Concepts clashed against each other. While the Czech concept was swallowed up by the much stronger German concept, the German and the Hungarian were unable to overcome one another. Thus, neither of these concepts could fully materialize, and the State apparatus of the dual Monarchy had to operate with compromises and half-solutions. This led to the intensification and aggravation of all problems which otherwise could have either been solved by the dictatorial methods of the Habsburg absolutism or by the Constitutional framework of Stephen's Crown.

Emil Franzel writes in his book, "Donauraum" (Francke Verlag, Bern, 1958), "Driven out of Italy and Germany, the Habsburg Empire was forced to turn toward the South-East. Bismarck himself suggested that Austria should transfer its center of gravity to Budapest ... The Constitution of Dec. 21, 1867 was the masterpiece of liberal ideologists. It contained the complete catalog of the basic human rights, limited the power of the government, introduced the responsibility of the cabinet, and contained directives concerning the equality of all nationalities. But exactly this point shows that the doctrine-makers of the liberal state were unable to bring life into the laws they had created. The spirit of the constitution would have requested that a nationality-law be drawn up which could have secured national autonomies from the town councils up to the ethnic universities. But the Parliament, in spite of its own Constitution, never settled this problem. That this Constitution was a work of idealists can also be seen by the fact that in many aspects it was left in a vacuum. It was the Constitution of a state which, in reality, never came into existence. The state, to which this Constitution was given, did not even have a name. It was called until its very end in 1917 the "Kingdoms and Coun-

176

tries represented in the council of Empire." This nameless State was not based in reality on either the Constitution or the Parliament ... but on the legality of the Crown, on the person of the ruler and on the subordinated executive power."

In order to better understand the problems which the Monarchy was unable, or did not have time enough to solve, we must examine causes and conditions which created them.

In Europe there were always peoples of different races, different languages, different religious beliefs and different cultures living together in the same organized framework of statehood. From the beginning of its history clear up to the 19th century, Europe recognized only two political and social units as absolute essentials: the State and the family. The relationship between these two units, State and family, was coordinated by the social system which grew out from the masses and which alone practiced politics: the nobility. In their hands lay the right and the possibility for organized action. They were the representatives of the State and were called the "Nation". Because everyone in the "patria" (fatherland) had about the same possibility for elevating himself through his own efforts and abilities into this class (with complete disregard to ethnic origin), the concept of "Nation" became politically sublimated, even in those countries where the nobility was filtered out of a homogeneous society.Thus the system of statehood was based on the dual polarity of a leading class on one side possessing all political powers, and the masses on the other.

This situation began to change with the French Revolution, which put the "people" as the ultimate source of law and power, in the place of the absolute Royal powers. In theory, that is. In actual practice only so much changed, that the "sovereign person of the absolute monarch" became distributed among the members of the bureaucracy, who did the ruling "in the name of the people".

The sovereignty of the people, as a concept, has no basis whatsoever in the social ideologies of Europe. As Harry Pross puts it ("Der Volksmithos ..." Neue Zürcher Zeitung, Jan. 17, 1959.), "The people is only a subsidiary concept ... as such it is unable to do anything, but those who act in its name can refer to it this way even more." Exactly because they were able to refer to it, and because they were able to justify their deeds with "the will of the people", those who did the acting, namely the politicians and ideologists, surrounded the concept of the "people" with a myth, and finally identified it with the nation-concept.

Thus were the modern national States created, not based on some political or social community, but based on the people as an ethnical, linguistical and cultural unit. Under the "sovereignty of the people" in the 19th century a catastrophic requirement of our age was established on the ruins of the feudal Europe: the united and indivisible national state-concept, corresponding with the ethnic borders. Because it was impossible to fulfill this requirement anywhere in Europe, since in every State people had been living for centuries who belonged to another ethnic group, the concept of "ethnic minority" came into the foregound.

How clouded this entire problem is can be demonstrated by mentioning that, for example, in the legal language of the Anglo-Saxon World "nationality" means citizenship, even today, while in practice it is the name of a cultural and linguistic   community, possessing historical individuality.

It must also be understood that the nationality problems of Europe cannot be compared in any way with the assimilative "melting-pot" tendencies of America, which brought forth the American Nation by blending together the sons of all the European nations. These Europeans who came into America did so with the open desire to become Americans. While most of the ethnic minorities found in the National States of Europe either ended up conquered or forced into group migrations in the foreign framework, and tried to preserve their own individuality in every possible way through clinging to their language, their traditions, their culture and their religion, which differed from those of the ruling majority.

Two opposing wills faced each other within each of the European National States: that of the ruling nation, trying to establish at any cost its own National State based on one unified ethnic origin, and that of the ethnic minorities struggling to preserve their own identity. The law and practice of democracy does not recognize ethnic autonomies. All it can do at best is to grant equal human rights. It does not recognize the ethnic groups as independent legal units, but it still demands from them absolute loyalty. Therefore, the ethnic minorities, even in the most tolerant States, must accept the status of second grade citizens.

Because they differ substantially from the ruling majority, the universal rights to them as a group cannot of themselves be satisfactory. In some countries (England, France), they can take part in the legislation only as members of one of the political parties, which are organized by and for the majority nation. In countries where they are allowed to form their own political parties, their influence on the policy of the State is very weak, if felt at all, because of their permanent minority status. Therefore, they feel that the country in which they live is only their homeland in a regional and not a political sense, and while they try to find a modus vivendi in order to survive, they always nourish the secret dreams of one day joining their own National State by moving the borders in order to fit their own geographical location.

It is understandable that during the last century a mutual distrust built up between majority and minority ethnic groups, all over Europe, which was the greatest obstacle in the way of any sensible solution. In the case of Hungary, the Hungarians have never regarded the Croatians as an "ethnic minority", but as a partner nation within the Federated union.

The Slovaks, who lived for a thousand years in the most intimate relations with the Hungarians, were alienated from them only under the ideological influences of the 19th century, and were torn out of their traditional community by the artificial creation of a Czech-Slovak State and Nation. While the dream of a Great-Serbia for a long time haunted the horizon, the Serbs of Hungary never wanted more than their minority rights as outlined in the Constitution. So far as the Germans were concerned, the Hungarians had no serious friction with this ethnic group, except under the influence of Hitler's imperialistic aggression.

However, it was entirely different in the case of the largest ethnic group in the country, the Roumanians.

VII

THE ROUMANIAN IMMIGRATION

Throughout history has the narrow flatland between the lower Danube and the Southern Carpathians served as the highway of Eastern aggression against the Carpathian Basin. This strategically important region was called for centuries the "Focsáni Gate". Huns, Avars, Bulgarians, Turks and finally the Red Army used this gateway in order to enter the Carpathian Basin.

For this reason, King Béla IV organized in 1235 a large Hungarian settlement on this territory, for the protection of the Focsáni Gate. This autonomous Hungarian settlement was called the "Bánság of Szöreny". Even today, more than 200 town and village names in the area remind us of their Hungarian origin. Thousands of Hungarian family names prove that assimilation process took place and the Hungarians became absorbed into the Roumanian, who migrated centuries later into this area. (Radu Rossetti: "Despre Unguri si Episcopiile Catolic di Moldova", 1905, Bucuresti, page 2-7 and Siculus: "A Moldovai Magyarok ... " 1942, University of Pécs, Chapter 14).

The Roumanians, or their original name, the "Vlach"-s, a Balkanian herds-people moved slowly from the Albanian mountains toward the East, and their appearance was first noticed in the 11th century, south of the lower Danube. The first scattered Roumanian settlements on the North Bank of the Danube, in the Hungarian "Bánság of Szörény", were reported in 1247. In the district Fogaras, their appearance was mentioned for the first time in a document dated 1206. At the end of the same century, two Vlach "voievodines" were established by the Hungarian Kingdom, called "Havasalföld (today Muntenia), and Moldova. Through their contacts with the Hungarians, these people soon came under the influence of Western culture, in spite of their Slavic-Orthodox religion. This influence, of course, left its mark only upon the ruling circles, who learned Western habits and manners through their contacts with the Hungarian nobility. The mass of Roumanians, being nomadic herds-people, could not be organized by force and kept on moving up and down along the Southern and Eastern slopes of the Carpathians. It took several centuries until they finally settled down to agriculture.

The endless wars which ravaged their country, and the despotic tendencies of their own rulers, forced them to be on constant alert and move into the mountains whenever danger arose. To escape danger and persecution by their own chieftains, they began to move in groups across the Carpathians, seeking refuge and protection in the Hungarian Kingdom, where they were organized into regular districts under their own selected leaders.

Both Roumanian voievodines came under Turkish influence and domination in the 14th century and their land served as a base of operation against the West. After the downfall of the medieval Hungarian Empire, these two Roumanian Provinces did not see any hope in resistance, and turning their back to the West, they became an active part of the Balkan. The Slavic-Greek influence of their religion proved to be stronger than their short affiliation with the West, especially after their own nobility died out during the wars and their place was taken over by Greeks. This Greek upper class, called "Fanariotes", introduced Byzantime corruption into state affairs, and in their greed, they degraded the people to the status of working animals. To escape this situation, more and more Roumanians began to migrate into Transylvania, where they were able to enjoy the privileges and the safety of a Constitutional State organization.

Lupu Vazul, Voevod of Moldova, reported in a letter to Istambul in 1643, that 1/3 of the population of Transylvania was Roumanian. According to the census made by the Jesuits between 1658 and 1662, Transylvania had a total population of a half million people, of which about 240,000 was Roumanian. The exodus kept on. According to the reports of Engel, the population of Muntenia in 1739 included 147,000 families, while in 1757 there were only 35,000 left. In the same time, from the 60,000 population of the city of Bucharest, 17,000 left the country bound for the West.

In Transylvania, the 1857 census found 1,089,054 Roumanians, and in the next fifty years this figure increased almost three-fold. The 1910 census showed 2,839,454 Roumanians, which made up 53.8% of the population. These figures clearly prove that the big "Magyarization" drive, claimed by the Roumanian politicians, was nothing but fiction.

As a result of the 1806 Russian-Turkish War, Russia annexed Bessarabia and the Eastern part of Moldova. The two voievodines united in 1859 under Alexander Cuza, who was forced to resign in 1866 under the charge of being a "Russian hireling". His successor, the Prinz Carl Hohenzollern-Siegmaringen, declared in 1877 the independence of the United Vioevodines and in 1881, the Roumanian Kingdom was proclaimed. This is the point where the history of Roumania, as such, actually begins.

The political, economic and cultural situation of the Transylvanian Roumanians within the Hungarian Kingdom has already been treated in another chapter. It was also mentioned that the Diploma Leopold terminated the Transylvanian principality in 1691 and revoked its Constitution. However, the status of the Province of Transylvania under Habsburg rule was still based on the same principles of the "union of three nations". Roumanian politicians in their separatistic efforts always referred back to the Diploma Leopoldicum, in spite of the fact that the Roumanians were not even mentioned in this document, because the Diploma Leopoldicum was not based on the national (ethnic) concept, but on the concept of feudal organization, in which the word "nation" (Hungari: nobiles, siculi et saxones) meant the organized groups and not the ethnic groups. The right concerning the use of the Hungarian language was not expressed in the document either, because in Transylvania, as in Hungary proper, the language of administration and public life was Latin. (Puscariu: Disertatiune despre impartirea politica Ardealului", 1864, Page 36.)

The identity of the political nation must not be confused with the identity of the ethnic nation. These two are not the same.

Toward the end of the 18th century and the first part of the 19th century, the social hatred of the Roumanians, who had been degraded into the status of serfhood by their own leaders, became transferred against the Hungarians, in spite of the fact that the Hungarian serf carried the same burdens on his shoulders. After 1848, when the serfs were freed, 1,615,574 acres of land was handed over to them, 80% of which went to Roumanians. Toward the end of the 19th century, due to the operations of the Albina Bank, financed by the Roumanian Kingdom, the land possessions of the Roumanians of Transylvania increased in great measure. In spite of the fact that the freedom and the prosperity of the Roumanians in Transylvania was safeguarded by the Hungarian, and not the Austrian Constitution, the leaders of the Rumanians declared their loyalty to the House of Habsburg and not to their Hungarian homeland. They tried to advance their future in a federated Habsburg Empire, in "The United States of Great Austria" (Aurel Popovici).

Dr. Vajda-Voevod, Hungarian nobleman and Roumanian political leader, who later became Prime Minister of Great-Roumania, wrote in 1913 in the "Österreichische Rundschau": "We, leaders of the Transylvanian Roumanians, can support only such policy, which keeps in view the future of all Roumanians. Without the presence of a strong Austria-Hungary, Roumanias on both sides of the Carpathians would be easy prey for Russian Imperialism."

In 1861, the Roumanian Cultural Society, the ASTRA, was created in Transylvania, which became the strongest tool of the Roumanian political movement. In 1881, the year of the Proclamation of the Roumanian Kingdom across the Carpathians, the Roumanian National Party was formed in Transylvania and worked hand in hand with the Liga Culturala in Bucharest on the common goal, that is, to undermine the Monarchy and to unite all Roumanians in a "great-Roumania".

However, not all the Roumanian political leaders were in favour of this policy. Many of them felt a deep distrust toward the Roumanian

Kingdom, where a Balkan-type corruption was in evidence at the highest administrative levels. After World War I, when Transylvania became part of Roumania, these politicians often expressed their displeasure. Stephen Pop Csicso said in an interview: "We are worse now, than ever before." (Adeverul, 1929, Febr. 4). and Vajda-Voievod admitted that - "law and justice were more respected in Hunary than in Roumania." (Patria, Oct. 26, 1928)

This did not change the overall Roumanian policy to disrupt the unity of the Carpathian Basin. The campaign toward this direction went on with an increasing speed and emotion, and finally resulted in the liquidation of Hungary after World War I.

For the sake of objectivity, it must be mentioned here that the oppression of the Hungarian minority in Transylvania did not come as an act of revenge from the Transylvanian Roumanians. On the contrary, the efforts of the Hungarians to keep their identity within the Roumanian Kingdom was regarded with sympathy by the Transylvanian Roumanians, who themselves had to fight sometimes for their rights against their own government.

The tendency of oppression came from Roumania-proper, as a long-range policy with the aim to eliminate as rapidly as possible the danger of ever having to give up Transylvania, the richest territory in South-Eastern Europe, which became nothing but a Province, ruthlessly exploited by its present conqueror, Trans-Carpathian Roumania.

VIII

TRANSYLVANIA, PROVINCE OF THE
KINGDOM OF GREAT-ROUMANIA

The peace treaties forced upon Europe after World War I paralyzed the historic and economic functions of the Danubian Basin. On top of this, they did not even serve their alleged purpose, that is, to solve the nationality problems. Only the roles changed, with this difference, that while the many different nationality groups of the Danubian Basin were able to co-exist successfully and in a constructive manner within the framework of the previous liberal Constitutional State, the new minority groups, created by the treaties, were mercilessly exposed to the most chauvinistic discriminations by the new national States.

Of the 325,411 square kilometers of territory of the Hungarian Kingdom, 232,448 square kilometers were divided up among these States, and from a population of 20,886,487 of which 54.5% were Hungarians, 13,271,370 were placed under foreign domination, including 3,319,579 Hungarians. Out of these, 1,704,851 became the subjects of the Kingdom of Great-Roumania. What this meant can be clearly realized from an editorial which appeared in the Roumanian newspaper, "Adeverul", on Dec. 10, 1912. "Our Roumanian State is not organized in such a manner that it could assimilate civilized countries like Transylvania or Bucovina. Those Roumanians who live in those countries would not put up with our Roumanian administration for six months."

The Peace Treaty included carefully outlined instructions for the protection of the ethnic minorities. Nevertheless, these instructions were completely disregarded by Roumania, and there was no place for the Hungarians to present their grievances but the League of Nations, which lent a sympathetic ear, but was unable to enforce respect for the so-called "minority rights".

Immediately after the take-over, the Roumanian Government launched a large-scale attack against the Transylvanian Hungarians. On the administrative level, all Hungarian public officials were replaced with Roumanians, more than 90% of whom were not even Transylvanians, but were sent out from Roumania proper to colonize the new territory. Since the darkest days of the Habsburg oppression, there was no precedent in the thousand-year-old history of Transylvania for such colonial-type administration.

On the economic level, Hungarian business enterprises were cut off from supplies and forced out of business by every possible means, even police brutality. The land-reform, executed by the Roumanian Government, took 2,718,146 acres of land from the Hungarians (mostly small land-owners and handed this over to the Roumanian population and the Roumanian churches. The owners of these properties were recompensed with valueless government bonds.

This action, which was directed only against the Hungarians, was camouflaged as a reform aimed against big landowners. The truth was that even according to Roumanian statistics, of the 5,461,200 acres of agricultural land in Transylvania, only 1,904,635 acres were owned by farmers possessing more than 100 acres. About 487,000 of this belonged to Roumanian churches and was never touched by the land-reform. Therefore, almost half of the land confiscated from the Hungarians was taken from small farmers with less than 100 acres. (M. Constantinescu: "L'évolution de la reforme agraire en Roumanie." 1925, page 247)

Parallel with the economic persecution, the Roumanian Government undertook an allout offensive against the Hungarian schools. Public education was completely in the hands of the State, and the Hungarian language was abolished and its use forbidden in all the public schools. In many cases, children were cruelly beaten for using their language among themselves during the recess.

Parochial schools, Protestant and Catholic, some of them established in the 15th and 16th centuries, were closed down and expropriated one after the other under different pretexts. While in 1918 there were eight parochial type colleges in Transylvania, in 1927, there were none. From seventy parochial high schools there were only 51 left, and from 1,088 elementary schools, only 830 survived the first ten years of Roumanian oppression.

The American Committee for the Rights of Religious Minorities gave the following report of the situation: "The administrative oppression, the violent enforcing of the Roumanian language, the closing down of the schools, the many interferences, the aggressive hostility by which the school problems are being treated, all these are aimed for the total destruction of the minority school system. The laws of 1925 serve as oppressive political and nationalistic tools against the minorities." (The Religious Minorities in Transylvania, 1925, and Roumania, ten Years after, 1928" The Bacon Press, Inc. Boston).

While the 1911, under Hungary, there were 2,813 public schools in Transylvania in which the language of instruction was Roumanian, in 1926 there were no schools left at all for the use of the Hungarian language. In a region where the population was 100% Hungarian, the public school situation was vividly illustrated in a report of the newspaper, "Brassói Lapok", Dec. 14, 1925. "The new teacher, Mr. Clemens Tratiu, who was sent recently by the government to the village of

Csikjenőfalva, in his efforts to enforce the new language regulations of the Government handed out such beatings to his pupils, that on the first day the parents had to carry home twenty-four badly beaten children from the schoolhouse, who were unable to walk."

The violent Roumanization program found other ways, also, to change the statistical figures. The registrars, when registering the birth of a Hungarian child, translated the names into Roumanian. Later, these names were referred to as Roumanians. After 1930, in certain areas, where the Hungarian population was in an overwhelming majority, the parents' choice in first names was limited to those which were not specifically Hungarian and could be translated easily.

A group of medical doctors, under the leadership of Dr. Peter Ramusatu, took blood samples of 20,092 Hungarian children. Some of these children, having had their names changed at registration, were declared Roumanians, and because their blood types were similar to the others', the doctors drew the conclusion and the theory, that the Transylvanian Hungarians were in reality assimilated Roumanians. The report handed in by this group received the award of the Roumanian Academy.

By the beginning of the 1930s, the two main strongholds of the Transylvanian Hungarians had fallen: the schools and the wealth. The nation, which was used for centuries to lead and organize, was turned into an ethnic minority and forced to survive in a new, hostile, morally and mentally inferior political and administrative framework. There was no place where the greivances could have been taken, since the State itself was the transgressor, by exercising discrimination under the law.

In this desperate situation, the Transylvanian Hungarians were forced to search for strength and resources within their own selves in order to survive. As a reaction to the increasing pressure a new attitude, a new national pride and consciousness became more and more evident within the Hungarian community of Transylvania.

The foundation of this new attitude of self-reliance was the large mass of the Transylvanian peasantry. The Transylvanian Agricultural Society, created by the big landowners before the war, became now the organization of the small farmers. Through intense education, the standard of production of Hungarian farmlands in Roumania increased by 200% above the average production of the country. The Transylvanian Agricultural Society provided the small farmers with registered breeding stock and improved seeds, and organized a network of producers' and consumers' co-operatives, credit co-operatives and homecraft product co-operatives. With the help of these organizations, in spite of the pressures and the burden of unequal taxation, the Transylvanian Hungarian farmers began to develop and prosper.

In this tight-knit Hungarian community, any service to the culture became a patriotic deed. The Transylvanian press, suffering under heavy censorship, lost its provincial character and rose to a European level. The Transylvanian Literary Guild and the Transylvanian Helicon gathered the writers and established a Hungarian Publishing Co-operative. A new and specifically Transylvanian literature was born, different from any other literature, imbedded deep in the history of the land and the realities of life. Struggling with poverty and with the Roumanian authorities, the Transylvanian Hungarian stage reached an unprecedented peak against all odds. Many Hungarian actors started their careers of world fame on the creaky boards of that old building the Roumanian Government graciously allowed to be used by Hungarians.

Just as it was in the days of the independent Transylvanian Principality of the 16th and 17th centuries, the Transylvanian Hungarian culture, separated from the mother-country, unfolded into a unique phenomenon of regional and national individuality, and, reaching across the borders of Roumania, joined the West, from which it became separated artificially. The Western connections became re-vitalized and intensified under the pressure. The Transylvanian Unitarian Church clung more then ever to its connections with England, and the Transylvanian youth movements joined hands with the Protestant Youth organizations of the Western World.

In spite of the Peace Treaties, which handed Transylvania over as a colony of the East, the Transylvanian Hungarian soul proved again, as so many times in history, that its choice and destiny are unalterably with the West.

The Transylvanian Jews took a great part in carrying the burdens of the Transylvanian Hungarian culture. Not only through money, but by giving noted writers and artists who were willing to carry the double load of minority status of being Jews and Hungarians at the same time.

The Transylvanian Germans, on the other hand, failed to establish any cultural or economic relations with the Hungarians and thus promote the formation of a unified front of ethnic minorities. It was the policy of the Roumanian Government to prevent the formation of such a unified front by granting special privileges to the small German minority and keeping them alienated from the Hungarians. Also, after Hitler's influence began to be felt, the Roumanians tried every possible way to obtain good relations with Germany.

While the revisionist tendency of the German policy toward the Versailles Treaty aroused opposition in Roumania, the other aspect of that policy, namely the ideology of discrimination against the Jews and other nationalities was greeted with sympathy and understanding. Anti-Semitism had deep roots in Roumania. The so-called "emancipation law", which granted equal rights to the Jews, was pushed through the

187

Roumanian Parliament only in 1881, when the European nations at the Berlin Congress stipulated that the Roumanian Kingdom would receive recognition only on this condition. After 1920, the Goga-Cuza anti-Semitic League became a serious political factor. C.Z. Codreanu formed a terrorist group called the "Legion of Archangel Michael" which a few years later became the nucleus of the ill-famed political party called the "Iron Guard".

Surrounded by a national myth, the Iron Guard gained prestige rapidly in Roumania, and in 1937, the party had 66 members in the Parliament. While King Carol II dissolved the Iron Guard and Codreanu was killed, still the government was formed by the leader of the anti-Semitic Lige, Octavianu Goga, which marked the beginning of the Fascist dictatorship in Roumania. Not only the Jews, but all the other ethnic groups suffered under this terrorist regime, with the exception of the Germans.

A book could be written on the most cruel and barbaric methods used by the Roumanian Government against the Hungarians in Transylvania. However, it is not our purpose to dwell on the past, but to find a way for the future.

While it is useless to search for scapegoats in order to blame them for the many mistakes of the past, it is worthwhile for the sake of the future to ponder the reasons which led to those mistakes.

Before World War I, the nationalistic movement of the Transylvanian Roumanians demanded autonomy. Not an autonomy within a Federated Hungary, but an autonomy within a Federated Habsburg Empire. Understandably, the Hungarians clung to the integrity of the Hungarian homeland, for which they had fought long and hard against the Habsburgs. Nevertheless, it is an open question whether or not they made a mistake in refusing the demands of the Roumanians. Giving in to these demands would have meant the disintegration of the Constitutional Statehood of Hungary, and the unlimited extension of the Habsburg rule, against which the Hungarians had fought for centuries.

As Silviu Drogomir, Roumanian writer and politician, wisely observed, there was another problem involved, that many seem to forget today. "The nationality groups (meaning Roumania, Serb and Ruthenian) would not be able to furnish any political leadership which could match that of the Hungarians. Therefore, even if territorial autonomies would have been established for the ethnic groups, the leadership within these autonomies would have shifted sooner or later back to the Hungarians. Just as it happened previously under the district system, where the majority of voters were non-Hungarian, but reluctant to cast their votes for their own kin." ("Un proces istoric" Tara Noastra, Oct. 1928, page 1375.)

Considering these facts, we can be justified in assuming that another fifty years of peace and prosperity in the Danubian Basin could have solved these problems in the normal way of social and political evolution. One more generation would have provided the Transylvanian Roumanians with adequate leadership in order to assume their rightful place in the Transylvanian community of nations, without force or violence.

However, World War I (which was not started by Hungary, but by the Emperor of Austria), and a long line of misunderstandings and misinterpretations, put an end to the unity of the Danubian Basin, as well as to the peace and the constructive and harmonious co-existence of the different nationalities, who for centuries shared the responsibilities of this living unit and built together its historic individuality.

The catastrophe of the war created a chaos and this chaos was ruthlessly exploited by Balkan politicians of an entirely different moral fiber and set of values. A corrupt administration came across the Carpathians and exercised a most destructive influence of the Transylvanian community. This corruption, and the extreme chauvinism which was expressed by that administration, filled even the Transylvanian Roumanians with disgust. Their leaders frequently admitted publicly their regret for the loss of their former status under the protection of the Stephen's Crown, which was the symbol of order, Constitutional legality and honesty. "No one in Transylvania has gained anything by the annexation to Roumania. Everyone lost. It is much worse now, than ever before." (Stephen Pop-Csicso, Adeverul, 1928). Many outstanding Transylvanian Roumanians stood up boldly for the protection of the oppressed Hungarians, as did Ghita Pop, who wrote in the newspaper Adeverul on Nov. 16, 1928: "The rights of the minorities, as outlined in the resolutions, are based on many centuries old experience and thought, and are identical with our own demands under the former Hungarian rule. These rights must prevail openly and without any ulterior motives. They must be granted to the minorities, not as a compensation for their votes, but as their natural and inalienable rights."

Toward the end of the 1930s, the position of the Hungarian minority became increasingly intolerable. The government of Hungary, in an effort to render aid, insisted on the revision of the Peace Treaties. The deliberations between the two governments failed to accomplish anything. The Roumanians, already affiliated with the Axis powers, turned to them for arbitration.

The Axis Powers brought their decision on Aug. 30, 1940, dividing Transylvania between Roumania and Hungary. According to the Roumanian census, the Northern part, which returned to Hungary, had a population of 1,007,170 Hungarians; 1,166,434 Roumanians; 60,046 Germans; and 160,234 other nationalities (mostly Hungarian-speaking people with non-Hungarian sounding names), while in the Southern part still under Roumania, there were 473,551 Hungarians left; 2,067,723 Roumanians; 481,128 Germans; and 133,000 of other nationalities.

Neither Hungary nor Rumania was satisfied with the Vienna Arbitration. They both expected another settlement after the war. The many reasons for the mutual dissatisfaction prove again that the Transylvanian problem cannot be solved by the shifting of borders.

The new border, cutting lengthwise across the middle of the country, with complete disregard to geographical, economic and administrative endowments, caused severe complications on both sides. Even so, there was very soon a great difference between the progress of re-organization on the two sides of the new border, which must be seriously evaluated and considered for future decisions.

The Southern part, filled with the overflow of the Roumanian bureaucratic apparatus which had to evacuate the North, was paralyzed by confusion, and absolutely unable to establish a normal administrative, economic and social order. In the same time the Northern part was re-organized by the Hungarians in a matter of weeks. Roads, railroads and other communication lines cut by the border were replaced and new roads, even new railroads, built to fit the new situation. Towns and cities, where it took the Roumanian administration 22 years to force its nationalistic blue-print upon the exterior looks of the streets, changed back to their original Hungarian individuality within a few days. The inspired labor and the creative power of the Transylvanian Hungarians, free again to be expressed, improved the country to European standards.

A few isolated cases of local transgressions excluded, which were immediately punished by law, there were no reprisals of any kind against the Roumanian population, while at the same time, in the Southern part of the country, the Hungarian minority was harassed in a most brutal manner by the angered Roumanian administration. Ministers, Protestant and Catholic alike, were arrested and beaten. Any manifestations of the Hungarian minority group, whether agricultural, commercial, or cultural, were severely repressed. Beatings of Hungarians in public places, and even in their own homes, were not only encouraged by the police, but in many cases carried out by them.

Even Germany knew that the Transylvanian problem was only solved on a temporary basis and set the date of final arrangements after "the victorious ending of the war." The representatives of the German Government promised the entire territory of Transylvania one day to Hungary, the next day Roumania, using it as a whip to force these two countries into giving more contributions and assistance in the war against Russia.

In this difficult situation, Hungary and Roumania followed two different paths. The Hungarian Government, knowing well that open defiance would bring German occupation and the fate of Poland, tried to get involved as little as possible in the war. Even so, the reluctance of Hungary brought on the occupation of the country by German troops in March 19, 1944, followed by the deportation of the Jews into Germany. The energetic intervention of Governor Horthy before his arrest saved only the Jews of Budapest.

During this time, the Hungarian Government tried to establish secret diplomatic connections with the Allied Forces, in the hope that aid could arrive from the Balkan Front. However, the fate of South-Eastern Europe had already been decided in Yalta and Teheran, and the negotiations could not change anything.

Roumania, under the leadership of General Antonescu, from the very beginning stood unconditionally and with full strength on the side of the Germans. But when, in the fall of 1944, the advancing Red Army reached the historic "Focsáni Gate", where the Germans had decided to establish permanent defense, Roumania suddenly changed sides and opened the way for the Soviet Union into the Carpathian Basin.

IX

TRANSYLVANIA UNDER THE ROUMANIAN
PEOPLE'S REPUBLIC

In the fall of 1944, the Russian Army moved across Transylvania. They were followed by regular Roumanian troop units and Roumanian guerilla bands, which terrorized the Hungarian population by murdering men, women and children and carrying out medieval-style executions in the Hungarian villages.

The new leftist leaders of the Transylvanian Hungarians turned to the Russians for protection. The Roumanian troops were ordered back to the border outlined by the Vienna arbitration, and the barbaric bloodshed was stopped.

The Soviet Army introduced military administration in Northern Transylvania, which was succeeded in the spring of 1945 by a Roumanian administration. With this step, Stalin, gave Transylvania back to Roumania even before the peace negotiations began. On one hand, he compensated Roumania for the re-annexation of Bessarabia and Northern Bucovina, but on the other hand there were also political reasons behind his decision. It is the usual practice of Bolshevism to prepare the introduction of communism by seemingly serving certain national interests.

In giving military protection against the Roumanian transgressions, the Soviet Union put the leftist leaders of the Hungarian minority under obligation to them. Stalin gave back North Transylvania to the Roumanians under the condition that they would respect the rights of the ethnic groups. With this step, he introduced into Transyvlania the Stalinist National Policy. This policy consisted of the recognition of ethnic autonomies and is based on the federation of these autonomies. These autonomies are "nationalistic in form, socialistic in substance." Which means that the nationality groups are Bolshevized in their own language and with respect to their national customs, but under the strict supervision of the almighty Party. Thus the nationality groups are held in tight dependency on political, economic and ideological levels, Communism is nothing but State Capitalism, where the State uses its executive power to arbitrarily determine the labor relations between itself and the citizens.

The other Soviet precept prescribes the following formula: "First socialization, then self-government." This means that the nationality groups receive their autonomy only after the Central Party leadership decides that they are completely socialized, in other words, when they are loyal communists who will carry out orders without objection.

The history of communism is full of examples that show what happens to nationality groups who refuse to obey. They are either exterminated or deported. Socialism on ethnic territories was built by Russian Party Organizations and they succeeded so well in "Russianizing" these territories that the Party Congress of 1961 was able to boast in their report that the administrative and public language had finally become Russian in every part of the Soviet Union.

At the Peace Conference of 1946, the communist members of the Hungarian delegation, in the name of "Socialist Brotherhood" prevented the official presentation of the Hungarian plans concerning the status of Transylvania. Thus the conference could do nothing but confirm Stalin's decision and officially give Transylvania to the Roumanians.

While Hungary showed great resistance against the introduction of communism, and was turned by brute-force into a communist state only after 1948, Roumania became a "people's democracy" immediately, without hesitation. Only Transylvania resisted, led by the Bourgeois Party of Gyula Maniu, called the Roumanian National Party. In the 1945 elections, for the first time in history, the Transylvanian Hungarians cast their votes for a Roumanian party (the Maniu Party), instead of for their own, which was under the new communist leadership. But the party of Maniu was soon outlawed and Maniu himself ended his life in prison.

On the cultural level, the Roumanians fulfilled for a time the demands of Stalin. Hungarian education was authorized in the lower and higher levels. The Hungarian University of Kolozsvár (Cluj) was allowed to continue its functions, with an Hungarian Medical School in Marosvásárhely (Tragu Mures). On the surface it seemed that the nationality problem was successfully solved. Nevertheless, the schools and all cutural institutions, newspapers, publishing houses, theaters, etc., were under the immediate direction of the Party. The Hungarian cultural life became "nationalistic in form, socialistic in substance." Everything was subordinated to the indoctrination and de-nationalization of the Central Communist Party's plans.

The Roumanian People's Democracy progressed with great speed toward the socialization of the country. The purpose was served by the nationalization of private property, the establishment of the colchos system, the subordination of the trade unions to the Communist Party, the introduction of the one-party system, and the effective liquidation of the "bourgeois elements" by murder, imprisonment and deportation.

According to figures not completely evaluated as yet, about 200,000 Hungarians have been killed, imprisoned and deported so far on the pretext of being "war criminals" and later, "conspirators", or simply "unwanted elements". Urban Hungarians were evacuated with only one suitcase and their homes, together with all their belongings were give to Roumanian colonists, mostly refugees from Russian-occupied Bessarabia.

The Greek-Catholic Church was liquidated by law. The leaders of the Roman Catholic, Presbyterian, Lutheran and Unitarian Churches were imprisoned or sent to forced labour camps. Aron Marton, the Roman Catholic Bishop of Transylvania was kidnaped by the Communist State Police on the open highway while visiting one of the church districts. After several years in prison, he is now being kept under house arrest in his residence. While all these persecutions against the Hungarians in Transylvania went on, the Hungarian and Roumanian Governments assured each other with enthusiastic words of the "Socialist Brotherhood" and the "indivisible unity of the Socialist camp".

In 1952, a new step was made in the direction of the Stalinist policy toward ethnic minorities, which might have a great effect upon developments in an unforeseeable future. Under Soviet pressure, the Roumanian Government organized an "Autonomous Hungarian Province" in the Eastern part of Transylvania. While in a Western sense it was not real self-government, it did mean the end of a certain fiction labelled the "unified and indivisible nation State of Great Roumania." The population of the Autonomous Hungarian Province included, according to the 1956 Roumanian census, 731,361 people, of whom 79.38% were Hungarians and 20.62% Roumanians.

The 1956 Hungarian uprising, which caused a great loss of prestige to the Soviet Union and disrupted the unity of the communist world movement, had its direct effect on Transylvania. We know positively today, that not only the Eastern European nations, but the youth of the Soviet Union itself, were sympathetic toward the Hungarians in their fight for freedom and were greatly influenced by this spontaneous outburst. However, due to the procrastination of the West, the Soviet Union, after having pulled out its troops once from Hungary, was able to return and localize the outburst by crushing the uprising. Roumanian stood on the side of the Soviet Union in those feverish days and immediately used the Hungarian uprising as a pretext for large-scale terrorist activity against the Transylvanian Hungarians. Mass arrests, executions and deportations were carried out and the prisons and forced labour camps were over-crowded again with thousands of Hungarians. The Roumanian Government received a free hand from the Kremlin in regard to its policy of terror against the Transylvanian Hungarians. This was mainly because in the Carpatho-Ukraine, annexed by the Soviet Union after World War II, there was still a population of 200,000 "unreliable" Hungarians, whose intimidation was in the interest of the Kremlin.

The Soviet policy toward Hungary after 1956 can be defined in the following three points: 1. To make the Hungarians realize by every possible means, that the West had given Eastern Europe up completely, and that there could be no hope of aid against communism; 2. To establish an example by the most cruel retaliation which would teach, not only the Hungarians, but others, too, that there can be no revolt against the communist system; 3. To create through small concessions (which could be revoked at any time), an atmosphere which would take the wind out of the sails of future revolutions.

This policy of Nikita Khrushchev was successful. It stabilized again the communist rule over Eastern Europe and, at the same time, exhibited the signs of "liberalization" for the benefit of the West, which led to many false conclusions and softened anti-communist public feeling created by the aftermath of the Hungarian uprising.

Gheorghiu-Dej, first Secretary of the Roumanian Communist party, gave the following directives regarding policy toward the minorities after his return from Moscow on Feb. 19, 1959: "The basic principles of the Marxist-Leninist Party recognize the equal rights of the ethnic minorities which must be expressed in the unity of fraternity of all the workers of Roumania." With this statement, Gheorghiu-Dej launched the last chapter of his de-nationalization program against the Transylvanian Hungarians.

On that very day, a student meeting was called at the Hungarian University of Kolozsvár, where the speakers of the Party declared that "the highest interests of socialism demand that the ethnic minorities learn the Roumanian language and learn to appreciate the Roumanian culture of the homeland." Two weeks later, it was pointed out that "the maintenance of a bilingual university is in opposition to the interests of socialism, and national isolationism in culture and science, just like any other manifestation of nationalism, is a poisoned weapon in the hands of the enemies of the people." A few days later, the student unions accepted a resolution which pronounced the fusion of the Hungarian and Roumanian Universities.

After this, the outlined de-Hungarization policy of the Roumanian Government advanced with great speed. Today, in 1965, there are no more Hungarian schools left in Transylvania. The axe also fell upon the publishing houses, press, theatre and all the other cultural institutions. The use of the Hungarian language is not only forbidden in public offices but everywhere, as we can read in the report of Mr. George Bailey, published in the "Reporter", Nov. 19, 1964.

On December 24, 1960, the Roumanian Parliament passed a resolution in which two districts were removed from the Autonomous Hungarian Province and attached to a Roumanian-populated territorial district. The population of these two districts was 92% Hungarian. At the same time, another large area was added to the Autonomous Hungarian Province on the other side, with an 88% Roumanian population. The name was changed from "Autonomous Hungarian Province" to "Autonomous Hungarian-Mures Territory" and the population of this new administrative unit changed in the following way: the Hungarian population was reduced form 79.38% to 63.97% and the number of Roumanians increased from 20.62% to 36.03%.

When, on Sept. 13, 1963, Gheorghiu-Dej visited the Autonomous Territory, the newspaper "Elore" reported the names of those leading officials who were responsible for the well-being of the people of that territory. There was not one Hungarian name among them.

Reports received lately from Western newspapermen visiting Roumania agree that the present popularity of the communist government in Roumania is not based so much on its slightly anti-Russian attitude, but mostly on its oppressive and discriminative policy against the ethnic minorities. Recently this policy led to some tension in the relationship between Hungary and Roumania. The explosion of this tension, just as in the days of Hitler, is being prevented only by the Kremlin. Just like the Third Reich, the Soviet Union tries to keep Roumania in line, and force Hungary into a more eager co-operation by constant threats of drastic changes in the status of Transylvania.

CONCLUSION

When some catastrophe destroys long established geographical units and successfully proven concepts of human co-existence, chaos sets in. To overcome this chaos, one must study the causes which led to it. This book has tried to fulfill this task in the most objective manner.

There are two opposing political and philosophical views in connection with the problem of Transylvania. Hungary claims Transylvania on the basis of historic rights. This right does not derive merely from a thousand-year-long possession, but from the fact that Transylvania created its own historic individuality and fulfilled an important European mission within the framework of the Hungarian State-Concept.

In opposition to this point of view, Roumania claims the land on the basis of the simple mathematical fact that the majority of the population is Roumanian.

The differences between there two viewpoints are irreconcilable, and therefore the Transylvanian problem cannot be solved permanently by the dictatorial assertion of the one or the other. Either way, the loser will keep on claiming his rights to Transylvania.

In order to find a suitable solution, we must recognize two cardinal laws, as the evident conclusions drawn from history:

I.   There can be no lasting peace in South-Eastern Europe until the unity of the Danubian Basin is restored.

II. Transylvania is an individual part of this unit, with well-determined specific functions. Therefore, it must rejoin this geographical and cultural unit.

The problem itself, as demonstrated in this book, has two equally important elements. One is the problem of the nationalities. The other is the problem of the political and administrative statehood.

The problem of the minorities can only be solved in an all-European context. The complexity of the problem is demonstrated by the fact that an international formula has not yet been found for its solution. Professor Ermacora sums up the activities of the United Nations on this subject with the following words: "The attempts to include directives and regulations concerning the protection of ethnic minorities into the Declaration of Human Rights failed. However, it was possible to include some such regulations into a draft dealing with civil and political rights. The United Nations prepared a whole series of studies and text-collections on this question. Finally, the General Assembly effectuated some concrete measures in the protection of some ethnic minorities." (Felix Ermacora: "Der Minderheitenschutz vor der Vereinigten Nationen," Europa Ethnica, 1961, No. 3.)

Neither the Charter of the United Nations, nor the 1948 Declaration of Human Rights contains clear provisions for the protection of ethnic minorities, but treats them in the spirit, and within the framework of the general and individual human rights. On the other hand, history has proved that the value of those obligations which are included into peace treaties or mutual agreements, depends always and everywhere upon the good will of the majority nation.

It is clear therefore, that all those problems which were allegedly the reasons for the fall of the Austro-Hungarian Monarchy, are not only still unsolved, but have increased to such proportions that it became necessary to bring international penal sanctions against government-organized genocide. (Prof. Ermacora: "Der Minderheitenschutz ...")

To solve this problem, the evolution of international law and, at the same time, the evolution of public opinion must reach the point where the ruling nation does not see any more "foreign elements" in the minorities, and on the other hand, the ethnic groups take full responsibility for the well-being of the country and do not isolate themselves as minorities. Today, the integrationist movements of Europe seem to point in this direction. History shows that where ethnic minorities were treated without discrimination, a slow and steady assimilation has taken place. Persecution draws resistance and increases national feelings. However, the thought of assimilation should not even enter the question. It should be recognized as man's inalienable right to speak the language he wishes to speak, to worship God in the manner he wishes to worship, and to belong to any cultural circle to which he whishes to belong, in his pursuit of happiness.

Insofar as the administrative and territorial part of this problem is concerned, that is, to which country Transylvania should belong, we have seen that the different arbitrary decisions made in our century have been unable to create a situation acceptable and reassuring to both sides. In this question, as in the question of the minority problem, an intermediary solution must be found. Today, under the given conditions, this cannot be done successfully in any other way than through national autonomies given to all three existing nations, the Hungarian, the Roumanian, and the German. Finally, to avoid any further territorial discussions, through the union of these three autonomous nations, the plan of a federated autonomous Transylvania must be worked out with extreme care.

In spite of the fact that up to 1918, this was the main demand of the Roumanians, today this solution would certainly be met by them with sharp opposition. At the same time, it would also raise protest from those Hungarians whose viewpoint is imbedded in historical principles, and therefore does not recognize the fact that today, Transylvania belongs to Roumania.

However, until the time arrives through the aforementioned

evolution of Europe itself, when national and territorial questions will be of only secondary importance, this is the only safe way to attain justice and liberty for all three Transylvanian nations. Such as arrangement would open the door again for Transylvania to continue to fulfill its European mission, outlined for it by the unchangeable laws of history. Namely, to again become the Citadel of the West, and the Bridge toward the East, culturally and politically, instead of being an exploited province and the powder-keg of South-Eastern Europe.

When making long-range historic decisions which will affect the lives of millions, one must carefully consider all the details involved. There can be no question of the fact that Transylvania is an independent living unit in itself, with a long-time historical individuality, which individuality has no counterpart on the globe. It is also clear that culturally, mentally and spiritually, Transylvania belongs to the West, while politically and geographically to the Carpathian Basin, which unit is again the Central and most important part of the larger unit, called the Danubian Basin.

Therefore, the Transylvanian problem is in itself, par excellence, a problem of survival to the Carpathian Basin, an acute problem to the Danubian Basin, and also the problem of the Western culture community. By no means can it be regarded as a Balkan problem or the problem of any other unit East of the Carpathians.

The final solution for Transylvania must be, in a long-range historic program, to find its way back where it belongs, where it has its roots in the past and its traditional mission for the future, that is, into the cultural, historical and geographical unit of the Danubian Basin.

Those who still stubbornly cling to the so-called "realistic policy" built on accomplished fact, should bear in mind that facts do change as time moves on. Only principles stand and the unchangeable laws of life which have molded those principles. It is much wiser to be guided in an ever-changing world by these laws and principles, than by temporary "facts" created by the hazardous whims of political intrigues. This is the only way we can hope for a better future, with "Liberty and justice for all", including the people of Transylvania, no matter what language they may speak.

BIBLIOGRAPHY

Hungarian:

M. Ferdinándy: Hungary History, Kossuth, Buenos Aires, 1957.
Homan-Szekfü: Hungarian History, Budapest, 1938.
Torjai-Szábo: Centuries of Transylvania, Munich, 1956.
Goldis: About the nationality problem, Arad, 1912.
Kovach: Hungarian History, Munich, 1951.
Mester: Autonom Transylvania, Budapest, 1937.
Siculus: Hungarians in Moldova, Univ. of Pécs, 1942.
Galdi-Makkai: History of Transylvania, Budapest, 1934.
Papp: Complaints of the Székelys in Csik, M. Szemle, 1928.
Zathureczky: Hungarian minorities in Roumania, M. Szemle, 1934.
Barabas: Hungarian Schools under Roumanian Rule, M. Szemle, 1928.
Endre Jonas: Trianon a European Problem, Munich, 1960.

Roumanian:
Sincai: Chronica Romanilor.
Onisifor Ghibu: Viata si Organisatia Bisericeasca si Scolara in Transylvania si Ungaria, Bucharest, 1915.
Activitatea Ministerul Instructiunii, 1922-26, Bucharest.
Breviar Statsitic al Republica Populara Romana, 1964.

International:
Oberschall: Die Sankt Stephans Krone, Herold, Wien, 1961.
E. Franzel: Der Donauraum, Francke Verlag, Bern, 1958.
Annuaire de la Societé des Nations, Geneva, Volume I.
Transylvania under the rule of Roumania, Bacon Press, Boston, 1920.
Religious Minorities in Transylvania, Bacon Press, Boston, 1925.
Roumania ten years after, Bacon Press, Boston, 1928.
Sidney Herbert: Nationalities and Problems.
C.A. Macartney: October Fifteenth, Univ. of Edinburgh, 1956.

A. Francé-Harrar: Die letzte Chance für eine Zukunft, Bayerische Landwirtschaftsverlag, Münich, 1950.
Raul H. Francé: Lebenslehre für Jedermann, Telos, Berlin, 1962.
Salvador de Madariaga: Portrait of Europe, 1952.
The Honorable Clayborne Pell, senator of Rhode Island: Senate speech, May 11, 1964.
Robert M. MacKisson, State Dept. Head of European Section: Letter to the American Transylvanian Federation, June 4, 1963.
Edward Crankshaw: THE OBSERVER, Aug. 4, 1963.
Federalist Union of European Nationalities (FUEN): Memorandum to the Roumanian prime minister J.G. Maurer, Nov. 2, 1964. Ref. No. 1-11-14-64.
George Bailey: THE REPORTER, Nov. 19, 1964.
Felix Ermacora: Der Minderheitenschutz vor den Vereinigten Nationen, Europa Ethnica, 1961, No. 3.
The Review of Reviews: 1927, No. 455. Page 494.
Fortnightly Review: November 1928.

TRANSYLVANIA:

THE HUNGARIAN MINORITY

IN RUMANIA

JULIA NÁNAY is a descendant of Transylvanian ancestors. She came to the United States subsequent to the Hungarian uprising of 1956. Miss Nánay graduated Magna Cum Laude, Phi Beta Kappa from UCLA in 1973 with a degree in political science. She has received two Master's degrees from the Fletcher School of Law and Diplomacy (Tufts University) in international economics and energy studies, 1974 and 1975 respectively and is currently working for Northeast Petroleum Industries in Boston, Massachusetts.

FOREWORD

In the course of my graduate studies at The Fletcher School of Law and Diplomacy, I became interested in the question of minorities. Having been born in Budapest, Hungary of parents who are of Transylvanian extraction, I was raised with an awareness of the problems encountered by a number of groups on the periphery of what is present day Hungary. I quickly came to realize that concern for these groups was more than just a passive exercise in futility. It was a very real part of the Hungarian consciousness. The attempt by surrounding states to assimilate these minorities, who until the end of World War I were incorporated for 1000 years in the Hungarian Kingdom, forming the majority, has served to fire already burning sentiments of nationalism.

The concept of minorities in the United States is a very complex matter politically, historically, traditionally, economically, legally, as well as emotionally. Many nations live together in the U.S.; nations whose race, language, history, traditions and religions differ. The U.S. is alone in the world in basing its population growth on multinational immigration. Therefore, its minority problems cannot be compared with those of any other area.

I have tried to present the minority question, in Transylvania as a mirror in which you can see and measure the use and abuse of plain politics in dealing with groups who were not immigrants to the land that serves as their home but were, in fact, the first settlers and original inhabitants of this land.

This study may be considered a small and modest portion of a much larger picture depicting how politicians handle the minority problem in Europe, particularly in Eastern Europe. I am very thankful to my professor, Uri Ra'anan, for his early comments and to Dr. Albert Wass and Dr. Paul Csonka without whose help and encouragement this work could not have been completed.

TABLE OF CONTENTS

situation in Transylvania.

Gheorghiu-Dej, Stoica and Kádár meet. Sentencing Hungarians in Transylvania after the Hungarian Revolution. Cultural, economic, educational sanctions after the revolution. The merger of the Hungarian language Bolyai University with the Rumanian Babes University.

Cultural socialization. Districts redrawn and population exchange further reinforced.

Nationality does not aim either
at liberty or prosperity, both of
which it sacrifices to the im-
perative necessity of making the
nation the mould and measure of
the State. Its course will be
marked by material as well as
moral ruin, in order that a new
invention may prevail over the
works of God and the interests
of mankind.

—Lord Acton

I.

THE BIRTH OF THE NATIONAL MINORITY QUESTION
IN TRANSYLVANIA

History can boast of few injustices as glaring as the decisions made
at Trianon. While the treaty makers of 1919 assigned one-fifth of the
population of East Central Europe to nations to which these people did not
want to belong, the measures forced upon Hungary without plebiscite,
were perhaps the harshest of all. On the principle of the people's
"pretended" right to self-determination, the thousand year old Hungarian
Kingdom was shorn of nearly three-quarters of its area and two-thirds of
its inhabitants.[1] With the dismemberment at Trianon, territories and
peoples formerly Hungarian were distributed among seven different
states: Austria, Czechoslovakia, Poland, Rumania, Yugoslavia, and Italy,
with Hungary left holding a very small remainder. While to the south, the
Serbians took Croatia and Slavonia as well as a portion of the Bánát
(Banat) to form with other territories the new state of Yugoslavia.
Rumania received the rest of the Bánát with the city of Temesvár
(Timisoara), as well as part of the Hungarian Plain and the much disputed
territory of Erdély (Transylvania Proper).[2] In effect, Rumania acquired an
area greater than that left to the sadly truncated Hungarian nation. Con-
sequently, 1,704,851 Magyars became subjects of the Kingdom of Greater
Rumania.

What occurred at Trianon in June 1920 was only one of many
fruitless efforts to resolve an issue which goes far beyond the question of
a mere border dispute. Regarding the world in terms of "spheres of influence," the victorious powers committed a grave historical blunder.
They ignored the ethnic map of the Danubian Basin and with a series of
dictatorial measures, passed off the problems of smaller nations as unimportant.[3] In short, the Paris Peace Conference did not light the liberty

torch for East Central Europe. It set flame to an already burning Hungarian national consciousness, which considered the Treaty of Trianon a humiliating form of degradation and refused for one moment to accept its "terms of shame". The slogan itself became one of "Tria-Non," "No, No, Never!" and the question of minorities and frontiers became a national obsession.[4]

The obsession had its roots in considerations that long preceded Trianon. Nationalism was a deeply embedded phenomenon in Eastern Europe, one that had acquired increasing significance before the victors met to pass out judgment. It was by no means a sudden wave of national passion that gripped the region in the interwar years but a protracted form of group allegiance. Before considering the aftermath of the peace settlement, it would be wise to examine Rumanian and Hungarian claims to Transylvania for a geographical and historical perspective. Not only will this prove helpful in furthering our understanding of the complexity of the national minority problem, but it will serve to clarify existing antagonisms in the area. Transylvania, after all, is one of the "problem children" of Eastern European nationalism.[5]

Transylvania's strategic importance derives from a multi-faceted appeal. Geographically, the region is an integral part of Central Europe; politically, it functions within Eastern Europe; culturally, it is very much attached to Western Europe; historically, it is an amalgamation of all three of these factors. Poised on the far eastern edge of Europe, her position was unparalleled in the defense of Western civilization from the Byzantine threat. Open towards the west, the southwest and the south, the province is enclosed from the northeast, southeast and the south by the Carpathian Mountains and the Transylvanian Alps. These mountains present a barrier some six hundred miles long, reaching altitudes of over 7,000 feet. There are few passes through the range and no wide roads leading into Rumania proper.[6] Consequently, the geographic division of Transylvania from the Regat (Rumania Proper) is almost complete, posing not only major problems of communication but also helping to preserve the area's Hungarian character. For while Transylvania is practically cut off from her administrative organ on the southeast, she is geographically linked to her neighbor on the northwest. This vital link with Hungary extends beyond mere natural unity. It provides a sort of spiritual force which keeps the flame of Magyar nationalism burning and in a sense, sharpens the xenophobic factor in Transylvanian-Rumanian relations.[7]

From the time of its formation in 896 A.D., down through the Middle Ages and modern history until 1918, Transylvania did in fact constitute an individual natural, political, and economic unit with the Hungarian Kingdom.[8] This historical antecedent is precisely the grounds for Hungary's claim to Transylvania. Rumania's argument is one of Daco-

Roman continuity which asserts pre-Magyar ties to the area.[9.]

It is interesting to note that prior to the end of the thirteenth century, three "ruling nations" existed side by side in Transylvania: the Magyars, the Saxons, and the Skékelys.[10.] The exclusion of the Wallachians (the name used in the middle ages for the Rumanians) from this triumvirate indicates that they were not yet a decisive factor in Transylvania. Their further exlusion from the "Union of Three Nations" in the fifteenth century and from the Constitution of 1542 eventually roused their resentment against the Magyars.[11.] In view of the fact, however, that the victims of the anti-Habsburg and anti-Turkish struggles were predominantly Magyars and Székelys, by the close of the eighteenth century the Wallachians formed the real majority in Transylvania proper. The recent Rumanian allegations, that they were in Transylvania prior to the Hungarians, can't be proved by any reliable historical document. The fact remains, however, that before the eighteenth century, they neither acquired the numbers nor the status which could give them equal recognition. The changing world order ushered in with the 1700's began the era of Rumanian national consciousness.

Having set the scenario for this unabated conflict, suffice it to say that the eighteenth century only sharpened existing frictions. After the turbulent years which followed Turkish and Habsburg domination in Hungary, the twentieth century did not bring with it any measure of relief. World War I brought added strife, and the order it endorsed saw a renewal of chaos.

Basing their title to Transylvania on Daco-Roman continuity, the Rumanians laid their cards before the victorious Powers at Trianon. Clemenceau drew first, and the others followed. A strong Little Entente on Germany's eastern flank was highly desirable from Clemenceau's perspective. Rumanian claims were sealed with approval and another boundary casually disrupted. Hungarian nationalism thereafter directed all its spiritual energies towards resurrecting the pre-War greatness of the Hungarian Kingdom. This strong revisionist tendency in the Hungarian political outlook was reflected in domestic and foreign policy, blurring any efforts to normalize relations with the successor states. The Treaty of Trianon reinforced the uncompromisingly conservative character of the Magyar nation, laying the groundwork for its semi-authoritarian future.[12.]

Hugh Seton-Watson diagnosed the Transylvanian situation as follows:

> Transylvania ... cannot be considered as a Rumanian province with a Hungarian minority or as a Hungarian province with a Rumanian minority. It is the home of both Rumanians and Hungarians, both of whom have lived there far longer than any historical records that can be considered reliable. Until the two nations can live together in

peace and friendship, it is inconceivable that the country can have any prosperity or security.

Prosperity undoubtedly envisioned an independent Transylvania or at least one which was loosely linked to both Hungary and Rumania for security purposes. While the simultaneous federalization of Transylvania with Rumania and Hungary was unlikely after World War I, prospects for a Kossuth type of Danubian Federation were also discarded.[13.]

Equality, unfortunately, is never desirable to those who hold positions of power. It was certainly unattractive to the Rumanians who savored the opportunity of dealing out repressive measures against their Transylvanian minorities.[14.] In the aftermath of Trianon, the campaign to subdue minority strength involved an extensive drive for "Rumanianization" more intense than any ever undertaken by Hungary.[15.] Countless measures were devised to dissociate the tightly knit Hungarian community.[16.] The Rumanians implemented a complete social revolution along national lines, displacing the Hungarian, German, and Jewish bourgeoisie. For while in Transylvania Proper Rumanians formed the majority of agricultural proletariat (shepherds, small peasants) prior to World War I, with the acquisition of this rich territory, they intended to carry out a campaign of forced cooptation at the expense of the groups which previously constituted the elite.[17.] The alienation of Hungarians, Jews and, although to a lesser degree, Germans from the new system forced these groups to unite in the face of possible annihilation.[18.]

Rumanian land reform expropriated 2,718,146 acres of land belonging to Hungarians.[19.] Primarily the holdings of small landowners, the properties were handed over to the Rumanian churches and people. The Orthodox Church was the principal beneficiary of these measures. Reform deprived the Lutheran, Protestant, and Catholic Churches of much of their lands. These losses constituted the greater part of their wealth.[20.]

Parochial education was also dealt a heavy blow. In light of the general impoverishment of the churches under land reform and oppressive taxation, denominational education was left to witness its own demise.[21.] Schools where Magyar was retained as the language of instruction were faced with considerable hardships. According to available data in 1931, the ratio of students to Rumanian language institutions of elementary school age was ninety-three per school wereas lack of adequate facilities to accommodate Hungarian children brought that ratio to three hundred sixty-five per school. The elementary school population ratio was one institution to 766 Rumanians and one institution to 1,187 Hungarians.[32.] Many children were thus forced to seek an education in institutions using the Rumanian language. In a survey of forty-nine towns in Transylvania where the proportion of Hungarians was 63% and where there were 68,000 children of school age in the year 1932-33, only 16,000 children or 24% were able to attend the Hungarian denominational schools. The state had limited enrollment to that figure.[23.] Oftentimes, moreover, the state refused to recognize minority schools as public institutions. Certificates issued by these schools were considered inferior to the ones issued by state-run Rumanian schools.

The inequities inherent in the "Rumanianization" of the educational process spilled over into other areas as well. By various methods of juggling data, conducting population exchanges among cities, gerrymandering district lines for political representation, Rumania was able to insure the existence of an indigenous urban majority in once predominantly Hungarian districts. The following statistics released in 1930 indicate the population shifts resulting from forced "Rumanianization":[24.]

Nationality	1910		1930	
Total	776,262	100.0%	963,418	100.0%
Rumanian	151,800	19.6%	338,000	35.3%
Hungarian	480,000	62.0%	368,000	38.4%
German	123,000	15.9%	127,000	13.3%
Others	19,000	2.5%	123,000	13.0%

Since government in Eastern Europe is the chief employer of labor and the main source of income for the citizens, the exclusion of minorities from its ranks can be a cruel form of injustice with devastating effects. Many Magyar speaking employees were barred from their jobs to make room for the Rumanian population. Language examinations were imposed on those remaining so as to find an excuse for their elimination as well. Statistical data for 1933 estimates the following breakdown in government employment:[25.]

Type of Employment	Total	Rumanian		Hungarian		Others	
County Administration	1,109	789	71.2%	209	18.8%	111	10.0%
District Administration	839	513	61.2%	142	16.9%	184	21.9%
District Notary	1,602	949	59.2%	344	21.5%	309	19.3%
Municipal Administration	1,532	901	58.8%	357	23.3%	274	17.9%
Municipal Notary	139	119	85.6%	11	7.9%	9	6.5%
State Supreme Court Judges	78	73	93.6%	4	5.1%	1	1.3%
Employees of State Court	153	130	84.9%	20	13.1%	3	2.0%
Superior and Municipal Judges	691	576	83.3%	65	9.4%	50	7.3%

Superior and							
Municipal Employees	2,926	2,193	74.9%	529	18.1%	204	7.0%
Superior Court							
Attorneys	62	59	95.2%	1	1.6%	2	3.2%
Attorneys' Assistants	78	62	79.5%	14	17.9%	2	2.6%
District Court							
Attorneys	13	13	100.0%	—	—	—	—
Attorneys'							
Employees	15	12	80.0%	3	20.0%	—	—
Total	9,237	6,389	69.2%	1,699	18.4%	1,149	12.4%

While Rumanians were given as the largest numerical element of the population, they were also the most backward. All the cities awarded to Rumania were founded by Hungarians or Germans. The cultural, ethnic and civic life of the region is, therefore exclusively a product of their energies. Turkish vassalage had left its toll on Rumanian civilization. Their approach to the treatment of minorities reflects the bitterness of former servility.[26.] Underlying the Rumanian population shifts in the interwar period was a desire to accelerate development. The strong Rumanian presence in county, district and municipal jobs in 1933 is indicative of a conscious effort to suppress the Hungarian minority.

Intelligently construed, the national idea should never lead to oppression. In Rumania, where the boundaries of the national government could not be made to coincide with those of each nationality, where diversity was abundant and homogeneity almost non-existent, where the will of the majority constantly felt threatened by that of the minority, the national idea led to divisiveness, persecution and resentment.

Hungary was unable to reconcile herself to the loss of her Transylvanian territories. Still nursing her wounds when World War II approached, she was being drawn closer to the folds of Magyar revisionism while attempting to resist fascism. Invariably, however, fascist Italy and Nazi Germany loomed in the foreground as the bastions of salvation against the Bolshevik threat and further Little Entente intrusion.

1940 was a decisive year for both Hungary and Rumania. In June, Rumania was forced to cede Bessarabia and northern Bukovina to the Soviet Union. In August, Bulgaria received southern Dobrudja. Hungary too began pressing her claims for Transylvania. Perturbed by the frontier disputes and the revisionist tendencies of Eastern Europe, at the request of the legal Rumanian government, Germany and Italy decided to resolve the issue of Transylvania by partition. The so-called Second Vienna Award gave northern Transylvania to Hungary and left the southern portion to Rumania. Rumanian census figures reported that the population of

214

Soviet Union

Körösvidék
Crişana

Máramoros
Maramureş

Hungary

Erdély
Transylvania Proper

Bánát
Banat

Yugoslavia

Rumania Proper

Bulgaria

The 1940 Vienna Award returned northern Transylvania to Hungary while leaving the southern portion for Rumania.

the area reannexed to Hungary was composed of 1,007,170 Hungarians; 1,166,434 Rumanians; 60,046 Germans; and 160,234 Others (mostly Hungarian speaking with non-Hungarian names). The portion still attached to the Regat had 473,551 Hungarians; 2,067,723 Rumanians; 481,128 Germans; and 133,000 Others.[27.]

This irresponsible carving up of territory generated disastrous consequences for both Rumania and Hungary. The partition created havoc where it should have restored order, exaggerated anomalies where it should have mitigated tensions. The boundaries imposed on Transylvania by the Axis dictators cut the region in half, inviting economic chaos and a renewal of ethnic strife. The line was drawn with complete disregard to geographical, administrative, and ethnic factors. There was a frantic scurry to transfer goods and people from one area to the other. The Rumanian Government immediately ordered all movable goods from the North to be brought to the South and introduced repressive measures against Magyars remaining in their territory.[28.]

While the complications arising from this division were immense for the two parties involved, the problem was momentarily resloved for the Germans. Transylvania was their whip to force their allies into submission, one day promising the prize to Hungary and the next, offering it to Rumania.

Thus, as World War II took its course, Germany was bolstered by two allies who were hopelessly opposed to each other, not particularly united behind Hitler, but commonly hostile toward the Soviet Union. Combating its primary enemy, Judea-communism, Rumanian nationalism envisaged a Greater Rumania for Rumanians. Encouraged by the reincorporation of northern Transylvania, Hungarian nationalism sought to recapture Hungary's former eminence. Although both were goaded on by the German Führer's promises, Hungary still cringed from involvement in the war. Not even visions of a greater Hungarian Kingdom could muster all-out support for the German effort. But what future hopes could not accomplish, circumstance was able to resolve. When Hitler's soldiers marched across the Hungarian frontier, all thoughts of recourse to neutrality were momentarily lost behind the gloomy shades of war. The extraordinary sequence of events in 1941 left Hungary no alternative but to cooperate. The Axis bonds were solidified with the Hungarian nation participating as an unwilling German satellite.

Rumania, on the other hand, supported Germany from the start. However, as the fighting progressed, her position became somewhat more ambiguous. German losses at Stalingrad in 1942 made Bucharest reconsider the alliance that had been formed. Hitler's defeat could be a serious blow to her expansionary aspirations. When, therefore, the Red Army reached the mouth of the Danube River, deep within the frontiers of

Rumania, panic and demoralization took hold of the populace. On August 23, 1944 Rumania suddenly switched camps and thrust the Soviet troops into the Carpathian Basin.

Triumphant in the Soviet victory, Rumania anticipated her share of the spoils, casting a hopeful glance toward Transylvania. In order to placate Bucharest for Soviet annexation of Bessarabia and northern Bukovina, Stalin annulled the 1940 Vienna Award. It was thus that northern Transylvania was reannexed to Rumania. Ec mem igosz, mert Románia nem kapta visna se olél Dobrudzsát, se Baszarábiat se Eczakbukovinát, amelyck 1938 bou veszei voltok.

When the issue of Transylvania actually came up for discussion at the Peace Conference in May of 1946, the United States favoured Hungarian retention of a northwestern strip of Transylvania including Nagyvárad (Oradea) and Szatmárnémeti (Satu-Mare). The Hungarian aide mémoire asked that Hungary receive a region which included those towns as well as the towns of Nagykároly, (Carei Mare) Nagybónya (Baia Mare) and Arad, but no participant ever bothered to read this mémoire. When the American Secretary of State, James F. Byrnes, advanced the proposition that in his de facto annexation of Transylvania Mr. Stalin should perhaps consider Hungarian demands, Mr. Molotov replied that the entire province had to be awarded to Rumania because "Mr. Stalin had so decreed."[29] The U.S. ultimately was not opposed to Mr. Stalin's decree. Foreign Minister Georges Bidault of France was absent. Those present conceded to Mr. Stalin's decree and the area was ceded.

The New York Times, in an article by C.L. Sulzberger, referred to the award as the "greatest political plum of any Rumanian Government" since the Treaty of Trianon.[30] One year and two months later, Mr. Sulzberger wrote: "While admittedly Transylvania is one of those areas whose perfect future is impossible to find, the manner in which its disposition was settled was just another indication that at times this peace is being made on strictly power politics lines."[31] For Hungary, the Peace Treaty of February 10, 1947 seemed to be nothing more than a reflection of Trianon, and the anxieties of the interwar period were transformed into silent bitter resentment.

II.

THE SOVIET APPROACH TO MINORITY PROBLEMS

Postwar Eastern Europe stepped into a new phase of development in which the model was not only provided by the Soviet Union but rigidly enforced by it as well. A revolutionary process was underway to remold societal, political, and economic conditions with special attention to the prescribed Soviet image. Socialist transformation demanded a complete reappraisal of the Western value system and a renunciation of traditional patterns of behaviour. It required a reassessment of what constitutes a Marxist outlook on nationalism.

Underlying the tangled catalog of Eastern European grievances was a network of intra-bloc hostilities. The Transylvanian question was far from reaching any substantive conclusion, and the fate of the Hungarian minorities was yet to be determined. Delineating Eastern Europe as a Soviet "sphere of influence" certainly left unresolved the issues plaguing national minorities. Their position after the war was even more precarious in terms of loyalties than it had been prior to Russian subjugation.

Transylvania was confronted with a curious web of allegiances. There was, of course, the omnipresent Communist party with its leading body, the Soviet Union. There was also Rumania and the party branch it would foster. Finally, there were the innate attachments to the fatherland of its various sundry nationalities. The most perplexing task of all was integrating these allegiances into a Marxian framework of proletarian internationalism.

In the process of achieving homogeneity, Marxism had to contend with a variety of contradictory themes: unity and diversity; tradition and modernity; continuity and change; consensus and conflict; political socialization and social fragmentation. It was constantly trying to reconcile differences between goals and achievements, theory and practice, ideals and realities. With the acquisition of Eastern Europe, the most serious confrontation of all occurred. Since Marx had failed to provide any working methodology for the treatment of minorities, the Soviets were hard pressed to reconcile Western nationalism with Communist internationalism. Because their approach to the Transylvanian question was dictated by a Marxist interpretation of the nationalistic syndrome, let us examine the context in which they viewed the problem.

Carlton Hayes defines "nationality" as a "group of people who speak either the same language or closely related dialects, who cherish a common historical tradition, and who constitute a distinct cultural society in which, among other factors, religion and politics have played important

218

though not necessarily continuous roles."[32] The combination of these factors conditions the individual's loyalties. Allegiance to one's nation-state is placed above all other loyalties in this scheme, presuming of course that this is the nation-state arising out of a "corporate will." A belief in the messianic role of this entity is central to the individual's thinking. Patriotism is associated with a love of the fatherland and the sacredness of the Patrie. Since patriotism and nationality both evoke a high degree of sentimentalism, it is only natural that they should be fused in a common frame of reference designated by nationalism.[33]

We have to approach Marxism with this theoretical construct in mind. In his treatment of the national question, V. I. Lenin observed, "Marxism cannot be reconciled with nationalism, be it even of the most just, purest, most refined and civilized brand. In place of all forms of nationalism, Marxism advances internationalism, the amalgamation of all nations in the higher unity..."[34] Nationalism, for Lenin, was strictly associated with capitalism and imperialism. Theoretically, the unity of the proletariat transgressed national boundaries and rejected any selfish love of the fatherland. But, in practice, the Soviet Union became the supreme and sacred fatherland where the leadership was to be buttressed by the complete and total allegiance of the masses.

The attitude of the Bolshevik leaders toward nationalism was in line with the traditional Marxist interpretation which cast shades of economics over every reformable facet of society. They recognized immediately that the people's right to self-determination could be exercised progressively or retrogressively, depending on the guidance provided by the Soviet Union. The more backward a people were in their economic developement, the more they would be reliant on the Soviet Socialist Republic. Nationalism was highly progressive as a movement in the colonial and semi-colonial world where the nation was still attempting to ward off the binding chains of capitalism. But once nationalism entered the stage of capitalism, its dependence on the Soviet Union was greatly weakened and in presenting obstacles to socialist transformation, it became retrogressive and undesirable.[35] If it was to survive in Eastern Europe, Communist internationalism obviously required the suppression of nationalism. Only its suppression could resolve the contradiction between consensus and conflict, theory and practice. Despite the grim facade of harmony and socialist cooperation which prevails today, the nationality problem continues to gnaw at the sides of the satellite regimes.

The Transylvanian situation after World War II was characterized by conflict and disunity. Conflict was a key factor owing to the geographical and historical conditions we have described earlier. Disunity was a direct consequence of a meshing of allegiances. Transylvania's integration into an internationalist Marxist framework was theoretically feasible, but the abolition of centuries of national conflict by indoctrination was practically impossible.

Stalin advanced cautiously at first, making friendly overtures in all directions. He was shrewd enough to realize that a rigid and dogmatic approach to ethnic problems would invariably result in mass alienation. Identification demanded a gradual reconciliation of existing contradictions, a slow process of synthesizing ideals and realities. He, therefore, introduced the Stalinist National Policy which recognized ethnic autonomies in Transylvania and urged their federated coalescence. The slogan now being "A Greater Socialist Rumania," these autonomies were to be "nationalistic in form, socialistic in substance."[36.] This substance was derived from directives issued in Moscow and implemented through Bucharest.

In December 1948, the Politburo of the Central Committee of the Rumanian Workers' Party advanced a resolution of the national question.[37.] It repeated Stalinist adherence to "equality in diversity among nationalities liberated from the class yoke." The resolution also referred to Stalin's speech of April 6, 1948 at the signing of the Soviet-Finnish treaty of friendship in which he spoke of equal sovereignties. Finally, it commended the Rumanian Workers' Party on its efforts to halt the persecution of minorities and promote friendly ties between Rumanians and other nationalities living in the new Rumania. Hinting at the spread of anti-Sovietism, the document acknowledged the need for its suppression.[38.]

Rumanianization thus gave way to Bolshevization. The various aspects of the "nationality" argument were utilized so as to effectively Bolshevize the diverse cultural units in Transylvania. Language, skillfully manipulated, became a vehicle for the dissemination of propaganda. The party created a rapport with the population by communicating with each group in its own language. Party supervision insured the tightening of dependency on the Soviet Union politically, economically, and culturally. Strict surveillance of the communications media also insured ideological dependency.

The Soviet Union recognized the importance of ideology in maintaining cohesion and as a means of legitimizing political power. In light of the Leninist conviction that human consciousness can be manipulated politically, it was necessary to saturate the population with every bit of information considered relevant to the party's ideology. The object was to influence national consciousness,and the role of the media in developing the national identity was not to be underestimated. Propagating the notion that the workers have no fatherland, the media were able to transform Marxist doctrine into a vehicle of nationalism. The Soviet Union became highly adept at reorienting its satellite states toward a new form of control in which socialist identity, political ideology, and organization were more important than parochialism, the family, and regional loyalty.

Rational is perhaps not the best description one could accord a totalitarian regime, but in its attempt to institutionalize revolution by pulverizing the existing associations in society, the communist regime acts with a great deal of rationality.[39.] Stalin appropriately began with the recognition that the social composition of Transylvania was rooted in diversity and characterized largely by overlapping associations. Compromise was necessary to solidify the communist stronghold. Once the regime was firmly entrenched, alternate courses of action would be available.

The ethnic composition of Transylvania (including Máramaros-Maramures, Körösvidék-Crisana, and the Bánát-Banat) in 1930 was returned according to race as 57.9 percent Rumanian, 24.4 percent Hungarian, 9.8 percent German, and 3.2 percent Jewish.[40.] The population breakdown for Rumania as a whole in 1930 was 72 percent Rumanian, 8 percent Hungarian, 4 percent German, and 4 percent Jewish. Ruthenians, Russians, Bulgarians, Turks, and Gypsies were also listed. While in Rumania as a whole Hungarians were distinctly outnumbered by the indigenous population, their numerical force in Transylvania was significant.

The revised statistics for 1952 indicate the population distribution for Rumania as a whole, but the criterion being used is that of mother tongue (language spoken best or most readily). The 1930 census emphasized race. The mother tongue-race distinction was evidently made to accommodate the inflated statistics which included many Jews and "Others" under Rumanian census figures. The distinction is purely arbitrary and a matter of semantics because, in fact, it is difficult to delineate the linguistic from the racial criterion of nationality.[41.]

The mother tongue categories of 1952 were 85.7 percent Rumanian, 9.4 percent Hungarian, 2.2 percent German, and 1.8 percent "Others". Comparing these with the 1930 figures for Rumania as a whole, there is a 13.7 percent increase in the Rumanian population, only 1.4 percent in the Hungarian, a 1.8 percent decrease in the German, a 3.1 percent decrease in the Jewish (in 1952 they constituted 0.9 percent), and a phenomenal 12 percent decrease in "Others". The exact population distribution according to nationalities (mother tongue being the criterion employed) for Rumania as a whole in 1952 was as follows:[42.]

Rumanian	13,597,613	85.7%
Hungarian	1,499,851	9.4%
German	343,913	2.2%
Yiddish	138,795	0.9%

Gypsy	53,425	0.3%
Serbo-Croatian	45,447	0.3%
Russian	39,332	0.2%
Ukrainian	37,582	0.2%
Czech-Slovak	35,143	0.2%
Turk-Tatar	28,782	0.2%
Bulgarian	13,408	0.1%
Greek	8,696	0.1%
Armenian	6,987	0.0%
Polish	6,753	0.0%
Albanian	735	0.0%
Others	15,639	0.1%
Not declared	523	0.0%
Total	15,872,624	100%

The decrease in Germans after 1945 can be accounted for by post-war Kremlin policies designed to eliminate the "German menace." While the Rumanian Government did not expel the German population, it inflicted harsh measures against them. Though many had fled with the retreating German Army, massive deportations to Siberia helped to deplete their remaining numbers. The minority was actually reduced to half its size. The reduction in figures for the Jewish minority is due in part to Nazi atrocities and in part to the postwar inclusion of Jews in the Rumanian category.

Any critical observer of Rumanian census figures learns to detect the inconsistencies. It is clear from the available data that Rumanians are intent on broadening the majority-minority gap. There is, moreover, a fine line to be drawn distinguishing race and language and an even finer line distinguishing language and nationality. Most attempts to define nationality have incorporated the language criterion. It is pivotal to the scheme Hayes devises. Schlegel and Fichte place undue emphasis on the linguistic component while C.A. Macartney specifically identifies nationality with language. The delineation of the two can best be interpreted by Hans Kohn's formula postulating a "corporate will". Reminiscent of the general will argument advanced by Rousseau, it is useful in perceiving the fine distinction actually made by the Rumanians. However, for all practical purposes, in terms of gathering census data, the validity of drawing this line can be questioned. By choosing to categorize minority groups according to language, Rumanian census officials were able to bypass the malaise inherent in the "corporate will". Individuals were not required to choose national alignments, but only to assert which language they spoke most readily. Many in the 1952 census were reticent to reply directly, preferring to be listed as Rumanian-speaking. In 1956 the race and mother tongue criteria of former years were replaced by the sharper language-nationality distinction. Individuals were then asked to identify not only their language, but their desire to belong to a specific nationality as well. They were called upon to clarify their "will" to belong, that is, to choose between the majority or the minority. The choice was not an easy one. The obligation to state before officials one's national priorities was enough to drive a wedge between a people and its culture and served superbly as an instrument for intimidation. Pressure on Hungarians to "denationalize" themselves became intense and unremitting.

The nationality and language figures for 1956 were as follows:[43.]

	Nationality	Language
Rumanian	15,011,190	15,086,923
Hungarian	1,589,443	1,651,953
German	382,400	391,388
Yiddish	144,198	34,263

The data were revised in 1960, apparently to account for some discrepancies in the earlier figures:

	Nationality	Language
Rumanian	14,996,114	15,080,686
Hungarian	1,587,675	1,653,700
German	384,708	395,374
Yiddish	146,264	34,337

There is a decrease in the Rumanian sector in the revised table both in terms of language and nationality, with an increase in Germans and Jews. The Hungarian figures stay much the same but still favour language after the revision. For every 1,000 people of declared Hungarian origin, there were 1,042 giving Hungarian as their mother tongue. Although it is somewhat bewildering to think that Hungarian would be the language of persons who were not of Hungarian origin, 4.2% of the Hungarian minority preferred not to admit to their Magyar origins.

While the 1956 and 1960 figures given above apply to Rumania as a whole, they are indicative of conditions in Transylvania. The most useful method for identifying population trends is by examining the available data[44.]

City	Population			
	1910	1930	1956	1966
Brasov (Brassó, Stalin)	41,056	59,232	123,882	140,500

Cluj (Kolozsvár)	60,808	100,844	154,752	167,930
Oradea (Nagyvárad)	64,169	82,687	99,007	111,657
Tirgu Mures (Marosvásárhely)	25,517	38,517	65,188	77,042
Timisoara (Temesvár)	72,555	91,530	142,251	152,552

The data for Hungarians and Rumanians in these cities are available for 1910 and 1930:

City	Hungarian		Rumanian	
	1910	1930	1910	1930
Brasov (Brassó)	17,831	24,977	11,786	19,398
Cluj (Kolozsvár)	50,704	54,776	7,562	34,836
Oradea (Nagyvárad)	58,421	55,039	3,604	20,914
Tirgu Mures (Marosvásárhely)	22,790	25,359	1,717	9,493
Timisoara (Temesvár)	28,552	32,513	7,566	24,088

During the interwar years, Rumania realized that something would have to be done to counterbalance the relative strength of the Hungarians in the towns. Population shifts proved useful in diminishing minority proportions. Since Bolshevization in the 1940s did not altogether nullify the Rumanian solution to nationality issues, population shifts to urban areas after World War II continued to be used to reduce Magyar numbers in Transylvania's cities. This is evidenced above by the tremendous increase in Rumanian settlers in Kolozsvár (Cluj), Nagyvárad (Oradea), Marosvásárhely (Tirgu Mures) and Temesvár (Timisoara). While some of the statistical growth was due to declarations of Rumanian nationality out of fear of reprisal, there was also a sudden influx of Rumanians from the Regat (Old Kingdom) to the major cities. Even as Hungarians were vigorously discriminated against in the issuance of settling permits, Rumanians were encouraged to immigrate. A survey of population shifts between 1910 and 1956 in twenty-five Transylvanian cities serves to illustrate the effects of forced Rumanianization.[45.]

	Hungarian Sovereignty		Rumanian Sovereignty		
	1890	1910	1938	1948	1956
Hungarian	58.3%	65.3%	46.6%	41.0%	36.0%
Rumanian	15.8%	15.6%	32.0%	47.9%	51.9%

The 1956 Rumanian census showed 6,069,535 people in Transylvania and the parts of the Hungarian Kingdom annexed to Rumania in 1920, all of this now being called simply Transylvania. This compares with 5,257,467 in 1910, the date of the last Hungarian census for historical Transylvania. The overall increase over a forty-six year span was less than one million. While part of the increase is natural, some of it is due to the settling of Rumanians from Bessarabia and Rumania proper in Transylvania, especially since German and Jewish war losses in the area were in excess of 600,000

In 1910 there were 1,661,805 Hungarians in Transylvania. Their number in 1956 decreased to 1,618,246 while Rumanian figures increased from 2,838,454 to 4,192,506. Historical Transylvania, of course, was smaller than today's area but most of the increase is due to a planned program of shifting population.[46] Irrespective of approximately 200,000 Hungarians who were forced to leave Transylvania after World War I, no other mass exodus has taken place. The statistics point to a methodical elimination of the Hungarian minority. If the population had been allowed to grow under normal conditions, it would most certainly have reached the two million mark over the given forty-six year span. It is altogether unlikely that the Hungarian minority would have decreased by 43,559 while the Rumanian population increased by 1,354,052.

Since the numerical increase of Rumanians in Kolozsvár (Cluj) is especially striking between the two wars, we should focus closely on post-1945 developments in that city. Kolozsvár (Cluj) is the capital of Transylvania and the largest city ceded to Rumania after Trianon and the annulment of the Second Vienna Award. It is today surpassed only by Bucharest in size.

Year	Total Population	Hungarian	Rumanian	German	Others	Footnotes
1910	60,808	50,704	7,562	1,676	866	[47]
1930	100,844	54,776	34,836	2,702	8,530	[48]
1948	117,915	67,977	47,321	360	2,257	[49]
1956	157,723	74,155	74,033	990	8,545	[50]

While the growth of Kolozsvár (Cluj) between 1910 and 1930 was the direct result of a threefold process of industrialization, urbanization, and Rumanianization, the increase after 1948 can only be explained by a deliberate attempt to swell the data in favour of the Rumanian majority or by forced population shifts. That is, the urbanization and industrialization which occurred after 1948 were greatly intensified by the drive for Rumanianization. Hungarians were driven from the urban to the rural areas to seek opportunities for employment, scarce as these opportunities may have been. It was no longer a threefold process passed off as a facet of modernization but rather a single campagin to totally assimilate or eliminate the Hungarian minority.

According to the statistics for Kolozsvár (Cluj), the total population increased by the same proportion in the twenty-year period between 1910 and 1930 as it did in the eight years between 1948 and 1956. Unlikely as this may seem, one is led to surmise that the information is significant but not wholly reliable. The 1948 figures are based on the 1939 census correcting for births and deaths but not for immigration. The increase between 1930 and 1948 was probably larger than these figures indicate. Thus, in the absence of sufficient reliable data on minorities, the detection of discrimination has become a process built on inconclusive evidence.

In the 1947 Paris Peace Treaty, the Hungarian minority was awarded certain rights partly as a result of Stalin's cautious approach to the ethnic problem and partly in appeasement of the American delegation's insistence that Hungary should be permitted to retain the Crisana-Körös region. Despite the treaty's attempt to formulate safeguards for minorities in Rumania, communist terror after 1946 was vigorously exercised against all non-communist segments of the population, especially that of the urban middle class. In terms of actual protection offered by the Peace Treaty for the minorities, let us examine a number of its provisions and some violations.

The agreement concluded in February 1947 between the Allies and Rumania asserts in Part II, Section 1, Article 3 that:[51.]

(1) Rumania shall take the steps necessary to secure to all persons under Rumanian jurisdiction, without distinction as to race, sex, language, or religion, the enjoyment of human rights and fundamental freedoms, including freedom of expression, press and publication, of religious worship, of political opinion and of public meeting.

(2) Rumania further undertakes that the laws in force in Rumania shall not, either in their content or in their application, discriminate or entail any discrimination between persons of Rumanian nationality on grounds of their race, sex, language or religion, whether in reference to their persons, property, business, professional or financial interests, status, political or civil rights or any other matter.

Much like the Treaty of Versailles, the 1947 agreement clearly contained safeguards to embrace all minorities regardless of ethnic considerations. Language alone was sufficient to bring a group under its protection. The Groza Government underwrote Rumania's guarantees toward her national minorities and pledged its adherence to the principles of "equality, democracy, and justice with respect to the entire population."[52.]

But despite Rumania's guarantee toward her minorities, there were many flagrant violations of human rights which drew an outcry of protest from the West. On April 2, 1949 the United States and Great Britain sharply criticized the Rumanian, Hungarian and Bulgarian governments. Forwarding all three a list of violations of guarantees included in the peace treaties, they ordered them to "stop the inhuman acts which accompanied their political and economic reforms."[53.] On July 11, 1949, the Soviet government rebuffed the Western powers for interfering. The matter was then referred to the Fourth Session of the General Assembly of the United Nations where it was held in abeyance until the International Court intervened. When told to appoint an arbitration commission to investigate the breach of peace treaties, the governments concerned simply refused to comply. The condemnation of these actions by the General Assembly on November 3, 1950 went unheeded. At one point, the International Court concluded that "the disregard shown by the Rumanian government for the rights and liberties of persons under its jurisdiction ... has indeed become so notorious as to evoke the condemnation of free peoples everywhere."[54.] Without replying to the Court's accusations, the Rumanian government proceeded to formulate a new constitution.

Particularly striking, both in terms of the peace settlement and the Rumanian constitution of 1952, are the provisions designed to safeguard the cultural rights of the minorities. In the constitution anyway, a conscious effort seems to have been made by the Groza Government to meet minority demands. Article 82 permits the use by each group of its own language and provides for the establishment of educational institutions at all levels to teach each group in its mother tongue. Administrative and judicial organs are authorized to use the language of the majority nationality in their respective area. There is also a stipulation for the appointment of civil servants from the majority group in each area. We can see why the Rumanian government organized massive population shifts. While these provisions were supposedly intended to protect the minorities, the official policies enacted by the leadership did everything possible to moderate their effect. The majority nationality in most areas was Rumanian, if not by nature then by force.

The constitution went on to assert that it was the duty of the State to protect the culture of national minorities "which ought to be socialistic in its content and national in its form." This was precisely the idea underlying the process of Bolshevization. It also characterized Stalin's approach to the minority problem. The government was actually permitted to dictate the socialistic content of minority culture. If this content did not agree with what was nationally desirable, the leadership could enforce whatever measures it considered necessary to make the two coincide. It is interesting to note that Article 81 designates "any kind of chauvinistic persecution of non-Rumanian national minorities" as "a criminal offence."[55.]

One of the most striking provisions of the constitution concerned the creation of the Hungarian Autonomous Region (Articles 19, 20, 21), an administrative district that had a 77.3% Hungarian majority (565,510 Hungarians). The other groups were as follows: 20.1% Rumanian (146,830), 0.4% German, 0.4% Yiddish, and 1.5% Gypsy.[56.] Marosvásárhely (Tirgu Mures) was designated as the capital of the Hungarian Autonomous Region. The 18 regions specified in the 1952 constitution now included this territory, embracing the parts of Transylvania with the greatest concentration of Hungarians.[57.] The National Federation of Hungarian Workers (MADOSZ) the socio-political organization of Hungarians in Rumania had at the end of hostilities urged the creation of such an autonomous region, and it was due in part to that effort, as well as to some insistence from Moscow, that the matter was thus concluded. It would not be wrong to presume that the pressure exerted by the International Court also had a role to play in its formation.

The main concentration of Hungarians, other than the strip of territory along the border, is in the eastern part of Transylvania where some 700,000 Székelys reside. This particular stretch of land, lying about one hundred miles east of the frontier, became the focus of Articles 19, 20 and 21. Modeled on the autonomous regions within the Soviet Republics, the Hungarian Autonomous Region embodied the principle of "genuine proletarian internationalism." It was the perfect area for experimentation with a "socialistic national culture." And, since ethnic identity is most intense along the border, this was the perfect area for conflict avoidance. The creation of an autononous region in the immediate vicinity of the Rumanian-Hungarian frontier would have enlivened an already burgeoning nationalism. As it was, the established region was somewhat removed to the east, alleviating the tensions Stalin sought to soothe.

The Rumanian government was thus able to meet Hungarian demands. It established an autonomous administrative territory, removed from the border with Hungary and surrounded by regions that were predominantly Rumanian. Contrary to an homogeneous state model which specifies that once a territory gains autonomy along nationality lines, it should be allowed to elect its own representatives at the regional and municipal levels, the Hungarian area functioned under much the same conditions as the other administrative divisions. The "autonomous administration" provision contained in the constitution was realized only in theory, not in practice. Articles 20 and 21 clearly stated that the laws of the Rumanian People's Republic governed the Magyar area along with the other regions of Rumania. Any statute drafted by the largely Hungarian People's Council had to ratified by the Grand National Assembly of the Rumanian People's Republic.[58.]

Then, a disruptive factor entered into the slowly stabilizing Rumanian picture. Even as communist officials from Moscow, Bucharest and Budapest flocked to the Magyar Autonomous Region to express awe and approval for the smooth functioning of "proletarian internationalism," the Hungarian Revolution erupted. Stalin's death in 1953 sparked the desire for de-Russification, but the revolt in 1956 stressed the need for further de-Magyarization. The momentary crisis in the communist leadership provoked by Khrushchev's call for de-Stalinization was followed by an explosive reaction on the part of the atomized Hungarian people, a reaction which breathed life into the limp body of Transylvania's minorities.

Revolutions as bloody as the October massacre of 1956 are not often recorded in the annals of history. 25,000 casualties were reported in an ordeal which commenced as a peaceful demonstration by students and ended as a full-scale battle by an entire nation against Soviet occupation. Far from increasing political stability or political liberty in Transylvania, it attested to the fact that nationalism in mixed areas makes for tension and mutual hatred.

The Rumanian government of Gheorghe Gheorghiu-Dej was alarmed. It confronted the occasion in the great Rumanian tradition of siding with the keeper of the key to power, namely the Soviet Union. During the upheaval in Poland in 1956, both Gheorghiu-Dej and Chivu Stoica, the Premier, had been in Yugoslavia to confer with Tito over the worsening situation in Hungary and its effects on the rest of the communist bloc.[59.] In Rumania's case, there was rightful cause for panic since any change in Hungary's posture could put pressure on that country for the recasting of Transylvania's frontiers. The disruption of equilibrium and the reopening of the border issue was the last thing Dej wanted to face. Upon hearing that students in Hungary were urging the formation of a Danubian federation, presumably incorporating Transylvania, Gheorghiu-Dej and Stoica cut short their visit to Yugoslavia.[60.] They hurried back to Bucharest on October 28, 1956. The possible installation of a liberated anti-communist government across the border was enough to trigger immediate Rumanian reprisals.

Despite stringent measures directly enforced to calm the revolutionary fever, demonstrations and student outbreaks swept across Transylvania and Rumania proper. On October 27, 1956, demonstrations were reported in Bucharest, Iasi, Kolozsvár (Cluj) and Temesvár (Timisoara). Rumanians too were eager to shed the armor of Soviet subjugation. The withdrawal of Russian army divisions stationed in their territory since the end of World War II would have been a much welcomed event. But for Gheorghiu-Dej, it was not a desirable prospect. Soviet troops, after all, insured his political survival. His sudden return from Yugoslavia was sparked by a comprehension that armed intervention in Hungary offered the only sure guarantee for keeping his government in power.

The mood was one of sullen defiance in Transylvania where invocation of the Stalinist dictate urging "revolutionary vigilance" increased the momentum of national patriotism. The "No, No, Never!" slogan of earlier days acquired a sharper edge as it cut deep into the fiber of Eastern European communism. Hungarian nationalists in Transylvania affirmed their belief that political and cultural matters were inseparable and that no culture can live if it is not developing freely in a sovereign state exclusively its own.[61.] The limited autonomy of the Hungarian Autonomous Region offered little in the way of satisfying minority demands. It seems as if the Peace Treaty of 1947 and the 1952 Constitution were purely illusory settlements of a problem which could find little hope for resolution in the Rumanian system.

The first published Rumanian comment on the 1956 incident was an editorial in *Scinteia* on October 28, 1956 wherein the Rumanian Worker's Party pleaded for minority support. In a series of articles written for *The New York Times*, Welles Hangen, the only Western reporter allowed into Transylvania at the time, unmasked the turbulent developments there. He described the Hungarian Revolution as a situation over which "Rumanian communist forces might not be so sanguine ... as they would like the outside world to believe."[62.]

Both Rumanian and Soviet army units were stationed in the Hungarian Autonomous Region and other parts of Transylvania. Their chief bases were at Temesvár (Timisoara) and Arad. When Soviet troops were ordered to Hungary from these bases to help quell the rebellion, reinforcements were quick to arrive in anticipation of resurgent Magyar enmity in the area. Hungary, it was said, was going through "the inevitable process of democratization."[63.] Hungarian rebels were denounced for their "hooligan acts of plunder and bestial hangings" as well as "acts of vandalism and crimes of unparalleled ferocity."[64.] Meanwhile, Rumanian communists spoke of "growing friendship among Rumanian and minority nationalities."[65.]

Irrespective of Rumanian claims of friendship, there was only tension and heightened animosity. Army units with sub-machine guns and rifles patrolled the streets of Kolozsvár (Cluj). On October 29, students in Bucharest were said to have torn up their communist membership cards in open protest. Students in Kolozsvár (Cluj). boycotted classes on Marxism-Leninism. Reports of outbreaks which included workers and farmers reached the capital. Arrests were widespread and frequent. The Rumanian government persisted in trying to minimize the importance of the whole affair but on October 31, a rumor leaked from Budapest that the police were firing on demonstrators in Transylvania.[66.] Rumania proceeded to bar foreigners from Temesvár (Timisoara), Arad,

Nagyvárad (Oradea) and Nagybánya (Baia Mare). Temesvár (Timisoara) and Arad were both used as military bases by the Soviet Union; Nagyvárad (Oradea) controlled the rail line to Budapest; Nagybánya (Baia Mare) was a potential source of trouble because of its large Hungarian population.[67.]

As riots gripped the country, Rumania's communist regime swore allegiance to Soviet opposition to the Hungarian nationalists. Allegiance meant revenge to Gheorghiu-Dej who threatened to "wage open war against any non-communist Hungarian government."[68.] Foreigners were confined to Bucharest. The Hungarian section of the university at Kolozsvár (Cluj) was closed temporarily. Welles Hangen was expelled on November 4, making information from the area hard to come by. November 4, 1956 was also the day the Russian army dealt the crushing blow to the revolution in Hungary. For Dej, however, relief was nowhere in sight. With the Russian army back in control, the strenuous task of reconstruction lay ahead.

In retrospect, several remarks can be made about the effects of the Hungarian uprising on the Transylvanian situation and on Hungarian-Rumanian relations. Gheorghiu-Dej hastened to aid the Kádár regime in the restoration of order and in the elimination of the menace of dissidents and counterrevolutionary elements. Of particular importance is Rumania's role in Imre Nagy's execution. For all apparent purposes, the removal of the Hungarian leader from the Yugoslav Embassy on November 23, 1956 with "permission" to go to Rumania was no more than a Soviet hoax to cloak his forthcoming execution. In June 1958, Nagy was executed with some of his colleagues after an investigation and a trial which provoked worldwide shock and indignation. The news of the killings was announced simultaneously in Moscow and Budapest. Although it has never been outrightly proven, Bucharest probably cooperated in the executions.

Gheorghiu-Dej and Stoica led two delegations to Hungary in November 1956 and January 1957 with the purpose of persuading Kádár to relinquish any claims to Transylvania and denounce as chauvinists and nationalists with irredentist aims those who participated in the revolution. Kádár met these requests when he visited Rumania in February 1958. In fact, owing to the weakness of his domestic position and to his reliance on Rumania for aid, Kádár could have done little else but renounce the Rumanian territories inhabited by Hungarians. His statement at a mass rally in Bucharest firmly posits his stand.[69.]

The Hungarian People's Republic has no territorial or any claim against any country. Anyone who makes such a claim is not only an enemy of the neighboring peoples' democracies which are living in fraternal friendship with us, but is above all a deadly enemy of the Hungarian People's Republic and of the Hungarian working people

231

who have suffered so much under their past rulers.

Noteworthy in this regard is the fact that the Rumanian government extended aid to the Kádár regime almost immediately after its inception, expressing support with a sixty million ruble loan.[70.] In her earnestness to establish a neighboring communist stronghold, Rumania was willing to go to any extremes. Some reports even suggested that Soviet deportation trains left Hungary through Rumania. It has also been acknowledged that the reorganization of Hungary's security forces was made possible with Rumania's help. The struggle against "bourgeois chauvinism" and "criminal-minded fascism" was thereby fully launched. Just two years after the events in Hungary, Rumania witnessed the withdrawal of the Red Army from her territories.

While the leadership in Rumania was basking in the full glory of their achievements, Transylvania felt the pains of governmental revenge. Several clergymen, Catholic and Protestant, were sentenced to imprisonment or death. Many Hungarians were arrested under the pretext of dissident activity. According to The New York Times, preventive arrests approached the 40,000 mark.[71.] In 1958, fifty-six of the Hungarian minority were tried. Ten were executed while others received long-term prison sentences.[72.] Edward Chrankshaw of The New York Herald Tribune reported that prison sentences ranged from ten to twenty-five years. The families of the imprisoned were often deported to other parts of Rumania, particularly to the marshes of the Danube Delta.[73.] In November 1964, George Bailey of The Reporter summarized the campaign of terror and repression which followed the revolt in these words: "Thousands of Hungarians were arrested, perhaps hundreds put to death. In one trial alone in Kolozsvár (Cluj), thirteen out of the fifty-seven accused were executed. This year some eight thousand political prisoners were released with considerable fanfare by the Rumanian government in a general amnesty. But as far as I could ascertain in my recent travels through Transylvania, not one of the Hungarians arrested during the revolt has yet been released."[74.] Mr. Bailey's figures are a bit higher than those of The New York Times. His article, however, provides an unequalled first-hand look at the Transylvanian situation in 1964. The article was written eight years after the revolution.

The institution to be hit hardest by the Rumanian axe was that of education. It was here that the first serious contradiction became manifest within a culture that was "socialistic in its content and national in its form." Article 82 of the constitution provided for the establishment of educational institutions at all levels to teach each group in its mother tongue. However, in 1959 it was declared that the maintenance of a bilingual university at Kolozsvár (Cluj) was "in opposition to the interests of socialism" and led to "national isolationism in culture and science (which) just like any other manifestation of nationalism, is a poisoned weapon in the hands of the enemies of the people."[75] The promotion of a socialistic culture necessitated the suppression of the national culture and required ethnic minorities to learn the Rumanian language.

Until 1958 education in the Hungarian language was available from the primary to the university level. With the instigation of this "socialist" policy in institutional reform, the number of Hungarian primary schools rapidly declined until it was decreed that only the eldest child could be enrolled for study in his mother tongue. This decree, of course, was in direct defiance of the constitution. Higher education also suffered. Undergoing a process of parallelization, it was obviously doomed to die a slow death. With the introduction of parallel sections that taught in the Rumanian language in minority institutions, the strategy was clear. Once the Rumanian section was established in the system, it could easily overtake and replace the whole Hungarian one.

In 1955-1956 there were, 1,022 four-year basic schools relying solely on the Hungarian language. By 1958-59, there were only 915 such establishments. Schools with parallel sections increased over the same period from 38 to 124. In 1955-1956 there were 493 seven-year basic schools where Hungarian was the language of instruction. In 1958-1959 there were 469. Schools with parallel sections increased from 10 to 77.[76] By the end of 1962, not a single completely separate Hungarian school remained in all of Rumania.[77]

Interestingly enough, Rumanian data for 1952-53 lists five universities in the country, with the Rumanian and Hungarian sections as Kolozsvár (Cluj) being counted separately. This reference to a distinct department at Koloszvár (Cluj) coincided with the granting of autonomy to the Magyar region in eastern Transylvania. The 1954 statistics refer to four universities.

In 1958 national minorities were being taught in fifteen languages in 3,250 schools and at Kolozsvár (Cluj) in Hungarian. In 1962-1963 this figure grew to 3,500 schools with the added emphasis "and at the medical faculty of Cluj University in Hungarian."[78] The change in wording is due to the coalescence of the Babes-Bolyai Universities.

The merger of the Hungarian language Bolyai University with the Rumanian Babes University in July 1959 was a serious blow to the Hungarian minority. The famous University at Kolozsvár (Cluj) now acquired the title Babes-Bolyai University of Science. Following this forced assimilation, several members of the faculty committed suicide.[79] Dej announced the merger at a conference of the Union of Student Associations in February 1959, possibly upon a directive from Moscow. The rector of Bolyai University, Lajos Takács, denounced "national isolationism." The rector of Babes University remarked that "the line between Rumanians and Hungarians, between Rumanian and

Hungarian professors and students, is an anachronism."[80] The scheme was unanimously "approved" at a meeting of students and professors on July 3, 1959. With the parallelization and phasing out process, the Hungarian Institute of Medicine and Pharmacy at Tirgu Mures (Marosvásárhely) lost its autonomy.

The French newspaper, *Le Monde*, dealt with the problem of the merger in 1967 in an on-the-spot report by Michel Tatu.[81] Although the distribution of classes in terms of language was not specified at the time of the merger, eight years after its occurrence only 30% of the classes were being taught in Hungarian. While there were 40 graduate students who were enrolled in Rumanian language and literature courses in 1960 with 29 enrolled in similar Hungarian courses, by 1965 the ratio fluctuated in favour of Rumanian course enrollment 218 to 39. This demonstrates an increase of 178 students studying Rumanian as compared to only 10 more studying Hungarian. This discrepancy over a five-year period is admittedly enormous. Moreover, the rector, three of the five prorectors, seven of the eight deans, and sixty-one percent of the teaching faculty were Rumanian. Today, proficiency in the Rumanian language is a prerequisite for admittance and all classes are taught in Rumanian, except those on Hungarian language and literature.[82]

An additional impact of cultural "socialization" was the systematic dispersal of Hungarian college graduates in non-Hungarian provinces. By 1964 it was estimated that the number of Hungarians living outside their own areas was between 35 percent to 50 percent.[83] The placement of most university graduates on a nation-wide basis, rather than according to personal preference, served to scatter Hungarian intellectuals throughout the Regat, thereby diminishing their threat as a concentrated force.

A logical outgrowth of the government's desire to minimize minority pressures was the reorganization of the Magyar Autonomous Region along more integrated lines. The plan for territorial adjustments was placed before the National Assembly at the end of December 1960. In March 1961, Article 19 of the Constitution was amended by the deletion of the phrase which referred to the region as being composed of a "compact Hungarian group." One-third of the Magyar Autonomous Region was attached to the overwhelmingly Rumanian province of Brassó (Brasov). The detached territory included the whole southern part of the former Hungarian Autonomous Region which consisted of two heavily Székely-populated districts. In its stead, three districts which contained a large Rumanian majority were annexed to the remaining Magyar territory from the southwest. The province was renamed the Mures-Magyar Autonomous Region, indicating that it was no longer a solely Hungarian controlled district. Recasting these boundaries inflicted serious casualties on the number of Hungarians, reducing the population by approximately 92,000 (15 percent) in the new province. The Rumanian population grew by 120,000 (15 percent), off-balancing the loss of the Hungarian strength.[84]

The reorganization of the Hungarian precincts through the process of gerrymandering district boundaries was just one facet of administrative discrimination. It was well known that the frontier provinces had the highest rate of industrialization in Rumania and, moreover, that these areas supported a large Hungarian contingent. With a stepped up drive to improve production, Transylvania was overrun by great numbers of civil servants, bureaucrats, and workers from the Regat. They swarmed to the border provinces and the newly created Mures-Magyar Autonomous Region. Here, as elsewhere, the formation of a large industrial bureaucracy of predominantly Rumanian composition squeezed out the Hungarian minority, forcing them to seek work in other areas. Countless numbers of unemployed Hungarians migrated to the Regat where they were greeted with further discrimination. Le Monde reported that in 1964 there were more than 250,000 Hungarians in Bucharest.[85] Many were again deported as forced labourers to the Danube Delta.[86] Management officials in the autonomous province, according to 1964 statistics, were 50 percent Rumanian.

In the Mures-Magyar Region as elsewhere in Transylvania, the use of the Hungarian language was prohibited in the courts and in official correspondences. Its use was even regulated on public conveyances and in stores. But when some Transylvanian Hungarians assembled in Hungary in 1963 to discuss these unfair practices, Kádár had them arrested and imprisoned on charges of "incitement to illegal organization." [87] In that same year, an appeal was sent to Moscow by a group of clergymen asking that the Soviet Union take Transylvania for itself rather than leave it at the mercy of the "Rumanian axe".[88] The signatories of this demand were sentenced to twenty-five year prison terms. It was indeed as Edward Crankshaw put it, "a smuggled cry to the West." But the cry went unheeded and the Hungarian population awoke to the precariousness of its position as a stranger in a strange land.

III.

NICOLAE CEAUSESCU SLIPS INTO LEADERSHIP

It was in the Soviet Union's best interests to give Rumania a free hand in the treatment of her minorities. There were, after all, 200,000 restless Hungarians in the Carpatho-Ukraine, annexed to the Soviet Union after World War II; there was as much potential for rebellion there as in any of the outlying areas of Hungary. Therefore, any easing of restraints in Transylvania could give rise to unrest among nationals in that Soviet territory. What is more, since the Hungarians were never considered as completely reliable elements in the socialist bloc anyway, the Kremlin's attitude toward Rumanian policies vis-à-vis its Hungarian minorities was generally one of complacent approval. It was only with Rumania's growing dissidence in the bloc that Transylvania was suddenly perceived as an attractive tool of Soviet efforts to keep its satellites in line.

Among Hungarians, the revolutionary spirit of 1956 gave way to resignation and at least temporary acceptance of defeat. Persecution led to assimilation; discrimination, to complete subjugation and humiliation. Official boundaries remained as the external symbol of minority existence but not of minority allegiance. The state had successfully imposed its control over a once significant nation enclosed within its territorial demarcation. The policies of the state were those of a national government seeking to eject all foreign elements from its system. Conformity was expected; opposition never tolerated. International peace was no closer to being realized than it had been in the Trianon days of "self-determination."

With the death of Gheorghe Gheorghiu-Dej in 1965, Nicolae Ceausescu slipped into the leadership slot and proceeded to rule from the pinnacles of party power. Deviating somewhat from Dej's Stalinist approach to minority issues, Ceausescu continued to condemn nationalism but eased up on the restrictions his predecessor had endorsed. He admitted that Hungarians should be allowed to maintain their national culture and even initiated some measures to help them do so. A joint publication agreement was reached with Hungary, whereby some Hungarian literature that had been banned previously could now enter the country, and a number of provisions were underlined for the translation of selected Rumanian texts into the Hungarian language. However, no book concerning Transylvania could appear in Hungary without the prior approval of Rumanian authorities. Censorship was strict and only books with non-political themes were available to the minority.

The significance of these measures was largely illusory. Little was accomplished in terms of actual contact with Hungary. Whether to increase his popularity or merely to breathe new life into a decaying situation, Ceausescu's actions were well within the boundaries of permitted freedoms for minorities destined for total assimilation. The liberalizing trend was well calculated. The Hungarian films which entered Rumania in a program of planned film exchanges were ofted dubbed in the Rumanian language and given subtitles in Hungarian. Theatrical companies from Hungary performed in Bucharest but not in Transylvania. Much of the cultural mainstream flowing into Rumania from Hungary was diverted to Bucharest where the Hungarian population was unduly sparse.

Ceausescu could afford to be more "liberal" in his approach. The pace of transformation had been decided by his predecessor, repressive measures had been taken and much of the opposition had been thoroughly suppressed or eliminated. All Ceausescu had to do was sit back and occasionally extend some show of benevolence toward the minorities.

This benevolence, however, did not alleviate the fears which pervaded the lives of the Magyar populace. The *Neue Zürcher Zeitung* clearly stated in December of 1967 that "the presence of the secret police is still strong. Political opponents and troublesome intellectuals are put behind bars without delay."[89] Surveillance was just as rigid as before, and the constant fear of being reported by informants prevented Hungarians from ever publicizing their true feelings. Transylvania today is probably the only place under communist rule where one still finds such echoes of the Stalinist era as fear of contact with foreigners.

1967 was an odd year in terms of national minority policies. Rumania underwent another reorganization of administrative divisions which completely erased the Mures-Magyar Autonomous Region from state maps. The program drafted in October 1967 abolished the sixteen regions which had been in existence since 1957 and provided in their stead 40 counties and 2,706 communes. The reason specifically advanced by Ceausescu for the drastic adjustments was to facilitate economic management.

Old regions were fragmented into several counties. The Mures-Magyar Autonomous Region forfeited its western districts to Mures County. The loss included the former capital at Tirgu Mures. Its eastern flank joined the Székely areas formerly belonging to the Brassó (Brasov) region. These divisions became effective in February 1968 with a few minor alterations. The Székely area was broken down into two counties where there was previously one. Kovászna (Covasna) and Hargita (Harghita), the two counties in question, were practically the smallest in all of Rumania.[90] Although both were predominantly Hungarian, the division subdued their influence. With greater party control of local governments and the state apparatus, their political role was negligible.

Despite the fact that the overall ratio of Hungarians to Rumanians increased in the new county divisions, the latter continued to enjoy a comfortable majority. The only exception was perhaps the case of Kovászna (Covasna) and Hargita (Harghita) Counties where Hungarians dominated in terms of proportions (88 percent and 79 percent respectively). To reduce the majority in Maros (Mures) County, Segosvár (Sighisoara) district was added to the detached western section of the former autonomous province. The ratio there was changed from 49 percent Hungarian - 45 percent Rumanian to 45 percent Hungarian - 50 percent Rumanian. This was a typical example of Bucharest's gerrymandering practices.

While the proportional strengthening of Hungarians in the otherwise tiny counties of Kovászna (Covasna) and Hargita (Harghita) was another conscious effort on Ceausescu's behalf to calm minority frustrations, it is interesting to note that after 1967-68, Rumanian statistical sources omit the mention of national minorities.[91.] Prior to that year, the usual assertion was that national minorities were taught in 3,500 schools and at the medical faculty of Kolozsvár (Cluj) in Hungarian. After 1967 mention is made only of five universities and in 1972 of six, with the founding of an institution at Brassó (Brasov). This was just another indication of the slow phasing out of minority education. The obvious conclusion one can draw from this reflects on the nature of a strongly multinational state. Ruled strictly by the majority nationality,it seeks to do away with any tensions between the nation and the state. The two, as in Rumania's case, became inseparable and the principle of national self-determination disappears somewhere in their coalescence, to become itself as illusory as any of the liberties granted to the minorities.

NOTES

1. Hungary was in fact reduced to 32.6% of her pre-War size and 41.6% of her population. See C. A. Macartney, *Hungary and Her Successors: The Treaty of Trianon and its consequences, 1919-1937* (London: Oxford University Press, 1937), p. 1. The German area in the west was given to Austria; the north to Czechoslovakia with some small areas in the extreme north going to Poland; the east, to Rumania; the south, to Yugoslavia with Italy receiving Fiume. In figures this meant that from a territory measuring 325,411 square kilometers prior to the War, Hungary lost 232,448 square kilometers to artifically created multinational states. From a population of 20,886,487, approximately 12,271,370 found themselves in these new states. It was the racial diversity of Hungary which led the victorious powers to summon the principle of the people's right to self-determination. A large segment of the population ceded to other areas was not Hungarian. A concept originally attributed to Marx and emanating from the Kantian autonomous will, the right to self-determination is a vital aspect of communist theory. Lenin summarized its essence as follows: "the political separation of these nations from alien national bodies and the formation of an independent national state." V.I. Lenin, "The Right of Nations to Self-Determination," in *Questions of National Policy and Proletarian Internationalism* (Moscow: Progress Publishers, not dated) page 52. Lenin did not speak of the formation of multinational states. The self-determination principle with assertions of Daco-Roman countinuity was used to justify the detachment of Transylvania form Hungary. The non-Magyars of the area were provided with the opportunity to exercise their right to self-determination, but Transylvania did not become the "independent national state" Lenin had envisioned.

2. As was mentioned earlier, the entire territory is now referred to as Transylvania.

3. The Treaty of Trianon came complete with provisions for the protection of the minorities in Transylvania. These provisions were to be enforced by the League of Nations which, due to the weakness of its organization, could not meet the claims of the minorities. Unanimous consent within the League prior to the taking of any effective action limited the scope of its activity. Supported by the system of the Little Entente, Rumania was in a position to manipulate the powers of the League in its favour and thus postpone indefinitely any measures aimed at safeguarding the rights of the minorities.

4. In Hungarian the phrase is "Nem, Nem, Soha!". The interwar years also produced the Magyar Creed. Authored by Mrs. Elemer Papp-Vary, it goes thus: I believe in one God (Hiszek egy Istenben), I believe in one Fatherland (Hiszek egy Hazában), I believe in one divine eternal

239

Truth (Hiszek egy isteni örök Igazságban), I believe in the resurrection of Hungary (Hiszek Magyarország feltámadásában), Amen. These are words which even today are inculcated into the youth of every generation to keep alive a faith in the "Patrie" and indeed, to hold up a belief in the reunification of Hungary.

The nationalistic sentiment generated by Trianon testified to the fact that the frontiers which are imposed on a territory do not insure peace nor do they subdue passions. The application of the principle of self-determination later clarified in the "corporate will" nationality argument only aggravated existing antagonisms. The resentment in the case of Hungarians in Transylvania was particularly acute in view of the fact that they were now trapped in a nation where, as foreign members, they were destined for assimilation or elimination. Both these alternatives were greeted by a staunch "No, No, Never!" — a stubbornness which was to cause Rumania many worries.

5. This is to coin a phrase from William F. Robinson, *Nationalism: Hungarian Problem Child.* (Munich: Radio Free Europe Research, July 5, 1967).

6. The famous Hungarian geographer and former Prime Minister, Count Paul Teleki, has written a great deal about Transylvania. In an essay entitled "Transylvania's Situation in Hungary and in Europe," he speaks of Transylvania as an "individual entity with respect to both time and place." Elie Kedourie, *Nationalism* (New York: Frederick A. Praeger, 1960). p. 125, remarks: "For natural frontiers do not exist either in the topographical sense favoured by Danton, nor in the linguistic which Fichte preferred; ironically, these two conceptions of Nature may even conflict as, for instance, in Transylvania, the topographical features of which endow it with perfect natural frontiers, but which is populated by a mixture of Magyars, Rumanians and others, long at odds with one another. Frontiers are established by power, and maintained by the constant and known readiness to defend them by arms." Rumania's readiness to defend her title to Transylvania during World War II as well as during the Hungarian Revolution of 1956 bears this out. Geographical unity no longer suffices for the maintenance of modern multinational nation-states. Political considerations override all other factors in the international power balance game.

7. Xenophobia, like patriotism, enters into nationalism but is not a part of its doctrinal composition.

8. C.A. Macartney, *Hungary and Her Successors, op. cit.,* p. 254, asserts that the Magyars entered Hungary at the end of the ninth century but did not occupy Transylvania until a century later. Another theory has it that the occupation of Transylvania came before the occupation of Hungary itself. The truth perhaps embodies all these suppositions. Magyar tribes probably crossed the Carpathians at several different

points in the ninth century streaming into Hungary and Transylvania at about the same time.

9. On the subject of Daco-Roman continuity, see Zsombor de Szász, *The Minorities in Rumanian Transylvania* (London: The Richards Press, 1927), p. 12. His account relates that in the second century, the Emperor Trajan destroyed the Dacian state he found in Transylvania and founded a Roman colony. But due to the filtering in of migrating peoples from Asia, after one hundred and sixty years, the colony was relinquished to the Gepides, Avars, Vandals, Huns, and Bulgarians. According to the theory of Daco-Roman continuity, Rumanians are the descendants of Emperor Trajan's soldiers and colonists who stayed behind and intermingled with the Dacian inhabitants. Hiding in the mountains for a thousand years, they reappeared in the twelfth century as a people who still spoke the language and practiced the traditions of the Latin colonists. The plausibility of such a theory is open to question, but R.W. Seton-Watson (the dubious and prejudiced professor of London - Ed.) See Seton-Watson, R.W., *Transylvania: A Key Problem* (Oxford: Classic Press, 1943). A more plausible explanation is given by Louis Élekes, "The Development of the Rumanian People" (*Hungarian Review,* 1941) p. 678. Élekes believes that "the origins of the Rumanians point to many different components.... All European nations have experienced a considerable mixture of blood so that in most cases the racial basis in no longer recognizable. This is naturally the case with the Rumanians who lived at one of the most troubled points of the continent and thus were exposed to many and varied foreign influences." Romanized elements persisting in the Balkans. Of further interest is a discussion of the continuity principle which appeared in Hungarian translation in the Hungarian periodical, *Előre* (Cluj-Kolozsvár: November, 1973), which is completely controlled by the Rumanian Communist Party. In it, the author emphasizes Rumania's Daco-Roman heritage which disclaims any union with the Slavs. The continuity movement, described as taking its roots in the eighteenth century, sought deeper ties with Rome. While it did not sever ties with the Byzantine culture, it popularized the notion that Rome represented the way of the past and the future. Founded in 1700, the Uniate Church was supposed to bridge the gap between Roman Catholicism and Greek Orthodoxy. Perhaps more of a political than a religious institution, it represents a Habsburg-Wallachian alliance at the expense of Protestantism in Hungary. With the advent of communism, the Uniate Church was reincorporated into the Orthodox sect in October 1948.

10. The Székelys populated Transylvania prior to the Wallachian migration into the area, which probably occurred sometime in the ninth

241

century. The origin of the Székelys is dubious with some historians postulating a Hun tradition and others saying they are descendants of the Avars. These arguments do not carry much weight in terms of which is more correct, since both the Huns and the Avars were Ural-Altaic tribes, speaking the same language with slightly different dialects. Saxon ancestry can be traced to the Moselle region in German. The first Saxons migrated to Transylvania sometime in the twelfth century. Undoubtedly, the Wallachian question is the most difficult one. The great Wallachian migration from the Balkans did not begin until the thirteenth century. By that time the Magyars and the Székelys had blended into one group, forming a significant majority in the region. While Rumanian official statistics do not differentiate between the Székelys and the Magyars, Ceausescu has often drawn the distinction in his speeches so as to show the existence of two small minorities instead of one large one.

11. The Wallachians were not included in the "Union of Three Nations" at Kápolna in 1438. Documentation is available from 1210 on testifying to the presence of Rumanians (Vlachs, Blachii, Wallachians) in the southern Forgaras district under their own chief or kenezs. The Tartar invasions of 1241-42 inflicted devastating wounds on Transylvania culturally, as well as economically and politically. Reconstruction required major concessions on the part of the government. To secure the cooperation of the nobility, the Hungarian kings donated estates to them. To replace the lost manpower, they allowed Rumanians to migrate to the Bihar Mountains and the Máramaros (Maramures). In order to encourage further migration, Wallachians were recognized as a "nation in the thirteenth century. But since the Rumanian kenezs were mostly Magyarized by the fifteenth century and no autonomous Wallachian region existed to speak of at that time, recognition was not accorded at Kápolna or in the Constitution. Wallachia and Moldavia united in 1859 and became the independent kingdom of Rumania in 1881. This preceded the Paris Peace settlement by a mere half century. It is as the Rumanian statesman Bratianu once said of Rumania in the course of a public lecture: "With us the Middle Ages began when they ended in other countries... . We were outside the civilization of Europe." See Zsombor de Szász, "Rumanian History," The Hungarian Quarterly, Autumn 1941, Vol. VIII, p. 205.

12. Revisionism in Hungary is discussed in C.A. Macartney, October Fifteenth: A History of Modern Hungary, 1929-1945 (Edinburgh: University Press, 1956, 2 vols.), vol. 1, pp. 3-24. See also the compilation of essays dealing with the question of nationalism in Hungary from feudalism to the present: A Magyar Nacionalizmus Kialakulása és Története (The Formation and History of Hungarian Nationalism) (Budapest: Kossuth, 1964). In particular, the treatment by Aladár Kis, "Az

ellenforradalmi rendszer reviziós kialakulása (1920-1933)'', pp. 302-315 and also Magda Adam, "Az ellenforradalmi rendszer revisiós külpolitikájához (1933-1941)'', pp. 356-395. Hungarian revisionism actually became blatantly manifest when Hungary joined the League of Nations and openly pressed her position in the international arena.

13. Lajos Kossuth (1802-1894) was the leader of the movement for national independence and governor of Hungary during the 1848-49 war of liberation. He proposed a Danubian Federation to be composed of all the nations in the Carpathian Basin and the northern Balkans. In 1850 he discussed this plan with Count László Teleki referring to the U.S. as a model organization. At the Moscow Conference in October 1943, Mr. Hull, representing the U.S., and Eden of Britain had blueprints for a Danubian federation but Russia refused to consider them. Transylvania in relation to such a federation was similar to Macedonia in relation to the Yugoslav federation. In both areas, cooperation among several states could have insured stability. The demand for this type of federation was echoed again during the 1956 uprising in Hungary.

14. In reference to the national persecutions which occurred in Rumania, anti-Semitic feeling ran about as high as sentiments against the Magyars since the Jews in Transylvania associated themselves with the Hungarian middle classes and most often considered themselves Hungarian. There was little guarantee of civil liberties for these minorities in the decrees issued from Bucharest and discriminatory taxation policies, language regulations, and land reform measures exacerbated the potentially explosive situation.

15. The so-called "Magyarization" drive followed the Compromise of 1867. In essence, "Magyarization" was an attempt at assimilation. Because the middle and upper classes were composed of Magyar speaking people, those members of other nationalities who were coopted to these classes gradually merged their national identities in a process of assimilating with the Hungarian speaking majority. "Magyarization" was not a contrived effort to forcibly eliminate national minorities.

16. The measures devised by the government were harsher in their implementation than in their actual content. Rumanians are known for the arbitrariness with which their decrees are executed so that the enforcement of any measure is left to the discretion of government officials. This was especially true in the inter-war years. The paper, *Brassoi Lapok* (December 14, 1925), reported an incident where a teacher in the village of Csikjenőfalva, "in his efforts to enforce the new language regulations of the government, handed out such beatings to his pupils that on the first day the parents had to carry home twenty-four badly beaten children from the school house, who were unable to walk." Incidents such as this

were probably sporadic and not daily occurrences. Nevertheless, this particular piece of evidence is indicative of the way "Rumanianization" functioned.

17. While prior to the changing world order of the eighteenth century the nobility was identified with the "Nation," under Rumanian control of Transylvania, the proletariat came to be identified with the Nation". This was very much in line with the Marxian call that the proletariat "must rise to be the leading class of the nation, must constitute itself as the nation." The proletariat had to assume the role of the socially progressive class which was previously reserved for the nobility (i.e., bourgeoisie). See Karl Marx and Friedrich Engels. *Manifesto of the Communist Party* (New York: International Publishers, 1932), p. 28. For a further discussion on Marx and nationalism refer to George Lichtheim, *Marxism: An Historical and Critical Study* (New York: Praeger Publishers, 1965), pp. 76-89; See also Robert R. King, *Minorities Under Communism: Nationalities as a Source of Tension Among Balkan Communist States.* (Cambridge: Harvard University Press, 1973), pp. 14-24.

18. While the Saxons, being a minority group themselves, sympathized with the plight of the other minorities in Transylvania, they could not bypass the Jewish question in view of their allegiance to the German fatherland. Fearing that Transylvanian Magyar-Jewish ties would endanger their relations with Nazi Germany, the Saxons sought closer cooperation with Bucharest. The latter had chosen to ally itself with Germany because of differences with the Soviet Union over the Bessarabian question. Saxon fears were confirmed when on April 5, 1926 Hungary signed a "Treaty of Friendship" with Mussolini's Italy in the wake of a growing concern over possible repercussions of German intrusion into Hungary. In March 1934 closer economic and political links were established with Italy and Austria, but Mussolini's preoccupation with Ethiopia in 1935-36 made Hungary uneasy about her heavy reliance on Italy. Events which were beyond her control restricted her choice of alternative solutions. With the Anschluss of March 1938 (German-Austrian union) Germany came drastically close to the Hungarian border, underlining the imminent threat of Nazi occupation. Finally, the Munich Conference of September 1938 established German hegemony over East Central Europe, making concession almost inevitable. As a result of the Austro-German alliance, Magyar-Jewish nationalism in Transylvania took on a distinctly anti-fascist character, losing some of its revisionist flavor. When Count Paul Teleki assumed the premiership in 1939, he suppressed the leading fascist organization, the "Arrow Cross."

19. Gyula Zathureczky, *Transylvania: Citadel of the West* (Astor Park: Danubian Press, n.d.), p. 44. Of 5,461,200 acres of land only 1,904,635 acres were owned by farmers possessing over 100 acres. Of this latter estimate, 487,000 belonged to the Rumanian churches and did

not fall under land reform. Almost half of the land expropriated from Hungarians, was, therefore, taken from those who possessed less than 100 acres.

20. C.A. Macartney, *Hungary and Her Successors, op. cit.*, pp. 303-306. As a result of land reform, 119 Catholic parishes were left without any land at all. In 1932 the Magyar Calvinist Church spent 64 million lei annually on its schools, of which the state contributed only 3 million. In 1935 even this subsidy was terminated.

21. Minorities were prohibited from establishing denominational Hungarian speaking higher schools or training colleges for elementary school teachers. Admission to denominational schools was made dependent on racial origin, judged by religion or an analysis of the surname. The surname in many cases had been Romanized and aided in disqualifying candidates. The Rumanian Law of July 1, 1930 introduced a school tax of 14% but this did not supply any allocations to Hungarian schools from the proceeds. It did, however, require these schools to pay the tax. See Tibor Eckhardt's speech to the League of Nations, "Roumanian Treatment of Hungarian Minorities," September 1934, Mr. Eckhardt was the Hungarian representative at the League of Nations.

22. Istvan Csatár, *Erdély és a Visszatért Keleti Részek* (Budapest: Halász Irodalmi és Könyvkiadóvállalat, 1941), pp. 107-108. Written at the time when the Second Vienna Award was still in effect, the English title is: *Transylvania and the Returned Eastern Sections.*

23. See Tibor Eckhardt's speech before the League of Nations, *op. cit.*

24. The 1910 Hungarian census was taken at the end of half a century when Hungary had done everything in her power to promote the knowledge of the Hungarian language. Based on mother tongue or the language spoken best, it does not coincide entirely with the Rumanian criterion used in 1930. Rumania based its census on race. This meant that Jews, for instance, who considered themselves Hungarian by mother tongue were shifted out into the "others" category. Their number came to 6.4% of the urban population in 1930. It is interesting to observe that in historical Transylvania which, by the way, was much smaller than the Transylvania of 1930, Hungarians were shown to outnumber Rumanians far more than in 1930. The 1910 census may have favoured Hungarians but even amidst the favouritism, the discrepancy between it and the Rumanian figures given for 1930 is immense. For a discussion of Rumanian census data, see Robert R. King, *op. cit.*, pp. 91-92.

25. Istvan Csatár, *op. cit.*, p. 88. The various categories are my translation. For a discussion of the many forms of discrimination against Hungarians, see András Hory, *Még Egy Barázdát Sem* (München: Ledermüller Oliver, 1967).

26. After the famous battle of Mohács in 1526, the Turks devastated

a large part of Hungary but then retreated. Pursuant to this decisive date, the Hungarians were able to establish a separate principality in Transylvania which, although paying tribute to the Turks, maintained its independence throughout the 16th and 17th centuries. In a series of campaigns lasting until 1699, the Turks were finally driven out of Hungary. Rumania's independence from Turkey was achieved between 1856 and 1866, a full century and a half after that of Hungary.

27. Gyula Zathureczky, op. cit., p. 49.

28. Robert L. Wolff, The Balkans in Our Time (Cambridge: Harvard University Press, 1956), p. 193. Wolff speaks of "long lines of trucks and long freight trains rushing across the new frontier into southern Transylvania..." He also mentions severe persecutions ensuing on both sides.

29. C.L. Sulzberger, "Big Four Quickly Cede All Transylvania to the Rumanians." (The New York Times, May 8, 1946), p. 1.

30. C.L. Sulzberger, "Rumania Gets Rule in Transylvania," (The New York Times, March 11, 1945), p.1.

31. The New York Times, May 8, 1946. This quote was taken from the article cited above. The administration of Transylvania was actually turned over to Rumania in March 1945. In April 1945, a Hungarian delegation went to Moscow with a proposal to cede 22,000 square kilometers of Transylvania to Hungary. The Soviets were not particularly interested in the Hungarian demands. The Hungarians were, after all, still considered former enemies. Moscow was reticent about making concessions to the Magyars. Molotov suggested that Hungary negotiate directly with Rumania, knowing full well that the latter would decline to do so.

32. Carlton J.H. Hays, Essays on Nationalism. (New York: The Macmillan Co., 1926), p. 5.

33. Patriotism enters into nationalism, but the doctrine of nationalism is more pragmatic in its essence than the patriotic flavor which accrues to it.

34. V.I. Lenin, "Critical Remarks on the National Question," in Questions of National Policy and Proletarian Internationalism (Moscow: Progress Publishers, not dated), p. 30.

35. Elie Kedourie, op. cit., p. 20 Kedourie describes the retrogressive-progressive distinction in very consice and vivid terms.

36. Gyula Zathureczky, op cit., p. 52.

37. Rezolutii; American Jewish Committee, The Jews in the Soviet Satellites (New York, 1953).

38. See also Ghita Ionescu, Communism in Rumania 1944-1962 (London: Oxford University Press, 1964), pp. 182-183.

39. For a discussion on rationality in the totalitarian regime see Zbigniew Brzezinski, "Totalitarianism and Rationality," (The American Political Science Review, vol. L, September, 1956).

40. Anuarul Statistic al Romaniei, 1937. According to the ad-

ministrative revisions made in 1945, Körösvidék (Crisana), Máramaros (Maramures) and the Bánát (Banat) constituted three out of the nine provinces in Rumania.

41. See Elie Kedourie's treatment of the linguistic and racial question in *op. cit.*, p. 71.

42. See Fred Pisky, "The People", in Stephen Fischer-Galati, ed., *Romania* (New York: Frederick A. Praeger, 1957), p. 54. Although an urban-rural breakdown is also available, we will not be dealing with those data here. The figures which have been given are advanced as well in Endre Haraszti, *The Ethnic History of Transylvania* (Astor Park: Danubian Press, 1971), p. 169. Since the major segment of the Hungarian population resides in Transylvania, the data reflect their strength in that area closely. The "not declared" category can be attributed to the fact that a number of individuals feared economic, social and political reprisal in declaring their nationality. This fear element may also account for significant shifts into the Rumanian category by some who were actually members of one of the minorities.

43. See the *Statesman's Yearbook* for these figures, 1957 and 1960-61. The data presented in 1960-61 are used in later years as well. I have chosen to limit the comparison to four national groups here since these suffice to illustrate statistical trends.

44. For the 1910 and 1930 figures see István Csatár, *op. cit.*, p. 95. For later data refer to *Statesman's Yearbook*, 1957 and 1967-68.

45. M. Eugene Osterhaven, *Transylvania: The Pathos of a Reformation Tradition* (Michigan: The Western Theological Seminary, 1968), p. 12.

46. One must always be wary when looking at Rumanian census figures since their absolute accuracy can be questioned. There may be discrepancies from one source to the next. One also has to be cautious because different criteria are employed from one census to the next, making comparisons a bit difficult.

47. "Population Conditions in Transylvania", *Journal de la Société Hongroise de Statistique* (Budapest, 1939). Also István Csatár, *op. cit.*, p. 95.

48. *Recensamentul General al Populatiei Roman din 1930*, Institutul Central de Statistics, Bucuresti, 1930. Also, see István Csatár, *Ibid.*

49. *Populatia Republicii Populara Romane le 25 Januarie 1948*, Institutul Central de Statistics, Bucuresti, 1948, Also see *Statesman's Yearbook*, 1949.

50. *Anuarul Statistic al R.P.R.*, 1960 Bucuresti. A brief look at these trends in Kolozsvár (Cluj) is provided by Osterhaven, *op. cit.*, p. 26. See also *Statesman's Yearbook*, 1957 which gives the total population for 1956 as 154,752

51. "The Hungarian Minority Problem in Rumania," *Bulletin of the International Commission of Jurists*, No. 17 in Gallus, Alexander, ed., *Studies for a New Central Europe* (New York: Mid-European Research Institute, 1964).

52. C.L. Sulzberger, "Rumania Gets Rule in Transylvania" *(The New York Times*, March 11, 1945), p.1.

53. Ghita Ionescu, *op.cit.*, p. 195.

54. International Court of Justice, *Interpretation of Peace Treaties with Bulgaria, Hungary and Rumania; Pleadings & c.*: Advisory Opinions of March 30th and July 18th 1950, p.28.

55. Constitution of the People's Republic of Rumania (September 24, 1952), Articles 17, 19, 20, 21, 81, 82, 84.

56. Robert R. King. *op. cit.*, *pp.* 150, 156.

57. In 1950 there were still 28 regions. The 1952 Constitution reduced the number of regions to 18, including the Magyar Autonomous Region. Approximately one-third of the Hungarian population of Rumania came under its jurisdiction. Based on an organic state model in which the territorial principle involved granting autonomy to certain administrative areas, the territory in question did not include the predominantly Magyar region of Kolozsvár (Cluj) (257,974 Hungarians) or Brassó (Brasov) (108,751 Hungarians) - figures are given according to the 1956 census. The Rumanian government obviously sought to keep the Magyar area as small as possible.

58. Robert R. King, *op. cit.*, pp. 150-152. Since the Autonomous Region had a Hungarian majority, it was able to adhere to the constitutional provision for choosing civil servants from the majority. As late as 1958, *Scinteia* asserts, 78% of the civil servants were members of national minorities, principally Hungarian, along with 80% of the deputies to the People's Council. See *Scinteia*, July 24, 1958.

59. Gheorghiu-Dej, as the First Secretary of the Rumanian Worker's Party, was much more powerful than Chivu Stoica, the Premier and President of the Council of Ministers.

60. The notion of a Kossuth type of Danubian federation was discussed earlier in this paper. It was raised as an issue during the uprising of 1956. On October 26, 1956, the student parliament of Miskolc was demanding federation while on November 1, 1956, *Magyar Szabadság* cited its establishment as "the most specific demand of our national foreign policy." Imre Nagy favoured some sort of cooperative union as well. See Robert R. King, *op. cit.*, p. 78.

61. Kedourie raised this idea, *op. cit.*, p. 117 and I have tried to confirm its relevance here.

62. Welles Hangen, "Rumania Arrests Unruly Magyars," *(The New York Times*, October 30, 1956), p. 17.

63. Welles Hangen, "Rumania Appeals to Her Minorities," (The New York Times, October 29, 1956), p. 9.

64. Welles Hangen, "Rumania Backs Soviet on Rebels," (The New York Times, November 3, 1956), p. 12.

65. "U.S. and Rumania Break Off Talks," (The New York Times, November 4, 1956), p. 34.

66. "Demonstrations Reported," (The New York Times, November 1, 1956), p. 24.

67. Welles Hangen, "Rumania Forbids Visits to Four Areas," The New York Times, November 1, 1956), p. 1.

68. Welles Hangen, "Rumania Backs Soviet on Rebels," (The New York Times, November 3, 1956), p. 12.

69. Radio Bucharest, February 27, 1958. See also Robert R. King, op. cit., p. 89.

70. Pravda, November 26, 1956. See also Ibid., p. 84

71. "Ethnic and Political Persecution in Rumania." The Congressional Record, August 8, 1964.

72. Ibid.

73. Edward Crankshaw, "Hungarian Minority Fears Rumanian Axe," (The New York Herald Tribune, April 15, 1963).

74. George Bailey, "Trouble Over Transylvania," (The Reporter, November 19, 1964).

75. Gyula Zathureczky, op. cit., pp. 55-56.

76. Robert R. King, op. cit., p. 153.

77. George Bailey, "Trouble Over Transylvania," (The Reporter, November 19, 1964).

78. Statesman's Yearbook, 1952, 1953, 1954, 1958, 1962-63.

79. Der Spiegel, No. 45 (October 31, 1966), pp. 158-162. The German paper reported several incidents of suicide. One incident was mentioned by George A. Hay, "National Minority Problems" in Kurt London, ed., Eastern Europe in Transition, (Baltimore: The Johns Hopkins Press, 1966), p. 133. Hay refers to the pro-rector, László Szabédi, his wife and five other university professors who committed suicide.

80. Robert R. King, op. cit., pp. 153-154. See also Scinteia, February 22, 1959. For details of the final merger see Scinteia, July 3, 1959 and The New York Times, June 10, 1959.

81. Michel Tatu, Le Monde, November 11, 1967. See also Robert R. King, op. cit., p. 154; also, M. Eugene Osterhaven, op. cit., p. 39; also, Scinteia, July 3, 1959.

82. Robert M. MacKisson, "Letter to the American Transylvanian Federation," June 4, 1963; also refer to The Congressional Record, Mr. Lindsay's speech on "Communist Mistreatment of Hungarians in Transylvania," July 22, 1964.

83. *The Congressional Record*, August 8, 1964.

84. The two districts detached from the Magyar Autonomous Region were Sepsiszentgyörgy-Sfintu Gheorghe (85.3% Hungarian) and Kézdivásárhely-Tirgu Secuiesc (90.2% Hungarian). The three districts added so as to form the Mures-Magyar Autonomous Region were Ludas-Ludus (22.1% Hungarian); Nagysármás - Sarmas (13.7% Hungarian); and Dicsöszentmárton-Tirnaveni (25.6% Hungarian). Rumanians in the new Region increased their ranks from 146,830 (20%) to 266,403 (35%). Hungarians decreased their ranks from 565,510 (77%) to 473,154 (62%). See Robert R. King, *op. cit.*, pp. 156-157.

85. *Le Monde*, July 4, 1964.

86. Gyula Zathureczky, "National Minorities, Step-Children in Communist Lands," in Gallus, Alexander, ed., *Studies for a New Central Europe*, op. cit., vol. 1, No. 2, p. 37.

87. *The Congressional Record*, August 8, 1964.

88. Edward Crankshaw, *op. cit.*

89. Neue Zürcher Zeitung, *December 3, 1967.*

90. Kovászna (Covasna) County was formed from the two Székely districts of Sepsiszentgyörgy (Sfintu Gheorghe) and Kézdivásárhely (Tirgu Secuiesc). It was the smallest county in Rumania. Harghita ranked fifth from the bottom. Their combined population according to the 1966 census was no more than 459,250. See Robert R. King, *op. cit.*, pp. 161-162.

91. See the trends depicted in the *Statesman's Yearbook*, 1960-1968.

BIBLIOGRAPHY

Andics, Erzsébet, *A Magyar Nacionalizmus Kialakulása és Története*, (Budapest: Kossuth, 1964).

Bratianu, G.I., *Rumanien und Ungarn: Demographische und Wirtschaftliche Betrachtungen* (Bucharest: Institutul de Stiinte Morale si Politice, 1940).

Central Statistical Board, Statistical Pocket Book of the Socialist Republic Of Rumania, 1966, 1967, 1969.

Cornish, Louis C., *Transylvania: The Land Beyond the Forest*, (Philadelphia: Dorrance & Company, Inc., 1947).

Csatár, István, *Erdély és a Visszatért Keleti Részek*, (Budapest: Halász Irodalmi és Könyvkiadóvállalat, 1941).

Déer, József and László Gáldi, *Magyarok és Románok* (Budapest: Athenaeum Irodalmi és Nyomdai Részvénytársulat Nyomása, 1941).

Fischer-Galati, Stephen, *The New Rumania,* (M.I.T. Press, 1967).

Fischer-Galati, Stephen, ed., *Rumania* (New York: Frederick A. Praeger, 1957).

Fischer-Galati, Stephen, ed., *Eastern Europe in the Sixties* (New York: Frederick A. Praeger, 1963).

Floyd, David, *Rumania: Russia's Dissident Ally*, (New York: Frederick A. Praeger, 1965).

Gallus, Alexander, ed., *Studies for a New Central Europe*, (New York: The Mid-European Research Institute, 1964).

Haraszti, Andrew, *The Ethnic History of Transylvania*, (Astor Park: The Danubian Press, 1971).

Hayes, Carlton J.H., *Essays on Nationalism*, (New York: The Macmillan Co., 1926).

Hayes, Carlton J.H., *The Historical Evolution of Modern Nationalism*, (New York: The Macmillan Co., 1949).

Hory, András, *Még Egy Barázdát Sem* (München: Ledermüller Oliver, 1967).

Ionescu, Ghita, *Communism in Rumania, 1944-1962*, (London: Oxford University Press, 1964).

Jorga, Nicolae, *A History of Rumania*, (New York: Ams Press, 1970).

Kádár, János, *Hazafiság és Internacionalizmus*, (Budapest: Kossuth, 1968).

Kedourie, Elie, *Nationalism*, (New York: Frederick A. Praeger, 1960).

King, Robert R., *Minorities Under Communism*, (Cambridge: Harvard University Press, 1973).

Kohn, Hans, *The Idea of Nationalism*, (New York: The Macmillan Co., 1961).

Kormos, C., *Rumania* (Cambridge: University Press, 1944).

Lenin, V.I., *Questions of National Policy and Proletarian Internationalism*, (Moscow: Progress Publishers, n.d.).

Lichtheim, George, *Marxism: An Historical and Critical Study*, (New York: Praeger Publishers, 1973).
London, Kurt ed., *Eastern Europe in Transition*, (Baltimore: The Johns Hopkins Press, 1966).
Macartney, C.A., *Hungary: A Short History*, (Chicago: Aldine Publishing Co., 1949).
Macartney, C.A., *Problems of the Danube Basin*, (Cambridge: University Press, 1942).
Macartney, C.A., *National States and National Minorities* (London: Oxford University Press, 1934).
Macartney, C.A., *Hungary and Her Successors, 1919-1937*, (London: Oxford University Press, 1965).
Macartney, C.A., *October Fifteenth, A History of Modern Hungary, 1929-1945 Parts I and II*, (Edinburgh: At the University Press, 1961).
Magyar Történelmi Társulat, ed., *Erdély* (Budapest: Athenaeum Irodalmi és Nyomdai Részvénytársulat Nyomása, 1940).
Makkai, László, *Magyar-Román Közös Mult*, (Budapest: Teleki Pál Tudományos Intézet, 1948).
Manuila, Sabin, *Aspects Démographiques de la Transylvanie*, (Bucharest: L'Institut Central de Statistique, 1938).
Meyer, Alfred G., *Leninism*, (New York: Frederick A. Praeger, 1972).
Molnár, József & Borbándi, Gyula, ed. *Tanulmányok a Magyar Forradalom eól* (München: Aurora Könyvek, 1966).
Montgomery, John Flournoy, *Hungary: The Unwilling Satellite*, (New York: The Devin-Adair Company, 1947).
Nyiró, József, *Mi Az Igazság Erdély Esetében?* (Cleveland: Katolikus Magyar Vasárnapja, n.d.).
Osterhaven, M. Eugene, *Transylvania: The Pathos of a Reformation Tradition*, A Reformed Review Occasional Paper (Michigan: The Western Theological Seminary, 1968).
Robinson, William F., *Nationalism: Hungarian Problem Child*. (Munich: Radio Free Europe Research, July 5, 1967).
Roucek, Joseph S. *Contemporary Roumania and Her Problems: A Study in Modern Nationalism* (Stanford: Stanford University Press, 1932).
Seton-Watson, Hugh, *The East European Revolution*, 2nd Edition (New York: Frederick A. Praeger, 1951).
Seton-Watson, Hugh, *Eastern Europe Between the Wars, 1918-1941*, (New York: Harper and Row, 1967).
Seton-Watson, R.W., *Transylvania: A Key Problem*, (Oxford: The Classic Press, 1943).
Seton-Watson, R.W., *A History of the Roumanians*, (Connecticut: Archon Books, 1962).
Sinanian, Sylvia, István Deák and Peter Ludz, ed., *Eastern Europe in the 1970's*, (New York: Praeger Publishers, 1972).
Sugar, Peter F., and Ivo J. Lederer, *Nationalism in Eastern Europe*, (Seattle

and London: University of Washington Press, 1969).

Szász, Zsombor De, *The Minorities in Roumanian Transylvania*, (London: The Richards Press, 1927).

Szekfű, Gyula, *Állam és Nemzet*, (Budapest: Magyar Szemle Társaság, 1942).

Teleki, Pál, *The Evolution of Hungary and Its Place in European History*, (New York: The Macmillan Co., 1923).

Toma, Peter A., ed., *The Changing Face of Communism in Eastern Europe*, (Arizona: The University of Arizona Press, 1970).

Transylvanus, *The Ethnical Minorities of Transylvania*, (London: Eyre and Spottiswoode Ltd., 1934).

Wickersham, George W., *Opinion: Regarding the Rights of Hungarians and Certain Hungarian Nationals Under the Treaty of Trianon* (New York, 1928).

Wolff, Robert Lee, *The Balkans in Our Time*, (Cambridge: Harvard University Press, 1956).

Zathureczky, Gyula, *Transylvania: Citadel of the West*, (Astor Park: The Danubian Press, n.d.).

ARTICLES AND PERIODICALS

The American Political Science Review
The Congressional Record
The Hungarian Quarterly
Irodalmi Ujság (Paris)
Magyar Élet (Toronto)
Magyar Hirlap
Le Monde
Népszabadság
Neue Zürcher Zeitung
The New York Herald Tribune
The New York Times
Pravda
The Reporter
Scinteia
Sovietskaya Rossiya
Der Spiegel
The Statesman's Yearbook
Világhiradó (Cleveland)

FROM MARXIST SOCIALISM TO NATIONAL-SOCIALISM
UNDER CEAUSESCU
by
Jonel P. Margineanu

(Mr. Margineanu was born in 1898 in a small village of central Transylvania, to a Rumanian peasant family. He received his education in Kolozsvár in a Rumanian language high school, under a Hungarian government. He finished college with a law degree under a Rumanian government in the same city. After practicing law for more than twenty years he was invited to join the faculty of the Babes-Bolyai University and was soon forced into retirement for "uncooperative attitude toward the government". Mr. Margineanu left the country in 1976, and settled in France. He is an ardent advocate of the "Independent Transylvania" movement and member of the Danubian Research Center.)

Though I am proud to be a Rumanian, I am even prouder today to be a Transylvanian Vlach, which is my nation's original name, meaning "shepherd". My forefathers were sheepherding people for more than a thousand years, moving their herds slowly northward from near Albania into our present homeland, in search of peace and better pastures. There is no doubt about our Latin origin and our migration, since we have left our footprints all over the Balkan peninsula in the names of mountains and streams, while our language bears witness to close connections with Albanians, Greeks, Serbs, Bulgarians and finally the Magyars. (See: Andre Du Nay, "The Early History of the Rumanian Language", Jupiter Press, Chicago, Ill, U.S.A., 1977.)

We do not have to hide behind false faces or invent a politically motivated history in order to become equal to other European nations. We do not have to claim to be "first settlers" in our land while all geographical names around us prove the opposite. We are native inhabitants of Transylvania (Erdély-Ardeal-Siebenburgen) together with others, having the same God given rights to this land as anybody else who belongs here. This does, and must, suffice for any one of us; Magyars, Germans, Vlachs. Together we are the proud heirs of a Western cultural inheritance which goes back many centuries into European history. It is a Transylvanian culture, special and unique in this world. It is the blend of different cultures coexisting here for many centuries forming a perfect foundation to a very special Transylvanian brotherhood; which, I am sorry to admit, because of overwhelming outside influences, never was able to materialize.

I was a teenage boy when the Hungarian gendarme called by father a "stinking Vlach", and a few years later I saw the newly arrived Rumanian gendarme beat up our neighbor and call him a "Hungarian Dog". It took time until I found out that neither the Hungarian nor the Rumanian gendarme "belonged" to us. They were both foreigners. One from Hungary, the other from Rumania. They were not Transylvanians.

There were times in my life when I felt that a Transylvanian brotherhood could be worked out, making our mutual homeland into a peaceful and wonderful place to live for all of us, no matter what language we spoke. First, it was during the late 1920's and early '30's, and again during the 1950's, when it seemed that perhaps old hurts and grievances could be forgotten and Hungarians, Germans, Rumanians could share the responsibilities of a brighter future, enjoying equal rights and carrying equal burdens.

Before World War II it was the plague seeping across the borders from Germany that obstructed the natural development of mutual understanding and trust between us, and contaminated the air with the miasma of hatred, turning our youth into ravaging wolves.

For the second time, my hope lay anchored in the new constitution of our socialist republic, which clearly stated:

In Art. 17: "The citizens of the Socialist Republic of Rumania, irrespective of their nationality, race, sex or religion, shall have equal rights in all fields of economic, political, social and cultural life. The State shall guarantee the equal rights of the citizens. No restriction of these rights, and no difference in their exercise on the grounds of nationality, race, sex or religion shall be permitted."

In Art. 22: "In the Socialist Republic of Rumania, the coinhabiting nationalities shall be assured the free use of their mother-tongue as well as books, newspapers, periodicals, theatres and education at all levels in their own languages. In territorial administrative units, also inhabited by population of non-Rumanian nationalities all bodies and institutions shall use, in speech and in writing, the language of the nationality concerned and shall appoint officials from its ranks."

However, in 1958 I found with dismay that these were only words used to camouflage the very opposite of everything I believed in and believed the constitution to stand for. One day a man by the name of Nicolae Ceausescu (at that time quite inknown to us Transylvanians) entered our bilingual university in Cluj-Kolozsvár with his leather jacketed storm troopers called the SECURITATE, and took the first brutal step toward the termination of the Hungarian section of that university. As a result, one of my Hungarian friends, the well-known poet, László Szabédi, committed suicide for fear of further physical and mental tortures. From that day on until today, Ceausescu and his "enforcers" have caused the death of many fine and dedicated Hungarian educators, and students, who bravely fought for their rights as set forth in the constitution. How great the number of those who were tortured and beaten to death, I do not know. It will be the job of future researchers to prepare the statistics of our awful shame as Rumanians and socialists as well.

Between 1959 and 1962, more than 2,000 Hungarian schools in Transylvania were merged with their Rumanian counterparts. The use of the Hungarian language in certain classes was retained only if a sufficient number of students were available who did not understand Rumanian. Such a requirement does not occur in a country where children grow up in a bilingual environment.

Then, in 1965, the Ninth Communist Party Congress adopted a new constitution, which declared:

"Rumania is a uniform national state, its territory now occupied by one nation which was formed by concrete historical events, and which resulted in the Rumanian Socialist Nation."

With this the practice of government policy shifted legally over from socialism to NATIONAL-SOCIALISM with a new Hitler at the head of his storm troopers - DICTATOR CEAUSESCU!

Methods and practices are the same as used in the Third Reich: Rumanians, descendants of the glorious Roman Empire and the brave Dacians, inhabiting the land for more than 2,000 years (What a shameful and ridiculous falsification of history!) are the only accepted and legitimate nation, the HERRENRASSE, the only culture bearers in this part of Europe, and the descendants of all intruders into this GREAT RUMANIAN "LEBENSRAUM" - Hungarians, Germans, Bulgarians, Jews, Russians, Serbians, Gypsies, Slovaks, numbering more than 5 million - must assimilate or be eliminated by force.

In order to eradicate every trace of Transylvania's cultural past, it was decreed that each document, book - even private letters, older than 25 years - is "national property". This decree was used in former Hungarian cultural centers, like Oradea-Nagyvárad, Cluj-Kolozsvár, Aiud-Enyed, Alba Julia-Gyulafehérvár, Targu Mures-Marosvásárhely, Odorhei-Udvarhely, etc., etc., to confiscate Hungarian museums, archives, libraries, including all church archives, and move them to a "central location", where most of the ancient historic material was systematically destroyed, while the rest was put away in damp cellars where they will rot away on their own. At the same time all historic markers, statues, coats of arms; even old Hungarian names engraved on tombstones, were removed or simply replaced by markers or names which could impress upon the foreign visitor an artificially created, non-existent, purely Rumanian past. Complete cemeteries were destroyed in order to erase the Hungarian past of certain towns. Tombs were bulldozed, bones hauled away by trucks and new cemeteries established at the same locations for future use of the recently imported Rumanian settlers, brought there from the "old country" (REGAT) to fill better paying industrial and administrative jobs, previously held by the native Hungarian population.

I am writing these facts with deep embarrassment as a Rumanian, and a believer in the socialist doctrine. I do not associate myself with these evil and barbaric deeds, and must emphasize again that I am a Transylvanian-Vlach, a "Rumun", and not a Rumanian from across the mountains.

I feel sympathy and brotherly allegiance to my Transylvanian co-patriots, like Mr. Jeno Szikszai and Mr. Lajos Kuthy, two splendid Hungarian educators in the city of Brasov-Brassó, who refused to sign a declaration praising the nationality policies of dictator Ceausescu, and denying any further need for Hungarian schools, and because of their brave refusal were tortured and killed - creating the illusion of suicide.

I feel great respect for Mr. Károly Király, a leading Hungarian socialist who had the courage to protest openly against theses inhumane anti-socialistic breaches of governmental power, knowing that he would be severely punished for his deed. His whereabouts are unknown today, perhaps he is not even alive.

As my good compatriot, Paul Goma, dissident Rumanian writer now living here in France, testified in 1978 in Frankfurt, Germany, on the international press conference dealing with human rights: "There is a clearly defined plan in progress today, executing anti-Hungarian measures beyond imagination by the use of arrests, interrogations, intimidations, terror and torture."

At the same time the Ceausescu government has published again and again new statistics on the country's population, based on arbitrary census figures. I personally know of Hungarian families in the community where I come from, whose names are; Fekete, Szóke, Puskás and Demeter, who are listed now as; Negrutiu, Seche, Puskasiu and Dimitru by the authorities. Even with all the falsifications and intimidations, the Ceausescu government admits the presence of 1,800,000 Hungarians. This figure does not include those deported into the swamps of the Danube delta, those living in Bucuresti, the Rumanian capital (about 200,000) and those in Moldova (another 200,000). I am certain that a fairly and honestly implemented census would bring up the total of Hungarians living within the borders of today's Rumania way above the 3,000,000 mark.

However, it is not up to me to list all the legitimate grievances of my fellow countrymen of Hungarian nationality. Their plight is made public and it must be the task of the United Nations and other international organizations to deal accordingly with this abominable oppression, practiced by a newly emerged national-socialist dictatorship.

Though my age lessens the possibility of seeing it with my own eyes, nevertheless I desire to look into the future, no matter how distant it may be. A future in which Transylvanian Rumuns as well as Transylvanian Magyars will be able to forget the past with all its ugliness and begin to build together something enduring, something worthy to be built; a Transylvania in which human dignity comes first, with everything this often misused expression truly entails.

I am sure that there are possibilities to work out solutions which could ensure such a future. But it must include the full mutual respect toward one another, as nations and as peoples, and complete trust based on this respect.

I am not stating that there are no other possible solutions, for possibilities are always unlimited. But to me, as a person, a socialist in my brain cells and a Rumun in my heart, the simplest and best solution seems to be the idea of an independent Republic of Transylvania, with as many autonomous administrative districts as needed, for each nationality group. This would create a rich and blessed country in which Rumuns, Magyars, and Germans would not compete AGAINST each other, but would be able to work TOGETHER in harmony.

I fully realize that the idea suggested here cannot be popular today with anyone of the concerned parties. My fellow Rumanians will regard it as treason, while the Magyars, rightfully embittered today, would not trust any solution suggested by a Rumun. They can see no other possibility for their survival than a return under the protecting shield of Hungary.

I must admit, there is solid argument underscoring this demand. Within the framework of a relatively tolerant Hungarian Kingdom, many nationalities, including us, Vlachs or Rumuns, were allowed to enter the country and settle in organized groups without ever being asked to give up our own national identity. On the contrary, we were aided and supported by Hungarians in maintaining our own religion, our own language, and in developing our own culture.

While on the other hand, under the brutal rule of today's national-socialist regime of Ceausescu, the Transylvanian Magyars are condemned in their own land to extinction. Regarded objectively, the intolerable political, economical and cultural situation within the National Socialist Republic of Rumania definitely turns the scale in favour of the Hungarian demands.

Nevertheless, as Hitler fell, so will Ceausescu, also. In today's world shiftless deceit of political propaganda, no matter how cunning, cannot fool public opinion for a long period of time. The eradication of 3,000,000 Magyars cannot go unnoticed, and sooner or later world opinion will react against Rumania. Then, perhaps, enlightened and knowledgeable leaders of the ruling powers, sincerely trying to make just and fair decisions, will realize the given similarities between Transylvania and Switzerland and will act accordingly.

MODERNIZED GENOCIDE

by Ferenc Kunszabó

[Condensed and translated from the Hungarian with the permission of the Catholic Hungarian Sunday, Youngstown, Ohio, U.S.A.

(Mr. Kunszabó is a young Socialist writer in today's Hungary. After visiting in Transylvania on three different occasions, he wrote a report on the situation of the Hungarians under the increasing pressure of an extremely chauvinistic Rumanian occupation. His report was published under the above title first in Hungary, then in Hungarian periodicals in Western Europe as well as in the United States.)

Just before the Easter Holidays in 1977, Jenó Szikszai,a high school teacher, was requested to appear at the office of the Brassó-Brasov political police. He was suspected of nurturing anti-people and anti-state convictions. The suspicion was based on the fact that in the 1930's he was going to college in Rome. Szikszai asked: What did he do to create the impression of being an enemy of the people and the State,since he had been teaching for decades in the Hungarian high school at Brassó, under the full supervision of the Rumanian government's school inspectorate?

"We are the only ones who ask questions here!" was the answer, and the beating began. Then they placed the text of his "voluntary confession" before him, in which he was supposed to admit that he was conspiring and had been conspiring for years against the Socialist State, that he was teaching Nationalism to the Hungarian students, and that his sin was planning to carry out a murder attempt against Comrade Ceausescu, the great leader of the Rumanian people. Szikszai refused to sign the confession. After more beatings, he was released with the order to return after the holidays for further questioning.

The elderly man knew that if he signed the confession he would die soon in one of the death camps of the Danube Delta. If he refused to sign, he would be beaten and tortured, and his friends and relatives would be harassed "to confess" against him. He discussed the situation with several of his friends, and on Easter Sunday, he committed suicide.

People who live under a milder political climate might get shocked at such brutality, and the manner of securing confessions. We are accustomed to this way of life. Therefore, my first reaction was, why did this questioning of Szikszai occur with the Rumanian political police exactly in 1977, some forty years after the case charged. Why now, after all these years? Especially since his case was not unique. At the same time, for example, another Hungarian teacher, Zoltán Zsufka was requested to appear at the Kovásna police. The accusation against him was that during World War II, as an Hungarian Army officer, he had beaten his recruits. Zsufka replied that there must be some mistake, since because of his age, he had only become an officer at the end of the war, and had been a recruit himself. While he was still speaking, a colonel entered the room, and turning to the interrogator he asked:

"Did you give the bandit his first beating?"

"Not yet", answered the examiner.

"Do you have a knout?"

"Just a billy club."

Having nothing better at hand, the colonel grabbed the rubber billy club and gave the "accused" a severe beating. Then the already typed confession was put in front of him. Now Zsufka had had enough of the beating and he signed the paper obediently.

The next day he registered a complaint, attached to a medical confirmation telling of the beating he had received. Again he was called to the SECURITATE (political police). They tossed another confession in front of him to sign, in which he admitted that his previous confession was false, and that he had never been beaten by anyone. After signing this paper, he was beaten again for willfully misleading the police with his previous confession. They let him go. (A few days later he was found in a nearby woods, shot through the head.)

These were not isolated cases during the spring months of 1977. The same harassments were repeated all over Transylvania. The reason for this became clear in the summer of the same year, Premier János Kádár of Hungary met with Ceausescu to intervene on the behalf of the Hungarian minority. By that time the Rumanian government had a briefcase full of documents proving that the Hungarian intellectuals in Transylvania were a group of chauvinist "reactionaries". They asked if Kádár was intervening on behalf of Fascists.

Then came the "Király case". A prominent socialist leader, son of a peasant, he was one of the most enthusiastic young Marxist-Leninists during the late 1940's and during the early 1950's, when Socialism was established in Rumania. He held many important positions in the Communist Party, as well as within the new State apparatus. In 1968, he became the First Secretary of the Kovászna District. By that time Ceausescu's chauvinistic policy had already been set into motion. First, he attacked and destroyed the Hungarian Universities, then he moved several hundred-thousand Rumanians into the Hungarian inhabited northern parts of Transylvania, and into the regions next to the Hungarian border. Király and many of his friends, as well as some of the sober Rumanians, thought this to be only a passing phenomenon and the Marxist-Leninist ideas would soon overcome this suddenly re-kindled Rumanian Nationalism. He was relying on this up to the end. It was his trust in the Socialist principles that made him write those much publicized letters in which he revealed the plight of his people under the ever increasing pressure of centralized chauvinism, asking for redress. Those letters caused his final downfall. Today no one knows whether he is still alive.

After my last trip through Transylvania in 1978, I came to the conclusion that what is happening there conflicts with the Constitution of the Socialist Republic of Rumania, the laws of the Rumanian State, the Human Rights Declaration of the United Nations and thus qualifies for the concept of "apartheid" as set forth in the text of prevailing international agreements. If not yet in its methods, the intentions and results deserve the definition of "Criminal Genocide."

I. International agreement for the prevention and punishment of genocide, dated December 9, 1948 states in Art. 1: "The signing parties endorse that genocide, whether committed in war or during peacetime, is a criminal act against international law, and they pledge to take effective measures against such violations". Art. 2 makes clear that "This agreement understands under the term 'genocide', any one of the following acts perpetrated with the intent to annihilate partly or completely any national, radical, ethnic or religious groups by: (a) killing members of that group, (b) causing severe bodily or mental injury to members of such group, (c) deliberately forcing on such group such living conditions aimed to cause the partial or complete physical annihilation of the group, (d) any measures aiming to obstruct the natural birth rate within a group, (e) the forced transfer of the children of one group into another group.

II. The 1965 International Agreement for the Elimination of all kinds of racial discrimination states in Part: I., Art. 1, Par. 1, "In the text of this agreement the expression of 'racial discrimination' includes all such discriminations, exclusions, restrictions or preferences which are based on race, color, origin, nationality and ethnic origin, as well as the intent, the result of which is the curtailment or complete annulment of the equal enjoyment or practice of the recognition of human rights and the basic freedoms in all political, economical, social and cultural fields."

III. Art. II, All of the document on the International Agreement for the combating and punishing apartheid, defines the term "apartheid", the following way: "Causing severe bodily or mental harm to members of a certain ethnic group by offending them in their freedom or dignity, or by subjecting them to tortures or other inhuman and degrading treatment or punishment.

The Socialist Republic of Rumania is one of the signers of these agreements, and is obligated by them to prevent the occurrence of all the above mentioned criminal acts within its borders. However, nothing was done, and as we can clearly see, the State itself, through its agencies, practices apartheid and genocide.

Though there are hundreds and hundreds of examples one could refer to in listing all the accusations against the Rumanian Government, I am not going to do so at this time. First, because the international practice of the previous decades has proved clearly that the actual and direct effectiveness of various agreements is almost nil. Secondly, because exposing the evidences of concrete cases would greatly endanger those involved as well as their friends and families. Government agencies are known to take harsh revenge under the camouflage of some created causes. We know of "fatal accidents", poisonings, and even people being incarcerated in insane asylums from where they have never returned. But most of all, I am not going to waste the time here to list pages and pages of brutalities, though these are everyday occurrences in Rumania. However, I do not see these as the most significant manifestation of officially instigated Rumanian chauvinism.

Firing squads, death camps, tortures, beatings by the police, arrests, and harassments, are such forthright, clear-cut activities all over the world, that it is easy for everyone to condemn them. Especially, since such condemnation has a deep-rooted tradition in past history, all over the world.

The Rumanians know this, and they don't want to provoke the reaction of world opinion by such deeds, although lately they haven't succeeded very well in hiding such activities, and under the influence of the ever-increasing national hysteria they are generating, it will be more and more difficult to do so. I regard as even more characteristic and more decisive their other method which I shall call here the perpetual and systematic torture of the mind and soul of the minority. They chose this method and operate it on a large scale because it is relatively quiet, almost a silent strangulation, that does not make a great clamour. Neither the European nor the North American ears are trained, as yet, to recognize the muffled sounds of murdered souls.

It began with the petulant outburst of Mr. Ceausescu in the Fall of 1971 during a nationality conference in Bucharest: "Rumania belongs to the Rumanians, and only to the Rumanians, because only Rumanians live here, even if some of them can speak foreign languages also."

All the Turkish, Bulgarian, Gypsy, Ukrainian, Ruthenian, Jewish, Serbian, Slovakian, as well as the German and Hungarian children are born into this atmosphere. The father goes to the State Office to register his child. He is required to do so by law. The community where he resides can be entirely ethnic, but the officials are all Rumanian who cannot or will not speak the language of the ethnic group they rule over.

The person behind the desk registers the date of birth, the sex of the child, and then comes the great question: "What shall be the child's name?" If the Hungarian father simply, "József", the man at the desk enters into the big book the name "Josif". If it is "János", he writes "Juon". So far it would not be too bad, because he has simply translated the name into the official State language, and in the long run it would even be to the advantage of the child to have a Rumanian name. However, since his name is written into the book in the Rumanian way, he will be regarded as Rumanian for the rest of his life. If later he tries to protest this to a census official, the authorities would call him a "Nationalist" and accuse him of "inciting against the Rumanian society."

Knowing all this, the father tries to find a name which does not stem from a common Christian culture and therefore cannot be translated into any other language. This is the reason that so many children in Transylvania carry names like Árpád, Attila, Csilla, Emese, etc.

Let us assume the father comes up with one of these names. The official raises his eyebrows. "There is no such name," he says and the discussion begins. Other officials gather around and six or seven people lash out abuses and insults on the lone Hungarian. It is understandable that in such circumstances many of the parents give up the idea of registering their children under Hungarian names and see to it that it is written down with correct spelling, a freedom they are supposed to have under the law.

It frequently happens that the father gives the Hungarian name, but the official writes something entirely different into the book, usually a Rumanian name, which has its Hungarian counterpart. It will come out years later when the child goes to school. By then it is too late to change it. It happens, too, that he simply refuses to write the name and tells the father to come back another time, after he has decided whether or not he wants to be a good citizen of the country. But let us assume that the father has succeeded in having the child registered under the name he has chosen. There is still ample time and opportunity to eliminate the national origin of the new citizen. Any official anywhere can change the child's first name at any time he is in contact with the official representatives of the administration, and needs to be listed, registered, issued a card, or anything else.

Now let us examine another common situation of childbirth. For a good ten years now, the Rumanian authorities have introduced the practice of bringing pregnant Rumanian mothers across the mountains into Transylvania for birth, under the pretext that there is no room in one hospital, and therefore the mother must be taken to another. In the same manner, the Hungarian expectant mother in Transylvania is told that there is not a place in the local hospital for her and she will be taken across the mountains into old Rumania. The child naturally, born in a hospital, is registered by that hospital and in the district where the hospital is located. Thus, when the next census is taken, districts which are supposed to be entirely Hungarian have a great many Rumanian children registered, while the children born to Hungarian mothers are registered somewhere else, where there is no minority problem.

This is the situation into which the children of the Transylvanian nationalities are born these days. At any rate, they are born into the world and begin to grow. He or she learns to speak the native tongue from the mother, then slowly the child gets out into the street - causing a new and permanent anxiety to the parent. This is true because there are no more entirely Hungarian towns or villages in Transylvania. For decades now, the government has been bringing in Rumanians, giving them free housing and the best of available jobs. This "Re-settling" is done in such a way that not only is the population of the towns and villages mixed, but even the population of the streets. The moment that the Hungarian child ventures out into the street, he encounters an "enemy world". The aim is to make that Hungarian child feel homeless and rootless, with no permanent place in which he belongs.

Minority children will converse among themselves in their minority language. Immediately some Rumanian children will shout at them, "What sort of vagrants are you? Can't you even talk properly?" And the quarrel begins. It ends with a fight. If the minority child is beaten up, the case is simple. The child runs home crying, the mother dries the tears and explains the facts of life. "Our name is 'shut up' because we are Hungarians." The trouble comes if the Hungarians beat up the Rumanians. The parents get aroused, and the police, as well as the entire State apparatus, is on their side.

I know of one such case which followed a street fight between Hungarian and Rumanian children. A Rumanian military unit was ordered into Kescivásárhely to "restore and maintain order".

Those who do not know the situation in Transylvania today may read these lines in disbelief, for in a normal society it seems unbelievable that Rumanian children would not tolerate the presence of children speaking a different language. However, the structure of Rumanian society today cannot be considered normal.

Every branch of the Rumanian media, with no exceptions, is deeply involved with nationalistic instigation and incitement, on a large scale, thus creating an atmosphere similar to Nazi Germany. Anybody can find this out just by listening for a few minutes to one of the TV or radio stations of Bucharest, or looking at the newspapers, magazines or any other printed matter.

There is, for example, the well-known poem by Vasile Alexandri, the "More Unirei", the first verse of which is used day after day in the Rumanian television: It says - "Come, Brothers, hand in hand - everyone who is of Rumanian blood - let us dance the hora - in this great Rumanian land - Let the weed disappear from our wheatfield, let the enemy go to hell - and not be anything among us - but Rumanian song and dance."

If anyone can be in doubt what is meant by the term "weed", it is clearly explained again and again. Even in the so-called "scientific publications" it is reiterated. For example: the Bucharest weekly, called "Contemorarul" brought an article in its 6th edition of 1978 in which two history professors, D. Berciu and C. Preda officially declared that the Rumanians have inhabited today's Rumania for at least five thousand years, and in the 10th century A.D. they bravely resisted the intrusion of the Magyars, as well as other barbaric intruders. The leader of the resisting Rumanian forces was the famous MENUMAQROTU, they claim. They refer, in fact to the MEN MAROT, a historically famous BULGARIAN CHIEF, who lost the battle against the Magyars in the 9th century, trying to defend a Bulgarian outpost on the lower Danube.

Branding the Transylvanian Hungarians as "intruders" is an every day occurrence, and it is no wonder that Hungarian children, or adults, are shouted at daily on the street, in the railroad station, public offices, etc., "You homeless vagrant, you dirty bandit, get out of here."

Since the Fall of 1977, this situation has been getting worse and worse. This is probably caused by the fact that the Bucharest TV station has started the program series, "We sing of Thee, Rumania".

The announcer and programmer of this series is the notorious chauvinist poet, Adrian Paunescu. I, myself, have watched his program, aimed at the children, on February 19, 1978. About the middle of his program, Paunescu's face suddenly becomes dark, his voice deep and somber, as he asks the viewers to pay special attention to the next number. A little girl appeared and told the audience that somewhere there is a fine, brave, intelligent, strong and handsome, honest, lovable, helpful and well-meaning Rumanian shepherd-boy who is being deceived trapped, and eventually will be killed by some cowardly, stupid, weak, ugly, selfish, dishonest, thieving foreigner. Guess who these foreigners are? Of course, the Magyars, the Germans, the Jews, the Hungarians, the Bulgarians. All the Rumanian children publications, radio as well as television, even the literary reviews bring out this story again and again in different versions. It is written and announced again and again, that those murderous, evil foreigners are Hungarian or German. These are foreigners in Rumania. These must be cleaned out like the weeds in the fields.

It is understandable that, under such centrally organized propaganda, the hate against the nationalities is daily increasing in Rumania. The minds of millions of Rumanian children are being poisoned with this hate, even in the schools, from kindergarten up. The "patriotic" teacher makes a play out of Paunescu's poisoned story. To give more emphasis to it, when it comes time to designate the roles among the children, the role of the "evil Magyar" and the "evil German" are always forced on the minority children.

This is the way and the surroundings in which the Hungarian child grows up today in Rumania if his father has succeeded in giving him an old Magyar name, one that cannot be translated. After kindergarten comes the school. Half of the class is Rumanian, the other half Hungarian. The principal, as well as most of the teachers are Rumanian. They make fun of the Hungarian names. They ridicule everything the Hungarian children say or do, and make the Rumanian children laugh at them and scorn them. But when "volunteer work" has to be done, the teacher turns to the minority side of the classroom saying, "Here, you may have the opportunity now to show that in spite of being an intruder, you still wish to be a good citizen of our Rumanian homeland!" In the case of some official celebrations or parades, it is always the minority children who are ordered out to be the enthusiastic and cheering crowd, and while doing a good job at it, the Rumanian children will say mockingly, "Look how enthusiastic you are. But no matter how much you try to show off, you are still nothing but a lot of dirty, stinking foreigners."

After the Hungarian child finishes the compulsory lower education, comes the middle school, which is not compulsory. The Hungarian children are told by the principal that now that they have learned to read and write it is enough for them.

In the early 1970's there were about a hundred Hungarian language middle schools where the Hungarian child was able to enroll. Today there are only approximately forty, and even these have only a very few subjects which are taught in Hungarian, the remainder are taught in Rumanian, with Rumanian teachers. Hungarian teachers are not allowed to give attention out of class to their Hungarian pupils. Whenever some of the children try to visit one of the teachers in their home in order to ask some questions, the dreaded SECURITATE appears on the scene and the teacher, as well as the student, and the parents of the student, are exposed to hours of questioning, and in most cases, beatings, in order to discourage such contacts between teachers and Hungarian students.

In case the Hungarian student had finished middle school, as well as high school, with excellent results (straight A's) he just might have a chance to enter college and become a professional. If he has been able to maintain his integrity through all of these adverse conditions and still call himself an Hungarian, he will have to be content with jobs that Rumanians do not want. If he weakens and denies his nationality and becomes more Rumanian than the Rumanians themselves, he can choose among the best, and for a few years at least, he will be indulged and a "pet" of the government.

However, if he still insists on being Hungarian, he will either be placed in a job, in some distant location in old Rumania where there are no Hungarians at all, or he will have to contend with some inferior work handed out to him by the authorities. If he was born and raised in an Hungarian village, he must return there and take what he can find. He is not allowed to move to a town, unless he first has a job in that town. All the better paying jobs in any Transylvanian town are already given to young Rumanians brought in from "across the mountains". Hungarians can only get jobs in a town if they are already residents there.

The vicious circle is closed. If you are Hungarian, you will be assigned into old Rumania to work. If you don't like it, you must stay where you were born, and take whatever you can find there - usually nothing more than manual labour, regardless of what your education might be.

Since the Hungarian has been born, he has to live, and if he wants to live, he must eat. Therefore, the young Hungarian, man or woman, shoulders the fate and tries to survive as best he can, unless he turns and becomes Rumanian. In this case, he will be placed immediately into some leading position, with special housing privileges, special salary, and will be kept in "public view" as an example for every Hungarian to see what treatment waits those who deny their national heritage and turn Rumanian.

However, within a short time those Rumanians who have stepped aside to give a high position to a turn-coat Hungarian, begin to voice their displeasure. Frustration grows to wrath, quite often making working conditions unbearable for these new Rumanians and many are driven to suicide. Ostracized by their own group, but never really accepted by the ruling majority, a vacuum is created around the individual, making existence intolerable. No matter how humbly a turn-coat tries to assimilate, in the eyes of the nationalistic Rumanian society he will always remain a "damn foreigner", a second class citizen at best. For these reasons, more than 1,700,000 persons in Transylvania have insisted, in the face of harassment of all kinds, on being listed as Hungarians. At least another million who do not have names which are indisputably Hungarian, or are forced by circumstances, by authorities, or job-opportunities, keep a discreet silence when they are listed as

Rumanians, while another 300,000 to 400,000 have been moved into Rumania proper, where no minorities exist, and have been "forgotten" as Hungarians, being counted in the census as Rumanians.

Taking into consideration that in the last sixty years the Rumanian population has increased 80% (according to official statistics) while the nationality groups have sharply decreased their numbers, one gets a clearer idea of the so called "equality" in this land boiling with supernationalistic hysteria.

In a land where:

you cannot purchase a railroad ticket if you ask for it in Hungarian;

you will not be served in a shop if you speak Hungarian, German or any other minority language;

the waiter will turn his back on you and customers at other tables make nasty remarks in response to hearing you speak, if you do not ask for food in the tongue of the "glorious Dac ancestors";

since 1920, all Hungarian, German, Bulgarian, Serbian, Croatian, Ukrainian, Ruthenian, Slovak, Turk or Russian monuments, relics, memorials, including statues of outstanding poets, scientists and artists, were systematically destroyed by the hundreds;

the telephone operators verbally chastise   in abusive language if the party is speaking Hungarian and are apt to remind the party they are in great Rumania   and not in some "Gypsy land";

if a member of a minority group attempts to sing a song in his own language he will be rudely reminded to "sing in the official language of the country, and not in the tongue of the bums";

a young mother may be beaten on the railroad. (I witnessed such an event, when one dared to speak Hungarian to her baby.);

old tombs are being dug up in some entirely Hungarian or German cities, the bones hauled away and dumped into clay pits, names removed from tombstones and entire cemeteries "Rumanianized" to make place for the newcomers;

every day teenagers are beaten on the streets and their portable radios broken if they dare listen to any other music but Rumanian. "When will you learn, you dirty bums, to listen to Rumanian music only as long as you eat Rumanian bread", is the leading slogan.

I could go on and on, since not a single day goes by when a member of a minority group in Rumania is not exposed at least once to some abuse, discrimination, scoffing or discouragement because of his or her national origin.

This is what I record as the most characteristic trait of modern genocide. The gradual destruction. The nationality schools were not all closed at the same time, instead in a methodical way they were closed, just as the street names, markers and signs were changed into the native language of the inhabiting population. As were the statues of Kossuth, Bem, Beethoven, Goethe, etc.

Repeatedly house searches were made and non-Rumanian books found in the homes were confiscated a few at a time over a period of time.

In other words, each incident is only one turn of the screw; just as much as the beaten minorities, their mental and spiritual resistance depleted, were able to take at one time; without drastic repercussion that might catch the attention of the international media.

This has been going on for thirty-four years.

What Hitler did to the Jews, and other non-German "inferior nationalities" with the speed of lightning, Ceausescu, the new and much slyer "FÜHRER" of Great Rumania is doing at a slow, but steady pace; however, just as cruel and deadly.

It is time we raise our voice in protest.

"Hands off the Hungarians", just as much as hands off the Germans, the Poles, the Rumanians or any other nationality on the face of the earth.

We must make the world know that in this hidden corner of Europe things are not straightened out at all. The two most ferocious wars of the human race were declared under the pretext of existing conflicts in these areas, however, both wars ended in such an unfortunate manner as to greatly aggravate and increase those very conflicts.

The balance of Europe was upset; the danger of an explosion was never as great as now. First we must tell, humbly and as pleasantly as possible to the great powers of France, England and the United States of America that they did not gain anything with their "reorganizations" following these wars; then we will be able to lay before Moscow, with proper tact and respect, what the geographical mixture of these small central and eastern European nations mean and what this historical ruin of mutual injustices and inextricable truths stand for.

Big nations usually do not have their antennas turned where they can receive the sound of the pains and miseries of small nations. The only way they will ever find out what is going on here, in the depts of human despair, will be if we are able to explain the situation without emotions, in a clear, authentic and sober way.

(See for special reference MICHAEL SOZAN's article - Slippery Rock State College - in CURRENT ANTHROPOLOGY, 18:4 - 1977 - 781-782, on OPPRESSIVE ETHNIC POLICIES OF THE RUMANIAN GOVERNMENT WHICH RESULT IN ETHNOCIDE.)

CONCLUSION

It seems obvious that during the centuries of Vlach (Rumanian) presence within the framework of the Hungarian Kingdom, it was possible for an unorganized, migrating herd people to turn into an established, settled, organized, economically secure and nationally conscious resident population, peacefully developing its culture, increasing in numbers without any restrictions, until locally, in some regions, it reached majority status. Thus, influenced by political powers from the outside, they were able to successfully turn against the host nation.

Since the opening of the secret files of the French Ministry of Foreign Affairs it is clear that in 1919 Rumania occupied the eastern part of Hungary under false pretenses. As a result of dishonest international manipulations and intrigues, and with complete disregard of the "Wilsonian Doctrine" (people's right to self-determination in the spirit of which the entire re-organization of Central and East Central Europe was supposed to be carried out) Rumania took possession of all the lands known today as Transylvania. Thus, the Rumanian occupation of Transylvania must be regarded as morally and legally wrong.

It seems obvious also that during the sixty years of Rumanian rule in Transylvania the native Hungarian population suffered extremely cruel abuse and discrimination as a "national minority" and became, together with the German and other minorities, economically and culturally deprived. Today the Hungarians of Transylvania are increasingly becoming the victims of a systematically planned cultural and biological genocide, carried out ruthlessly by the Rumanian government.

In view of the above, it is obvious that something must be done in order to remedy the situation, which is the shame of the entire civilized world.

First of all it seems mandatory to re-evaluate certain concepts, and the very principles upon which these concepts were established.

The accepted definition of "national minority" refers to a group of people who have migrated into the established country of another nation, and failed to assimilate. Based on this principle, if Germany would occupy Denmark, or France would occupy part of Germany, neither the Danes nor the Germans annexed by France could be regarded as "national minorities" within the occupying nation, but as a nation or part of a nation subdued by another nation as a result of an act of force. The same would be valid in case that Mexico should overrun California or Cuba would invade Florida. Americans inhabiting these states could not be regarded as "national minorities" residing in Cuba or Mexico, but as Americans, separated by foreign occupation from the rest of their country.

Exactly the same is true in regard to the Hungarians in Transylvania.

They were, and ethnographically still are, part of the majority nation inhabiting for eleven hundred years the Carpathian Basin. They held an established statehood there for all these centuries, building this complete geographical unit in Central Europe into a lasting and functioning economical, political and cultural entirety, long before the Vlach immigrants, forefathers of the Rumanians, began to seep into the eastern part of their country. On the ethnographical map of the Carpathian Basin, this Hungarian majority still constitutes an almost uninterrupted unity, dotted with smaller and larger foreign settlements. Therefore, as the original inhabitants of the Carpathian Basin, the Transylvanian Hungarians must still be regarded as part of the Hungarian nation, since their present day minority status was not the result of peaceful evolution but of global armed conflicts which found them, unfortunately, on the losing side.

From this it follows that the cultural genocide, the forced relocation, the forced Rumanization, and the total discrimination to which the native Hungarian population of Transylvania, numbering more than three million, is being subjected today by the government of the Socialist Republic of Rumania, need to be treated as breaches of several treaties, and acts against humanity, and must be resolved as soon as possible in order to put an end to unnecessary human suffering caused by hatred, ignorance and chauvinistic bigotry.

Since the Socialist Republic of Rumania not only refuses to fulfill its legal obligations toward the Hungarians in Transylvania, as outlined in the treaties but is in the act of carrying out a clearly defined genocide: it has furnished proof of Rumanian incompetency and inability to rule with justice and fairness over a land of diverse population. Therefore it is the responsibility of the Powers, which countersigned and thereby guaranteed those treaties, as well as the responsibility of the entire civilized world to politically restructure the Carpathian Basin in such manner that the geographical, economical and cultural unity of this region be restored, and thereby the long coexisting nationalities may again have the chance to live and develop together in peace.

This aim might be achieved:

1. By returning Transylvania, the eastern part of the Carpathian Basin, to the Hungarian motherland, granting administrative and cultural autonomy to the native Rumanian population of Transylvania within clearly defined Rumanian autonomous districts.

2. By creating an independent Transylvania under United Nations charter, consisting of as many autonomous Hungarian, Rumanian, and German districts as necessary to give the most possible freedom of self-government to the greatest possible number of people.

3. By the creation of a federation of independent states, which would

include Austria, Hungary, Croatia, Slovenia, Slovakia and Transylvania, thus restoring in a modernized form the best proven economic framework of the Carpathian Basin.

Experts on the Transylvanian problem agree that a fourth solution, namely the dividing up of Transylvania, somewhat similar to the "Vienna decision" of 1940, combined with a population exchange, would further disrupt the geographic and economic unity of the land. However, if no other peaceful solution can be reached, it would still bring an end to the human suffering, discrimination, brutality and cultural and biological genocide, caused and practiced today by the government of the Socialist Republic of Rumania.

ETHNOGRAPHICAL MAP OF HUNGARY By I. Zólyomi

BORDER OF HUNGARY DURING
THE LAST THOUSAND YEAR

Border of Hungary after the
Trianon and Paris Treaty

THE HILLS OF THE HUNGARIAN AND
RUMANIAN IN THE CARPATHIAN
BASIN FOR THE HISTORICAL HUNGARY

RUMANIA

BUCURESTI

TRANSILVANIA

HUNGARY

BUDAPEST

POZSONY

FIRMÉLY
TRANSILVANIA

HUMETUM

MAGYARORSZAG
Hungary